Patents, Copyrights & Trademarks For Dummies®

Cheat Sheet

W9-BWQ-232

The Perilous Patent Path

Because a patent is the most expensive and complex type of IP (intellectual property) right, first analyze whether you can protect your IP with a copyright, trademark, or service mark, or by keeping it under wraps as a trade secret. If you and your IP professional decide that a patent is the way to go, and you have the time and money to see the process through to the conclusion, here's the patent process in a nutshell.

1. Make sure the invention is really yours and doesn't belong to your boss, your spouse, or your business partner.

2. Do a patent search to make sure that no one else has already come up with your formula, process, or invention.

3. Check that your invention passes the three-part test — it's new, useful, and wouldn't be obvious to someone knowledgeable in the field.

4. Prepare a patent application, including:
   - A short abstract of the invention
   - The claims
   - A description of the best implementation of the invention, including a drawing, if applicable
   - A brief description of each figure of the drawing
   - A brief discussion of the general field, background, and circumstances of the invention
   - A summary of the invention
   - References to any prior applications

5. File your patent application, paying special attention to filing deadlines.

6. Manage publication of your application.

7. Pursue and prosecute your application through the Patent Office.

8. Appeal adverse decisions.

9. Get the patent (if you still want it).

The Skinny on Copyrights

A copyright protects an Original Work of Authorship (OWA) — think short story, computer program, or song lyrics, for example — which must have tangible form, be a result of significant mental activity, have no inherent technical function, and be the author's original creation. Here's the skinny on copyrights:

- As soon as you create an OWA, you automatically have a copyright, which prevents others from copying, publishing, or performing your work.

- Make sure that you own the OWA. In other words, you didn't produce it as an employee, or as a work made for hire.

- You can register your copyright, which makes prosecuting copycats easier.

- When you register your copyright, mark your work as a copyrighted work to discourage infringers and give yourself legal advantages.

For Dummies: Bestselling Book Series for Beginners

Patents, Copyrights & Trademarks For Dummies®

Cheat Sheet

Making a Mark with Commercial Identifiers

There are three types of commercial identifiers that distinguish your product, service, or company from others:

- ✔ Product identifiers, commonly known as brands, or *trademarks,* which distinguish your product from others.

- ✔ Service identifiers comprised of *service marks, certification marks,* and *membership* or *association marks.*

- ✔ Company identifiers, called *trade names,* which are typically business names and logos.

A good commercial identifier has the following characteristics:

- ✔ Original (do a search first)
- ✔ Unique
- ✔ Recognizable
- ✔ Memorable
- ✔ Pleasant associations

Keeping Trade Secrets

Trade secrets can take many forms, such as your customer and supplier list, your next marketing campaign, a particular process or formula, or your finances. How can you protect them?

- ✔ Have all employees, contractors, consultants, advisors, and suppliers sign a confidentiality agreement.

- ✔ Restrict access to areas of your office or plant.

- ✔ Mark documents with a confidential legend.

- ✔ Limit circulation of confidential documents.

- ✔ Lock away sensitive material.

- ✔ Include warnings and directives in your employee manual.

Acronyms to Know

ARIPO	Western Africa Patent Office
EAPO	Eurasian Patent Office
EFS	Electronic Patent Filing System
EPO	European Patent Office
EU	European Union
IP	Intellectual property
MPEP	*Manual of Patent Examining Procedure*
OA	Office action (by a patent or trademark examiner)
OAIP	Southeastern African Patent Office
OHIM	European Trademark Office
OWA	Original work of authorship (protected by copyright)
PCT	Patent Cooperation Treaty
PVPA	Plant Variety Protection Act
PVPO	Plant Variety Protection Office
TMEP	*Trademark Manual of Examining Procedure*
UPOV	Convention for the Protection of New Varieties of Plants
USC	United States Codes
USPTO	United States Patent and Trademark Office
TEAS	Trademark Electronic Application System
WIPO	World Industrial Property Organization
WMFH	Work made for hire

Copyright © 2004 H. Charmasson
All rights reserved.

Item 2551-4.

For more information about Wiley Publishing, call 1-800-762-2974.

For Dummies: Bestselling Book Series for Beginners

Patents, Copyrights
& Trademarks

FOR

DUMMIES®

Patents, Copyrights & Trademarks

FOR DUMMIES®

by Henri Charmasson

WILEY

Wiley Publishing, Inc.

Patents, Copyrights & Trademarks For Dummies®
Published by
Wiley Publishing, Inc.
111 River St.
Hoboken, NJ 07030-5774
www.wiley.com

About the Author

Henri Charmasson is an attorney who specializes in intellectual property cases, and a product-branding consultant to major corporations. He's also an entrepreneur and inventor with his name on a dozen patents. In a distant life, he was an electrical engineer who designed aerospace and computer hardware.

Henri has authored several books and articles on patent, copyright, and trademark topics, including an authoritative treatise about the art of naming companies and branding products.

Born and raised under the sunny skies of what he refers to as "French-occupied" Provence, Henri fled his native land for two reasons: first, to catch the California boom of the early '60s; second, to escape De Gaulle's arrogance (not necessarily in that order).

Dedication

To Lisette, Luc, Keith, Brielle, Marcel, Mathieu, and Danielle.

Author's Acknowledgments

A million thanks to Maxine Levaren who skillfully translated my pedantic legalese prose into plain English.

Publisher's Acknowledgments

We're proud of this book; please send us your comments through our Dummies online registration form located at www.dummies.com/register/.

Some of the people who helped bring this book to market include the following:

Acquisitions, Editorial, and Media Development

Project Editor: Mike Baker

Acquisitions Editor: Tracy Boggier

Copy Editor: Laura Peterson

Assistant Editor: Holly Gastineau-Grimes

Technical Editor: John Murphey

Senior Permissions Editor: Carmen Krikorian

Editorial Manager: Jennifer Ehrlich

Editorial Assistant: Elizabeth Rea

Cover Photos: © Getty Images

Cartoons: Rich Tennant, www.the5thwave.com

Production

Project Coordinator: Maridee Ennis

Layout and Graphics: Andrea Dahl, Michael Kruzil, Heather Ryan, Jacque Schneider, Julie Trippetti, Melanie Wolven

Proofreaders: Carl William Pierce, Kathy Simpson, TECHBOOKS Production Services

Indexer: TECHBOOKS Production Services

Special Help: Jennifer Bingham, E. Neil Johnson, Laura K. Miller

---

Publishing and Editorial for Consumer Dummies

Diane Graves Steele, Vice President and Publisher, Consumer Dummies

Joyce Pepple, Acquisitions Director, Consumer Dummies

Kristin A. Cocks, Product Development Director, Consumer Dummies

Michael Spring, Vice President and Publisher, Travel

Brice Gosnell, Associate Publisher, Travel

Kelly Regan, Editorial Director, Travel

Publishing for Technology Dummies

Andy Cummings, Vice President and Publisher, Dummies Technology/General User

Composition Services

Gerry Fahey, Vice President of Production Services

Debbie Stailey, Director of Composition Services

Contents at a Glance

Table of Contents

Introduction

● ●

*H*ave you always thought you might be the next Thomas Edison or maybe another Danielle Steele? Has your company recently developed a bold new corporate logo or eye-catching trademark? Perhaps you're think-ing of a new concept in software, one that can revolutionize the entire manu-facturing process. Or maybe you've just dreamed up the latest in "latest things" — something to rival the zippy little scooters flying around your neighborhood.

If so, you've come to the right place because having the great idea, creating the magnificent work of art, or coming up with the next fad is only the first step to cashing in on your creativity and hard work. Next up is protecting your intellectual property.

But, obviously, you know that. You've been enticed to pick up this book (and buy it, I hope) by those three not-so-little words: patents, copyrights, and trademarks. I'm guessing you want to find out more about these matters. Well, you're about to find out everything you need to know (but were afraid to even think about). You're entering the exciting world of intellectual prop-erty rights. Well, maybe the term *exciting* is pushing the envelope a bit, but give me a break, I am an IP attorney after all.

Welcome to IP Avenue! I'll try to make your visit as pleasant and enlightening as I can.

About This Book

The book you now hold in your hands explains, in layman's terms, the basic nature, function, and application of intellectual property (IP) rights, including how you can acquire those rights, wield them effectively against your com-petitors, or exploit them lucratively through licensing agreements and other rewarding schemes.

To make this book effective for anyone interested in intellectual property, each of the main types of IP protection — patents, copyrights, and trademarks — is covered in its own complete part.

After checking out the information presented in these parts, you'll have a solid grasp of the processes involved in acquiring, registering, maintaining, and protecting the intellectual property rights due you and/or your company. You'll be able to make informed decisions and speak confidently with the IP professionals you meet along the way. And you'll have the tools and knowledge to take care of much of the work involved in the various research and registration processes.

However, this book is no substitute for legal advice from a specialized professional. When you deal with intellectual property and IP rights, you face many complex legal issues. Remember that there's only one definite answer to any legal question. "It depends." So make sure that you have a competent professional advisor to guide you through the legal muck.

Conventions Used in This Book

I use the following conventions throughout the text to make things consistent and easy to understand.

- ✔ New terms appear in *italic* and are closely followed by an easy-to-understand definition.

- ✔ **Bold** highlights the action parts of the numbered steps.

- ✔ Actual trademarks and servicemarks will appear in all caps when they're used as such, in keeping with legal usage.

- ✔ Sidebars, which are text enclosed in a shaded gray box, contain information that's interesting to know but not necessarily critical to your understanding of the chapter or section topic.

- ✔ I regularly use the abbreviation IP to refer to intellectual property. It's one of those IP lawyer things I just can't shake.

- ✔ Throughout the book, I provide *estimates* of fees you may run into in your quest to sew up your intellectual property. Many U.S. Patent and Trademark Office fees are changed at least once a year (usually in October). Some changes can be substantial. The fee estimates here are based on the most recent published fee schedule at the time of this writing. Failure to pay the full applicable fee can result in a missed deadline and lapse of your application, patent, or trademark registration. Always check the current fee schedule on the USPTO Website before sending a payment.

- ✔ When I use the term *you*, I am, of course, referring to you the reader. But for those tasks, jobs, and other assorted legal hoops where I advise you to consult an IP professional — and there are many of them — *you* often refers to both you and the professional.

Foolish Assumptions

In order to channel the sea of IP information into a single book that's helpful to you, I make a few assumptions about you, the reader. See whether one or more of these shoes fit:

- ✔ You have a penchant for entrepreneurial adventure.

- ✔ You're running a business. Even the smallest commercial enterprise, such as an outdoor coffee cart, can benefit by making intelligent use of IP — creating an inspiring business name, for example.

- ✔ You're a budding or accomplished sculptor, painter, playwright, choreographer, musician, or songwriter, or you're involved in some other type of artistic activity.

- ✔ You're a writer, publisher, or computer programmer, or you're in another profession that takes advantage of the products of your creative mind.

- ✔ You're a scientist, engineer, or an inventor.

- ✔ You were born on a day ending in the letter *y*.

- ✔ You're a college student who's considering a career in the field of IP law.

- ✔ You're a business lawyer, an executive, or are in middle management and wish to understand some aspects of IP rights.

If I've hit the mark with any of the previous descriptions, this book is for you.

How This Book Is Organized

Patents, Copyrights & Trademarks For Dummies is organized so that you can easily access the information that you need. I've organized the material in six parts, each with several chapters related to a common theme. I now give you a preview of coming attractions with a brief statement about each section. Projector, please.

Part 1: Covering Your Assets: Intellectual Property Basics

Part I talks about intellectual property and briefly describes how patents, copyrights, trademarks, trade secrets, and other IP tools protect your IP assets. I also include the basics of dealing with IP professionals, such as agents, attorneys, and examiners.

Part II: If You Build It, They Will Come: Patenting Your Product

Part II deals with perhaps the most complex type of IP protection — the patent. Here, I explore what types of inventions qualify for a patent and whether you should patent your invention based on costs and other considerations.

I show you how to better your odds of getting your patent by doing a search to see whether your invention is really original and useful. I then explain, in detail, how to go about getting that patent — getting professional help, preparing your patent application, following up on your paperwork, and dealing with the patent examiner.

Throughout Part II, I also show you how to protect your invention during that perilous period when your application is active (and somewhat public) but not yet protected by a patent. All that for the price of admission!

Part III: Knowing Your Copyrights

Part III talks about the wide variety of creative works, from symphonies to software, that can be protected with a copyright. And I give you some good news and bad news. The good news is that you may already have exclusive rights to some of your works; you just need to make sure to keep them. The bad news is that if you created something original while employed by someone else, they may have exclusive rights. But I help you maneuver that maze here in Part III.

Part IV: Making Your Mark: Protecting Your Commercial Identity

Part IV gives you the lowdown on commercial identifiers — basically, the process of putting an exclusive brand on your goods and services. I define the various types of identifiers (such as trademarks and servicemarks), show what makes a good mark (and what should be avoided), and talk about how a good commercial name can give you a leg up on the competition. I also show you how to search to make sure your mark is unique and how to register and use your trademark or servicemark.

Part V: Exploiting and Enforcing Your IP Rights

Part V gets into what you can do after you've acquired your U.S. patent, copyright, or trademark. I tell you how to protect your IP overseas, how to employ your IP to the greatest possible advantage to make some money, and how (and when) to go after those who infringe on your rights — the bad guys.

Part VI: The Part of Tens

The icing on your IP cake, this section contains some valuable information that you absolutely need in convenient top-ten packaging. What kind of valuable info, you ask? Good question. Here's a good answer: Things not to do in a patent application, frequently asked copyright questions, blunders to avoid when selecting a business name, and some great IP resources.

Icons Used in This Book

The bull's eye marks tips and tricks that you can put to use to make your life easier while you're protecting and profiting by your IP.

This icon highlights something you need to keep in mind while working on your patent, copyright, or trademark.

The Warning icon alerts you to common mistakes that can trip you up and to other factors that may prove hazardous to your market image or your financial or legal health.

This icon indicates projects or examples from real-life IP cases. At times, the names have been changed to protect the innocent — and infamous.

Throughout this book, I provide you with examples of actual text — paragraphs and passages — that you can use in legal documents. I flag this information with the Legal icon.

This icon tells you that the info is a bit more complex than most of the fine and fascinating points I raise throughout the book. Although this information is still interesting, you can skip it if you want and not miss out on any need-to-know advice.

Where to Go from Here

One good thing (of the many good things) about a *For Dummies* book is that you don't need to read it from beginning to end to access the information you need. This book is designed to let you get in and get out, only focusing on the information you need. Simply turn to the part, chapter, or section that contains the info you want to know. Only interested in creating a catchy new product name? Turn to Chapter 15. Want the scoop on copyrights? Turn to Part III. It's easy — you won't need a compass to get around. Of course, you can read the entire book (and truthfully, I'd be thrilled if you did).

I do suggest that you read Chapter 1, which provides an overview of the main IP components, if you have questions about which IP tool can best meet your needs. After that, let the index at the back and table of contents at the front of the book be your guide. And then just follow the signs, which in this case are headings and those handy little icons.

Part I
Covering Your Assets: Intellectual Property Basics

The 5th Wave   By Rich Tennant

"I still like his knives the best."

In this part . . .

If you're currently reading this page, you probably have an invention, a creative work, a trademark, or some other piece of intellectual property that you want to guard against all the copycats out there. Well, you've come to the right place. In this part, I give you an overview of intellectual property (IP) in all its glory and tell you why protecting these assets is important. I map out each IP instrument — patents, copyrights, and commercial identifiers — showing how they each protect a different type of IP asset. I also talk about ways to treat your IP as a trade secret, by restricting access to information, using confidentiality agreements, and taking advantage of other tools at your disposal. And I top things off with info on hiring an IP professional — when, why, and how — working effectively with an attorney or agent, and estimating how much the whole process can set you back.

Chapter 1

Examining the Tools in Your IP Box

*W*elcome to the world of intellectual property (IP). If you've created, invented, or named something that you're selling, you already have intellectual property. And that property could be quite valuable. What if you'd invented the Segway scooter or written the first *For Dummies* book? Wouldn't you like to be able to cash in on it? Exploiting your IP assets for your own financial gain and, at the same time, pursuing those bent on infringing your precious but fragile rights to those assets (IP rights) is what this chapter and, in general, this book are all about.

Buying into Intellectual Property

What is intellectual property? Although I've encountered many true and effective definitions, including information with a commercial value, proprietary product of the mind, and things protected by patents, copyrights, and trademarks, none of them is quite complete. Here's the one I like best:

Intellectual property is intangible creations of the mind that can be legally protected. Because IP has no physical form, I can give you a better idea of what it is by providing examples of what it isn't. Intellectual property is not

- ✔ The new and wondrous machine that you developed in your garage. It's the invention embodied in that machine.

- ✔ The marvelously efficient cholesterol-reducing pill you see advertised on TV, but the formula and the process used in manufacturing that pill.

- ✔ The portrait that an artist made of you, but the aesthetic expression of the artist's talent reflected by the painting.

- ✔ The riding mower you reluctantly start up every Saturday. It's the brand name that embodies the reputation of the product and its manufacturer.

Now, if you'd be so kind as to refer back to my scintillating IP definition, I want to expand on it. Intellectual property is made up of two components:

- ✔ **Assets:** IP assets are intangible creations, such as the invention, the formula and process, the expression of an artist's talents as reflected in a painting, and the brand name.

- ✔ **Rights:** IP rights are the legal protections that secure each IP asset against its unauthorized use by others. One or more of the following legal protections can be used to secure IP rights:

  - **Patents:** Obtaining a patent protects the invention from outright thievery.

  - **Trade secrets:** Keeping a formula or manufacturing process confidential safeguards it against imitators.

  - **Copyright:** Holding a copyright shields artistic expression against copying by others.

  - **Trademark:** Adopting a trademark as a brand name keeps it and its market reputation yours and yours alone.

Some IP rights — copyrights and trademark rights, in particular — attach themselves automatically upon the creation or use of the IP assets without you ever having to lift a finger or spend a cent. Obtaining other IP rights — patents, specifically — requires you to put up a pretty good fight and spend plenty of money.

What happens when you don't protect your IP rights? Sorry, Charlie, but an unprotected IP asset is up for grabs — anyone can copy it, steal it, or change it for the worse (possibly damaging your good reputation). The bottom line is that your unprotected IP will fatten the bad guy's bottom line.

A little IP history

Patents were invented (ha-ha) by a bunch of short-breeched fellows in powdered wigs, mostly lawyers, who met in Philadelphia in the 1780s. However, incorporating intellectual property (IP) into the laws of the United States was nothing close to a slam-dunk. Thomas Jefferson was viscerally opposed to all shades of monopolies, including patents. Ironically, our Jeffersonian Democracy was put in place in Philadelphia in the absence of the Sage of Monticello. At the time of the Constitutional Convention, Jefferson was ambassador to France, busily courting the Parisian ladies. It was Alexander Hamilton who deserves credit for including a patent and copyright clause in Article II of the U.S. Constitution.

But there's more to IP assets and rights than mere talk of patents, copyrights, and trademarks, and that's what this chapter is all about. You first must verify that you own that IP asset you want to protect, make sure that it's original, and know how to secure all the IP rights that can apply to it. And last but not least, you have to know how to get the professional advice that you need. Curtain, please.

Exploring the Patent Process

I may as well start with the most well-known (though not the most practical) form of IP protection — patents. A *patent* is a temporary legal right granted by the government as a reward for a unique invention, giving the inventor a way to keep others from stealing the fruits of his or her labor — the invention.

While I'm on a roll, how about another definition? Patent law defines an *invention* as a technological advancement that is useful, new, and isn't obvious to a person with ordinary skill in the field of technology. Inventions can take many forms, from a machine or device to a method or process, from a new composition to a new use of an old product, from a man-made organism to a new plant created with or without sexual fertilization (you know, the birds and the bees thing).

If you're wondering whether your latest and greatest invention actually fits the invention bill, check out Chapter 4, which details the types of patents and the inventions covered by each.

Obtaining a patent

You must file an elaborate application that completely describes your invention in order to get a patent from the United States Patent and Trademark Office (USPTO — I cover the nuts and bolts of this application in Chapter 7). The USPTO rigorously examines your application (see Chapter 8 and Chapter 9 for all the gory details). If you pass the test, you're granted permission to pay a hefty fee so those nice people at the USPTO can afford to print your patent and take a long, well-deserved summer vacation. After all, they think they earned it by making you sweat blood for the last two years. (Chapter 10 covers that info, minus the vacation itinerary.) Yes, that's the minimum amount of time it takes to get your application approved if, of course, the moon is right and the gods are with you.

Make no bones about it, the patent process is costly in terms of both time and money (and blood, sweat, and tears). So if you're thinking you may want to head down this road, you need to be sure that it's the best path for protecting your IP. (Check out Chapter 5, which provides you with other options and an exercise to help you decide whether a patent's the right choice.) The first stop in your journey will likely be to conduct a patent search before pouring a bunch of money into a doubtful application. (Chapter 6 provides a road map for that side trip.)

Putting a patent to good use

Emblazoned with fancy lettering and a big shining seal with blue ribbons, a framed patent makes an impressive conversation piece on your living room or office wall.

Oh yeah, you can also use it to threaten imitators with a lawsuit if they're using and abusing your invention. Basically, a patent is nothing more than a license to sue someone. If the copycat answers with an obscene gesture, you can mortgage everything you own down to your grandfather's dentures and file an infringement lawsuit. If the Force is with you, the litigation goes well for your side, and your adversary is flush with greenbacks, you'll make a bundle. Find out what else you can do with your patent in the section "Putting Your IP to Work at Home and Abroad," at the end of this chapter.

Yes, a patent has teeth, but those teeth come at great expense. So looking at your other IP rights is a good idea, too. You can also buy insurance policies that cover some of your litigation costs. I discuss that issue in detail in Chapter 20.

Copyrighting Your Creations

Although derived from the same constitutional mandate as patents, copyrights resemble them only superficially. A *copyright* is a temporary right giving a creative person exclusive control over the use of an original work of authorship.

Okay, one more definition: An *original work of authorship* (OWA) is a textual, graphic, plastic, musical, dramatic, audio, or visual creation that you created. A few examples of original works of authorship (for the complete scoop, turn to Chapter 11) are

- ✔ Any writing (including a computer program)
- ✔ A drawing, painting, or computer-generated image
- ✔ A sculpture
- ✔ An architectural design
- ✔ A song, a symphony, or an opera
- ✔ A play
- ✔ A video or audio production (including movies, video games, television or radio broadcasts, or recordings on cassette, CD, or DVC)

Even when the same thing was done before, you can obtain a copyright if your work wasn't copied from or influenced by the pre-existing work. For example, just think of how many books have recanted the life stories of the Kennedys. A copyright protects the form in which an idea or concept is expressed, not the idea or the concept itself.

Copyright basically doesn't extend to abstractions or to something technical or functional. For example, an idea for a new TV program isn't protected by copyright. The way the idea for the show is developed and played out is protected. The copyright on a cookbook prevents anyone from copying the way the various recipes are expressed in words or images, selected, and arranged. It doesn't prevent you from freely using the very same recipes and even incorporating them step by step into your own cookbook (because the steps are actually a technical process) as long as you don't express them in the same style, compile them in the same order, or arrange them in the same format. I go over this idea/expression distinction in great detail in Chapter 11.

Computing copyrights

The copyright law is always 10 or 20 years behind technology. In an attempt to catch up, Congress characterizes computer programs as copyright-protectable writings. This legislation gives programmers, and the entire software industry, an effective security tool. In a computer program, the choice of words or lines of computer code and their respective positions in an instruction represent the creative portion of the program and are critical to its operation. The fact that others cannot copy this specific language greatly expands the scope of copyright protection for software. I explain in Chapter 11 how the courts separate the unprotectable functional aspect of the program from the protected way its various components are expressed. Although patents also are available to protect innovative processes within a given computer program, the industry relies heavily on copyrights to protect its software.

Getting your hands on a copyright

Check this out: After you've created an original work of authorship (like the doodlings you used to decorate your geometry manual while Miss Squareroot attempted to explain the quadrature of the circle), all you need to do to get a copyright is relax and have a glass of chardonnay to my health. Or better yet, send me a check for this worthwhile advice.

Seriously, that's it! Copyright attaches automatically as soon as the work is shown in a perceptible and reproducible form without the need for any formality. That means that as soon as you've printed out your great American novel, it's already copyrighted. That's a big advantage over patents. If, however, you may want to sue someone for infringement, or worse yet, someone sues you, you need to prove that it's actually your original work. That's why you should make it official — apply for a registration of your copyright with the Copyright Office and submit a copy of your creation as proof of your authorship.

Going after the bad guys

You can use your copyright in much the same way you use a patent — to pressure and sue an infringer — except that copyright litigation tends to be much less expensive than patent disputes.

Claiming Your Identity: Trademarks and Other Commercial Handles

Trademarks are only one species within a class of IP assets called *commercial identifiers* that you use to distinguish your company, product, or services from others. The three basic types of commercial identifiers (which I cover in more detail in Chapter 14) are

- ✔ **Company identifiers:** A company is identified by its legal name (for example, General Motors Corporation) and often by the logotype that adorns its buildings and letterhead (General Motors or the familiar blue-and-white GM emblem).

- ✔ **Service identifiers:** The services that a company offers to the public — such as automotive-maintenance or fast-food restaurant services — usually are identified by a servicemark. It can be a word or phrase (Mr. Goodwrench, McDonald's), logotype (the arched *M* you see on a ubiquitous fast-food chain), or the shape and decoration of a building (the KFC brand of restaurant service outlets).

- ✔ **Product identifiers:** Trademarks (brand names) are the most familiar product identifiers and can also take the form of a single letter, or a mere design or symbol, such as the swoosh mark on a popular brand of athletic gear.

  Any fanciful and nonfunctional characteristic of a product or package can act as a product identifier — for example, the ribbed bottle of a large soft-drink company or the pink color of a glass-wool insulation material. These nonfunctional characteristics often are referred to as *configuration, design marks,* or *trade dress,* which, like trademarks, can be registered at the state and federal levels.

Commercial identifiers constitute the IP rights that I consider to be most neglected, misunderstood, and underestimated by entrepreneurs in their new industrial, commercial, educational, or scientific ventures. Watching as new businesses spend *lots* on money on chancy patent applications always puzzles me when they're obviously neglecting the wondrous marketing tools provided by good commercial identifiers.

Company image, product fame, or a reputation for providing quality service are critical aspects of a business that can be greatly enhanced by and benefit from the right choice and use of pleasant and motivating monikers, logos, and distinctive and attractive packaging. However, coming up with an identifier that's a hit with customers isn't easy, so I devote the whole of Chapter 15 to providing some insight in making such a selection.

Likewise, I detail all you need to know about the ins and outs of developing marks and names that the courts will protect, and explain how the degree of protection awarded to company identifiers and other commercial names depends mainly upon the distinctiveness of the name, all in Chapter 14.

A great name can be the most valuable asset of a company and deserves a lot of attention and appropriate protective measures, such as federal registration and proper usage. But a great commercial identifier won't do you any good if it duplicates an existing identifier, so before you begin the registration process, discussed in Chapter 17, you'll want to do a search to make sure no one else is using your brainchild (or something close). I explain trademark searches in Chapter 16.

Keeping It Quiet: Trade Secrets

Kiss and tell only on a need-to-know basis . . . keep it under your hat. The best way to keep a commercially advantageous piece of information like a manufacturing method or customer list away from your competitors is to take advantage of laws that protect *trade secrets,* a very important and inexpensive IP right. Don't let anyone in on a trade secret other than the people who necessarily need to know about it.

Not every type of commercially advantageous material can be safely and practically kept under lock and key. Whenever that happens to be the case, and you can't keep some information as a trade secret, you need to rely on other types of IP rights — patents, copyrights, or trademarks — for protection.

In Chapter 2, I explain how you can implement a trade-secret strategy and how the law provides for enforcement of trade secrets in case of negligent or intentional disclosures. I also discuss the trade-offs between patents and a trade-secret policy.

Putting It in Writing: Looking at Contractual IP Rights

A category of legal contracts, explained in Chapter 19, are specifically intended to deal with IP rights. They provide contractual IP rights to all parties. For instance, a company may acquire the contractual right to manufacture a patented product while the inventor obtains rights to a percentage of the sales proceeds called *royalties*. Even if you are not an inventor or computer programmer, you may acquire contractual rights to inventions or software that you can exploit in place of or in addition to their creators.

Similarly, after you acquire your patent, copyright, or commercial identifier, you can profitably sell or lease it to others. You can transfer your IP rights through an *assignment* (the outright purchase or sale of the IP right) or a *license* (an agreement allowing another individual or business to use your IP rights). For example, if you want to publish a book, you must either buy the copyright from the author using an assignment or obtain the author's permission to publish the work under a license.

When you hire employees or commission independent contractors to do a job for you, you can enter into written and signed agreements stating that any technological advancement or original work of authorship that results from their employment or commission belongs to you. See Chapter 12 for information on assigning and licensing copyrights and Chapter 14 for information about commercial identifiers.

The contract should always be in writing and be signed by all parties to the agreement.

You can also acquire contractual rights to intellectual property by buying a *franchise* for a specific type of business — fast-food and dry-cleaning franchises are among the more common ones. In Chapter 19, I explain how a franchise constitutes a classic and convenient way of exploiting a bundle of IP assets and related IP rights.

Putting Your IP to Work at Home and Abroad

You can use IP assets and rights in many ways. Developing and protecting your intellectual property assets and rights can give you an edge over the competition by discouraging unscrupulous competitors, developing new revenue sources, and increasing the value of your company. (I talk about each of these aspects in detail in Chapter 2.)

But because IP rights are rare exceptions to antimonopoly and antitrust laws and regulations, their use is strictly limited. ***Remember:*** When you misuse your teddy bear to beat your little sister, your mom confiscates the bear. The rules haven't changed with regard to IP rights. The usual penalty for an abusive misuse of an IP right is forfeiture.

When you take advantage of your IP assets within the confines of your own company, basically exploiting your own invention, you face little risk of running afoul of the law. However, when you're forced to use your IP rights against others outside of your company who infringe upon them, you need to be more careful. Trust your IP litigation attorney to know how to stay within the bounds of the law. Check out Chapter 3 to find out how to select and work with an IP professional. IP specialists, like any other attorneys, are bound by strict confidentiality obligations and are subject to discipline and loss of their license to practice if they breach these obligations. Therefore, you can reveal your most sensitive knowledge or information to your attorney. There's no need to make her sign a confidentiality or non-disclosure agreement because she's already bound by law to complete discretion.

You'll be happy to know that almost all industrialized countries have IP laws that are roughly parallel to the ones in the United States. Because acquiring a copyright doesn't require any application or other formality, you can readily defend and exploit your copyright all across the planet, at little cost.

By contrast, patents and trademarks require local applications and examinations in almost every foreign land, which I detail in Chapter 18. Costs tend to be even higher abroad than they are in the United States, and proceedings can drag on for years. A foreign patent program is not for the fainthearted and requires substantial financial resources.

Chapter 2

Protecting Your Intellectual Property

. . . .

In This Chapter

▶ Taking an inventory of your IP assets

▶ Developing new IP

▶ Planning an appropriate IP protection strategy

. . . .

*I*n any serious endeavor, logic and pragmatism pay off. That's what I learned in business school. You can be logical by following a well-defined plan. You need to be pragmatic by using your resources efficiently and remaining within budget. Although you may not yet be involved in any kind of business activity, the minute you start dealing with intellectual property (IP), you're talking about assets that can be financially valuable. Therefore, developing an IP acquisition and protection strategy is a must for a business venture of any size. Briefly, your IP strategy should include evaluating your IP assets, deciding what type of IP rights would best protect them, doing a search to make sure that they can be protected, and going for every form of IP protection available to you.

Examining Your Motives

When you implement an IP program, getting carried away and spending beyond your needs and means are easy mistakes to make. One of the biggest errors is going after a patent when a copyright, good commercial identifier, or trade-secret policy would better serve your needs at a cheaper cost. If you're motivated by pride, and your goal is displaying a patent on the wall behind your desk, you need to find an easier ticket for your ego trip.

I know of only three good reasons for developing and protecting an IP asset:

✔ Gaining an edge over your competitors

✔ Creating a revenue source

✔ Enhancing the value of your business

IP rights can be aptly compared with an interest in real property. You can keep others off of your lawn, you can sell, lease, or otherwise share a piece of land with others, and you can count your little garden plot as an asset. Likewise, someone who buys real property simply to look at the deed or brag about it to others isn't the shrewdest real estate mogul.

Don't hesitate when assessing whether you should be motivated by pride or profit in implementing an IP protection program. Profit wins, hands-down!

Keeping your competitors at bay

Almost every IP right gives you a way of excluding others from doing something that interferes with or competes against a vital part of your business. When you can tolerate competition and still maintain a reasonable income, you may forget about IP protection and spend your resources on marketing or some other more productive and lucrative activity.

However, I can't conceive of a business that wouldn't benefit from acquiring at least some IP rights. At a minimum, your business can capitalize on the protection afforded by a trade-secret program, which could prevent, or at least deter, former associates or employees from using any of your manufacturing or marketing methods or stealing your customer list. At most, acquiring a patent, copyright, and/or trademark can give you a huge competitive advantage on the market and considerable legal clout to stifle copycats.

Developing a new revenue source

After you acquire IP rights, you can generate income with them by licensing someone to manufacture your product or by leasing your commercial identifier to another organization to market products under your brand name. You can also franchise other folks to manufacture or sell your goods and services under your guidelines. Under any of these arrangements, you make money any time someone makes, sells, or uses your goods or services.

Finding manufacturing ventures that close down after securing solid protection for a product or technology and then license the IP rights to others isn't unusual. They may even license those rights to former competitors.

Licensing IP rights is like renting out a piece of real estate. You maintain title to the property (the IP assets and IP rights) while collecting rent on a periodical basis in the form of royalties. One typical situation is when a young entrepreneur launches a new line of sporting or casual garments, enhances his product line with an attractive brand name and logo, and then licenses the brand to other clothing manufacturers as soon as the brand is established. The entrepreneur then gets out of the business except, of course, for opening envelopes containing the quarterly royalty checks and laughing all the way to the bank. As you can see, when they're planned and marketed well, IP rights can be an essential part of your product line.

If you don't want to get out of the business completely, you can maintain the right to continue manufacturing your product by granting only nonexclusive licenses to one or more manufacturers. However, the royalty rate is lower than for an exclusive license. I cover this approach in Chapter 19.

Adding value to your business

When the time comes to sell your business, you can get more for it if your

- ✔ Products are protected by patents.
- ✔ Proprietary computer programs are covered by copyrights.
- ✔ Brand names are unique, motivating, and not copyable by competitors.
- ✔ Goodwill is transferable to the buyer under your business name.

But, you don't have to sell your business merely to capitalize on its IP-enhanced value. If you need to raise more capital or borrow money, your IP can provide a nice boost to your net worth, making your stock more attractive to investors and offering added collateral security for the lender to consider.

Implementing an IP Program

Developing an IP acquisition and protection strategy is a must for business ventures of all sizes. Although such a strategy probably is more elaborate for a major corporation than for a small business, the recommendations that I make in the sections that follow apply to all commercial and professional enterprises, regardless of size. These components, taking stock of your IP assets and mapping out a strategy for protecting those assets, are the essential part of an effective IP acquisition and protection program. (By *acquisition*, I mean developing and safeguarding your own IP assets and IP rights and only occasionally buying some of these rights from someone else.)

Business people often are unaware that they may actually be using IP assets already developed or created by themselves, their employees, associates, or contractors, including inventions and other technological advances, computer programs, and other original works of authorship. Because these assets go unrecognized (and unprotected), they often remain in the hands of their developers and creators or fall into the public domain. Nothing is more frustrating than discovering that an asset you thought you owned belongs to a former employee or contributor who becomes your toughest competitor.

However, with the proper preventative measures packaged as a well-planned IP program, you can keep these assets. The first step in such a program is preparing proper written agreements to be routinely signed by your employees, associates, and contractors. The second step is defining and applying a trade-secret protocol. Finally, you must look at each IP asset and protect it by going for every applicable IP right available.

Taking stock of your IP assets

Begin implementing an IP protection program by taking an inventory of the intellectual property you already have. Begin with the following steps:

1. **Identify all the innovations in products or manufacturing methods that you and your associates or employees developed during the last couple of years — older technology has already fallen in the public domain.**

   This gives you a list of all your assets that may benefit by patent or trade-secret protection.

2. **Gather all the software, instructional manuals, or promotional literature developed or published under your direction or authority for the last five or six years — which is the grace period you have to go after copycats.**

   These items are good candidates for copyrights.

3. **Look at all your commercial names and logos, including business identities and product brands.**

   This itemizes all your assets that should be protected by a registered mark.

After you gather this information, you have at your fingertips an inventory of the IP assets that you can protect with a variety of IP rights.

But, before investing in protecting what you already have or acquiring more IP assets, you need to make sure that your assets are the best they can be. You can always improve inventions and processes, and you can often boost the marketing and legal strengths of commercial names with some adjustments and selective use (see the "Preserving company identity and brand names" section, later in this chapter). Likewise, before investing your hard-earned cash in acquiring IP asset protection, make sure your widgets, assembly lines, and logos are in the best shape possible. Copyrightable material — such as manuals, books, graphics, and computer programs — are the exception here. Copyrights attach as soon as the work is put on paper (or saved to disk). Nevertheless, make sure you revise and update these documents to include any improvements you've made to the assets they represent.

Identifying trade secrets

After taking stock of your IP assets, you need to define and apply a trade-secret protocol. Although you may think that you don't have any trade secrets because you and your staff are always open, candid, trusting, and trustworthy, you may have information that isn't readily available to the public that gives your company a competitive edge. Good for you!

Okay, so I'm not talking about any cloak-and-dagger scenario or about those skeletons in your file cabinets, but take, for example, your customer list: How would you feel if one of your former associates, or perhaps the employee who maintained that list, jumped ship, hooked up with your closest competitor, and started using that list to solicit your largest customers? Other examples might include someone revealing the identity of your supplier of a hard-to-find component, the parameters of a tricky manufacturing process, the way your financial resources are allocated, or the details of your next marketing campaign. Shall I continue? (See the "Protecting technological advances" section, later in this chapter, for more tips about determining whether you need to take the trade-secret route or go with a patent or rely on copyrights.)

You can maintain and enforce the confidentiality of this type of information only by establishing a *trade-secret protection policy.* Such a policy may involve:

- ✔ Having all members of your staff, your contractors, outside consultants and advisors, your critical suppliers, or anyone else who may be exposed to any sensitive information sign a confidentiality agreement.

    You may even be wise to add some customers and casual visitors to the list of folks signing a confidentiality agreement.

- ✔ Restricting access to certain areas of your place of business.

- ✔ Marking some documents with a confidential legend.

- ✔ Limiting the circulation of confidential documents.

- ✔ Locking away sensitive material.

- ✔ Including appropriate warnings and directives in your employee manual.

Company or contractor: Who owns the copyright?

A common and distressing scenario occurs when a freelance computer programmer (not an employee, but an independent contractor) contributes a substantial and critical piece of software without a proper contractual arrangement. The company commissioning the programmer may then be unable to make lucrative use of the software because the programmer refuses to cooperate. Worse yet, the company may find itself on the receiving end of an infringement complaint filed by the programmer if it unknowingly or unwisely does something restricted by the programmer's copyright.

I can imagine you scratching your head, realizing that you've stumbled into one of these legal nightmares. However, one way you can prevent such a disastrous situation is using a well-drafted agreement signed by anyone you ask to contribute any type of IP component to your projects. In Chapter 12, I give you detailed information about using this type of agreement in connection with copyrights.

You don't necessarily need to adopt *all* these measures, but you do need to exercise reasonable precautions. You need to ensure that any leak that may occur can only be the result of gross negligence or breach of duty for which you can get some legal remedy. No breach of duty can occur when your rules aren't clearly set and understood.

Courts will enforce reasonably drafted and implemented trade-secret protection policies by issuing restraining orders or injunctions against anyone breaching policy and against the beneficiaries of the indiscretion. Compensatory damages can also be awarded.

There is no application, registration, or other type of governmental involvement in devising a trade-secret policy no long wait; no expensive filing fee; just some advance planning, discipline, and a bit of legal work by your IP attorney to draft a few confidentiality agreements.

Managing third-party contributions

A common business mistake is thinking you automatically have the rights to property you obtain through the labors of others, including your employees. Acquiring an asset and obtaining the IP right that attaches to it are two different things. You must take some precautions and legal steps to get all the rights to what you acquire from others.

The law distinguishes between objects that are the embodiment of their underlying IP asset and the IP rights protecting that asset.

For example, if you hire a painter or a photographer to produce a portrait of you, and you pay for those professional services and for copies of the artwork, you may expect to acquire all rights to the use of those materials. You may feel free to make copies, distribute those copies to your fans, or draw a mustache and devil horns on some of them. You'd be dead wrong. Those acts are restricted by the copyright that automatically attached to the artwork the minute it was put in a perceptible or reproducible form, in this case, a canvas or photographic film. Because you didn't specifically buy the copyright, in most cases, the artist or photographer retains control over how that material can be used, including, in some cases, making any alterations.

I tell you much more about copyrights in Part III. For now, I just want to let you know that what you think you're paying for isn't always what you get.

If you're the contributing third party, you need to insist upon retaining some rights to use the material that you contributed; otherwise, you may paint yourself into a corner. One day, you may need to incorporate part of that material into another project, only to find that you no longer have the rights to what you created because all aspects of your art have been assigned to your former customers. Under those circumstances, you have to adopt a new style and develop a new stock of frequently needed material.

Covering copyrighted creations

Even though all original works of authorship are automatically copyrighted, registering them is important if you want to profit from them and also be able to take infringers to court. To do that, periodically gather and evaluate all textual, graphical, and audio-visual material, including technical and promotional works, photographs, computer programs, and microchip masks. You then need to register your copyright claims in the U.S. Copyright Office (see Chapter 13 for all your registration needs). You also need to establish a procedure for periodically updating your applications for registration.

Calling in the big ©-police

Here's an eloquent demonstration of the effectiveness of a well-planned IP protection policy. I know of an advertising agency whose art department produces sketches that are used as part of a promotional campaign aimed at potential customers. Every few weeks, they collect and bind copies of all their artwork and then duly deposit and register them as unpublished works.

One of the agency's competitors got hold of one of the proposals, underbid the agency, and copied the artwork onto a massive billboard. Only a few days later, the agency's attorney, armed with a copy of the copyright registration and without having to go to court, convinced the customer to take that billboard down and reclaimed the advertising contract for his client.

Protecting technological advances

As a means of promoting inventiveness and other forms of technological breakthrough, a company needs to ensure that all valuable contributions are protected and encouraged by:

- ✔ Implementing a recordkeeping system to document all new developments
- ✔ Devising a reward program for its creative employees

Preparing complete written disclosure of potential inventions and submitting them to a patent attorney or agent is important. The attorney or agent helps you determine on a case-by-case basis whether you need to file a patent application or treat the breakthrough as a trade secret. This decision is extremely critical in further helping you achieve your desired scope of protection within the constraints of your company's budget.

In general, whenever you know that your inventions can't be readily reverse-engineered — your competitors can't figure out what's going on by breaking it down or analyzing it — you can keep the inventions confidential and thus protected by a tight trade-secret policy. Chemical compositions are prime candidates for this type of treatment. Someone may be able to detect every chemical element in a new plastic material or eyedrop medicine, but is unlikely to determine the amount of each element or the mixing process with any level of practical precision. In many cases, keeping the formulae, dosage, and mixing parameters as a trade secret insures protection against imitators.

The main advantages of treating an invention as a trade secret are:

- ✔ The invention need not be disclosed to the public in a patent application.
- ✔ The life of a trade secret is not limited to the 20 years normally associated with a patent.
- ✔ The costs for preserving a trade secret are relatively insignificant compared to the amounts involved in obtaining and maintaining a patent.

But, with trade secrets, you unfortunately run a substantial risk that another party may independently discover the same thing and even secure a patent for it. When that happens within one or two years of your original discovery, the patent owner may be able to exclude you from the market.

Inventions that are practiced by way of a computer program can get a certain degree of protection under the program copyright (see Chapter 11), either by itself or in combination with a trade secret. In Chapter 13, I show how to safeguard a trade secret when you register your copyright.

Preserving company identity and brand names

Commercial names, specifically a company's business name and logo and more significantly its brand names, determine how a company is perceived in the marketplace. In fact, these commercial names are vehicles upon which all a company's marketing programs ride.

Few brand names that you see every day are outstanding. In fact, many are downright mediocre. At worst, some brand names are counterproductive because they impede rather than bolster the promotion of the goods and services they identify. How are you faring? Do you have gems in your commercial-name jewel box or merely lumps of coal in your stocking? You'd better find out and act accordingly.

If budgetary constraints limit your ability to protect your product and polish your commercial image, I recommend favoring the latter. Establishing a good brand-name program is cheaper than obtaining patent protection, and you get much more bang for your buck. (Chapters 14 and 15 have the scoop on creating effective commercial identifiers and avoiding bad ones.)

Screening your commercial names

Be methodical in assessing your commercial names by:

- Taking a hard look at all your current commercial names and logotypes
- Rating their promotional value according to the criteria defined in Chapter 15
- Phasing out the ones that don't make the grade and replacing them with more judiciously selected monikers

Registering commercial names

Registering your commercial names on the federal register and, for extra protection, on some state registers (described in Chapter 17) greatly enhances their legal clout when you have to weed out copycats. Consider registering

- All your brand names as trademarks
- Your business identities as servicemarks
- The copyrights of all logotype graphic components in the Copyright Office as visual art

Protecting distinctive product and package configurations

Don't overlook the fact that an attractive and nonfunctional product shape or ornamentation, such as the unique shape of a bar of soap or a whimsical design on the side of an athletic shoe, can be recognized as source identifiers and registered as a trademark, just like a brand name. For example, the fanciful shape of a perfume vial and the bright stripes across a pesticide package are distinctive packaging that can be registered as trademarks.

Even the recognizable sound of a motorcycle exhaust, the unique smell of a detergent, and the springy feel of a textile product can influence a buyer and so can be deemed registrable, nonvisual marks.

If you don't have these kinds of unique identifiers for your product line, put your designer to the task of creating them. The more unique and distinctive you make your product, the easier it becomes for you to prevent your competitors from copying it.

Developing contractual procedures

Contractual engagements with your associates, employees, contractors, advisors, and eventually visitors, which are essential for implementing your IP protection strategy, always need to be secured in writing. You need to consider contractual agreements with:

✔ Potential inventors and others who contribute to your technological assets. Agreements with these people ensure your ownership of their work products.

✔ Computer programmers, writers, artists, photographers, music writers, producers of audio-visual works and sound recordings, microcircuit mask designers, choreographers, architects, and others who contribute copyrightable works to your business. These kinds of agreements:

  • Make you or your company the legal author and copyright owner when contributors' creations come to life.

  • Obligate these contributors to transfer any copyright they acquire to you or your company.

✔ All associates, employees, representatives, and some of your contractors, suppliers, visitors, and customers who guarantee the confidentiality of your trade secrets.

For these agreements to be effective, a competent IP attorney must draft them. Don't rely on a personal-injury or criminal-law practitioner or even a business attorney because they may not know the latest developments in IP law. These well-meaning but often unqualified lawyers routinely rely on forms plucked from outdated manuals or may even use the wrong form for the job altogether.

An IP specialist can save you money and keep you out of trouble when drafting agreements to implement IP programs by:

- Combining necessary contractual agreements into a single document
- Ensuring that the contractual agreements extend to employees and agents of the parties signing them
- Forbidding personal use of confidential material by the parties and other similar acts
- Making sure that the agreement conforms to local rules and regulations
- Charging a fair fee for actual legal work and not merely for clerical tasks

Having the president of a company with which you have a contract agreement sign a confidentiality agreement in the name of her company doesn't necessarily obligate her personally. She potentially can leave the next day and start a competing business using your confidential material. But, your well-versed IP attorney knows just how to draft the agreement to avoid this and other problems.

Chapter 3

Dealing with Professionals and Picking Up the Tab

In This Chapter

▶ Knowing when you need an accredited intellectual property professional

▶ Finding and selecting a professional at home and abroad

▶ Keeping an eye on the bottom line

*1*f you're like most people, the idea of hiring a professional, especially one who has an Esq. tagged after her or his name, can send cold shivers down your spine, put goose bumps on your arms, and set your heart palpitating like that loose muffler on your grandfather's Edsel. (The thought even starts me quivering — and I'm an attorney.)

Yes, attorneys are expensive, probably more so than you think, especially if they specialize in intellectual property (IP) cases. To get an idea of the total costs, just take a peek at the section "Assessing the costs," later in this chapter. But hang on — I show you ways to mitigate the high cost of professional services. First, you have to accept that you'll need a professional's services sooner or later and make the best of an unsavory but highly beneficial reality. What counts is that you know what kind of help you need and how to get it.

Getting the Help That You Need

Let's face it, you need professional help, and no, I'm not questioning your mental fitness. You need professional help when diving into IP waters because acquiring and using IP rights to protect and exploit IP assets are essentially legal procedures. And as you know, laws are characterized by nuances, exceptions, and loopholes. IP laws are no exception. Over the last 20 years, the need to harmonize U.S. intellectual property procedures with those of other industrialized countries and the huge volume of IP applications and filings have brought many changes in IP law. These changes require increasingly complex and expensive procedures. The days when a garage inventor could navigate a patent application through the United States Patent and Trademark Office (USPTO) with the help of a how-to manual are over.

Law students spend years studying this stuff, bringing a level of expertise to the table that most people can't easily duplicate. By steering you clear of legal pitfalls, the IP professional saves you the time, grief, aggravation, and expense of having to refile a defective application or other paperwork. More importantly, a professional makes sure that you don't miss any critical deadlines and lose the opportunity to acquire the IP protection you need.

This book, helpful as it is, is no substitute for engaging the services of a competent IP specialist.

Identifying the right person for the job

Because IP is such a vast and complex field, many professionals limit their practice to narrow specialties, such as patent applications, IP litigation, or entertainment copyright cases. It's up to you to retain the professional most qualified to handle your case.

Registered patent attorney and agents

Registered patent attorneys and agents are accredited by the USPTO to represent individuals and companies in matters related to patent applications.

To be registered, attorneys and agents have to meet the following criteria:

✔ Have a technical or scientific education or experience (typically an engineering or scientific college degree).

✔ Pass a rigorous examination about patent application procedures.

Using a patent attorney

Any attorney admitted to the bar in a state can interpret the law, apply it to your case, give you legal advice, and represent you before judicial or administrative authorities, including the USPTO and the Copyright Office. However, only an attorney registered to practice in the USPTO can represent you in a patent application. In almost all foreign countries, IP matters are handled by agents and rarely by an attorney, solicitor, or barrister.

Using a patent agent

Because a patent agent's fees are generally lower than an attorney's, you may wish to hire an agent. However, you must clearly understand the limitations of his or her authority.

A patent agent can conduct an anticipation search on your invention and give you an opinion of whether your invention is patentable. He or she can prepare and file your patent application and represent you throughout the examination of the application.

However, a patent agent can't interpret any law beyond the issue of patentability, tell you whether your invention infringes upon an existing patent, or advise you about what your patent will cover and how it'll be construed by a judge in any future infringement lawsuit.

A patent agent is at a real disadvantage when it comes to drafting the claims in a utility patent application. (In Chapter 4, I show you why the claims are the most important part of a patent application.) Because an agent has no training in litigation, he may not understand how your claims may be interpreted by the court if you need to stop an infringer at some point.

If you can live with these limitations, consult a patent agent, but you may want to look for a "backup" attorney in case you run into an issue that falls beyond the agent's authority or expertise.

Non-registered IP attorneys

Certain well-intentioned business and corporate lawyers won't hesitate to tackle intellectual property matters (other than patent applications), which they're authorized to do, but not necessarily competent to handle. Many are very knowledgeable and will do their best but are clearly out of their league when it comes to the latest developments in IP law.

Be particularly careful if you approach an attorney who's not an IP specialist. Question the legal eagle about her competence and experience — something you should do whenever consulting an attorney. You may, for instance, ask her whether she has read this book! (My publisher will love that line.)

A young entrepreneur consulted an IP lawyer when he was threatened with an infringement lawsuit for the use of his company and brand name, which he thought his business attorney had *cleared* (searched). When the IP lawyer phoned the business attorney, he discovered that the business attorney had checked for the availability of the name in the records of the local secretary of state, which only showed that no corporation existed by that name in the state. The search didn't discover that the name was already used as a trade name elsewhere in the United States. The entrepreneur had to change the corporate name, letterhead, signs, stickers, labels, and packaging, at significant cost and loss of *goodwill* (business reputation) already accumulated under that name.

Qualifying an IP professional

To ensure that the person you hire is the right one for the job, interview several candidates and ask some hard questions before you make your final decision. Lawyers and agents will gladly supply you with references and samples of their work and answer these questions:

✔ What is your technical background?

✔ How long have you been practicing in this field of law?

✔ Are you familiar with my area of technology?

✔ Have you assisted clients in obtaining patents related to my invention?

✔ How many patent applications have you handled?

✔ How many patents have you obtained?

✔ Do you draft licenses and other IP contracts?

✔ Do you issue infringement opinions?

✔ Who else, besides you, will be working on my case?

Unaccredited individuals and companies

Some individuals and companies offer various IP services, such as patent, copyright, and trademark searches (see Chapters 6, 12, and 16). Many advertise extensively in the Yellow Pages and professional publications. Although they can do some legwork for you, their services are limited and don't extend to any kind of legal matter. For instance, a company may conduct a trademark availability search and come up with a list of similar marks and trade names already in use. However, it can't give you a legal opinion as to whether the use of that mark infringe on the rights, if any, of the users of the uncovered marks and trade names. In Table 3-1, I provide a breakdown of the sequences offered by various IP professionals

Table 3-1	Authority and Competence of IP Professionals and Service Companies			
Action	*Registered Patent Attorney*	*Registered Patent Agent*	*Attorney Not Registered to Practice with USPTO*	*Unaccredited Individual or Company*
Conduct a preliminary search on your invention	Yes	Yes	Yes	Yes
Give you an opinion of whether your invention is patentable	Yes	Yes	Yes	No
Prepare and file a patent application on your behalf	Yes	Yes	No	No

Action	Registered Patent Attorney	Registered Patent Agent	Attorney Not Registered to Practice with USPTO	Unaccredited Individual or Company
Represent you throughout the examination of the application by the USPTO	Yes	Yes	No	No
Give you advice on issues of patentability	Yes	Yes	Yes	No
Give you advice on issues of patent coverage	Yes	No	Yes	No
Conduct a mark availability search	Yes	Yes	Yes	Yes
Interpret mark availability search results	Yes	No	Yes	No
Help you register a mark	Yes	No	Yes	No
Help you register a copyright	Yes	No	Yes	No
Represent you in court in any IP matter	Yes	No	Yes	No
Give you legal advice on an IP matter	Yes	No	Yes	No

Finding and Retaining an IP Professional

The best and safest way to find a competent IP professional is by referral from someone who has used that professional's services in the past and been satisfied. You do have some other options, though (listed in order of preference):

- Ask for a referral from an attorney you know and trust.
- Consult an attorney referral service (see the Yellow Pages).
- Sift through listings of IP professionals in the Yellow Pages under "Intellectual property law," "Patent attorneys or patent lawyers," "Patents or patent searches," and "Trademarks and Copyrights."

When you're ready to retain or hire an IP professional, insist on an engagement contract or retainer agreement that clearly spells out all the services, terms, and conditions of your professional relationship.

Here is a partial checklist of the most important things to include:

- ✔ What the IP professional will do for you.
- ✔ How much and when you have to pay for the services.
- ✔ What additional costs and fees you may encounter.
- ✔ How you can terminate the agreement and hire another professional.
- ✔ Who the IP professional will represent: you, your associate or partner, your company, or the man on the moon.

This last point is particularly important. You may ask your IP professional to do something that isn't beneficial to your associate or your company. An eventual conflict of interest that wasn't properly anticipated can lead to a nasty legal fight.

Giving up a piece of the action

Fledgling entrepreneurs are always short of cash and often eager to offer their IP professional a part of their business, technology, or invention as payment for services. If you're tempted to do so, here are a few things to think about first:

- ✔ A part-owner of your company or its assets may have some say about how the business is run. Have a clear, written understanding about these matters to prevent a costly dispute.

- ✔ You don't yet know what your business or IP is worth, so you may be giving up too much for the services you're trying to secure. Later, you may find yourself without enough remaining assets or ownership of the business to obtain the capital and resources you need. Don't sell yourself short. Wait and see where you're going before making that kind of trade.

- ✔ A part-of-the-action fee arrangement is fraught with many dangers for an attorney

or patent agent because the likelihood that a conflict of interest will eventually develop is high. This places the IP professional at a disadvantage because of the strict duty of loyalty imposed by professional codes of ethics. Although it's not your problem if the professional runs into trouble with his state bar association or the USPTO, I'd seriously question the prudence, integrity, and professionalism of an attorney who takes such a risk. Get the entire financial arrangement in writing and get a second opinion from another attorney.

- ✔ Giving a piece of your invention or company to someone must be done in a legal business framework. Accepting anything of value, including legal services, in exchange for a percentage of future earnings from the invention is a serious violation of state and federal security laws. You can go to jail for that.

Staying within Your Meager Means

Legal services are expensive and eat up the lion's share of the money you spend to protect your intellectual property. I'm going to give it to you straight here (you may want to be sitting down), but don't panic — I also give you some advice on keeping your IP protection expenses within your budget.

Assessing the costs

Here's the skinny on some hefty prices. Don't be surprised if your IP specialist quotes you hourly rates between $200 and $500. Registered patent attorneys charge $250–$450 an hour, while registered patent agents can charge $200–$300. Keep in mind that fees and costs, including government charges, often change and may not be the same in all places. The following sections contain some sample budgets for common basic services, using average attorneys' rates.

Patents

Before applying for a patent, and after reading Chapter 6, you may decide to conduct a preliminary search to explore what has already been done in your field and to get a professional opinion about whether a patent is right for you. Here's what a search will cost:

Invention preliminary search (no attorney opinion)	$400
Review of search results and attorney opinion	$500
Total	$900

Assuming you don't encounter any complications, a formal utility patent for a simple mechanical invention will cost you about $5,000. A more complex invention may run $10,000 to $20,000. Here's a detailed breakdown for a U.S. utility patent covering an electro-mechanical device of medium complexity:

Preliminary interview and draft of application	$4,500
Drawings and filing fee	$1,000
Review of examiner report with attorney	$500
Answer/amendment	$1,000
Publication and other miscellaneous fees	$800
Issue fee and cost of copies	$750
Total	$8,550

Any complication, such as interference or opposition, doubles or triples these figures. Appealing an adverse ruling may call for $5,000 to . . . who knows? It depends on how high you want to climb the judicial ladder.

Copyrights

Here's the good news — relatively speaking. The registration and deposit of copyrighted material costs less than $1,000, unless you face complex issues of ownership or copyrightability.

Registration of a copyright for a computer program:

Preliminary interview and preparation of application	$450
Filing fee and miscellaneous charges	$60
Total	$510

Trademarks and other commercial identifiers

When you select a mark or trade name, you want to make sure it won't infringe upon a commercial identifier already in use (see Chapter 16). Here is what each availability search may cost you:

Word mark availability search (no attorney opinion)	$350
Legal review of search results and attorney opinion	$400
Total	$750

A trademark or servicemark registration can set you back $1,000 to $3,000.

Here are the details for registering a design trademark in two classes:

Preliminary interview and draft of application	$850
Filing fees and drawing	$850
Review of examination report with attorney	$450
Answer/amendment	$900
Total	$3,050

Protection abroad

You should budget between $50,000 and $150,000 for overseas patent protection and between $10,000 and $20,000 for trademark registration. All this to cover only 10 to 20 foreign countries. See Chapter 18 for more on international patents.

Managing the expenses

Your IP attorney can help you properly allocate your resources and minimize IP-related expenses. Here is a short list of what she can do for you:

✔ Give you short-term and long-term estimates of all fees and costs.

✔ Show you how to strategically spread the protective measures over a number of years so you don't have to blow the entire budget all at once.

✔ Devise the least expensive approach for protecting your intellectual property — such as applying for a copyright, configuration mark, or design patent application instead of the more expensive utility patent, or by implementing a trade-secret protection program using confidentiality agreements and other procedures.

✔ Tailor your IP protection program to your basic needs. However, if you need to go into the witness protection program, this book won't help.

✔ Give you some peace of mind and a bill for her services — not necessarily in that order.

Patent agents can only give you cost estimates. They can't plan an IP protection strategy involving more than patent applications because of their limited area of practice.

Doing it yourself

Throughout this book, I point out some things you may do yourself. However, the savings may be minimal and may not be worth the risk you're taking. My experience and my malpractice insurance carrier tell me not to rely on what the client has done on his or her own. An IP pro would rather start from scratch than try to unravel the mangled mess of an inadequate patent application. The best thing you can do is carefully prepare the background material, as I suggest in Chapter 7.

Paying the piper

You can pay for IP professional services in one of three common ways:

✔ An hourly fee

✔ A fixed amount for the whole job

✔ A combination of the above

If you agree to an hourly fee, request a complete estimate of all the costs over the life of the project, such as filing fees, copying and mailing costs, foreign agent charges, and maintenance fees. *Maintenance fees,* also called *annuities,* are paid to patenting authorities during the life of a patent. In some countries, the annuities are due from the date of filing the application.

Exercising caution with TV invention-development services

Gee, by now those commercials touting invention-development and marketing companies probably sound pretty enticing, don't they? What a savings they represent compared to the fees I just quoted you! My advice? BEWARE! This industry is riddled with abuses. Many of these companies prey upon the ignorant, the naïve, and the elderly, taking inventors' money and never returning a cent to their trusting victims.

Several states and the federal government have had to intervene, shutting down some of these long-established firms. A few states, namely California and Michigan, even adopted laws that severely restrict the ability of these companies to siphon money from their clients.

If you do choose this route, be as prudent as you are when selecting an attorney. Insist upon proof of prior performances by asking how much money the company has doled out in the past and how many customers have received those disbursements. Ask for references and check them out thoroughly. Interview and compare. And keep in mind that only a licensed IP attorney can give you valid legal advice. Remember that if it sounds too good to be true, it probably is!

If you're going to pay a fixed fee, ask about other expenses, such as government charges, drawing costs, and copying charges that may not be included. In all cases, clarify how and when you must make the payments.

Working with Foreign IP Professionals

You must have a representative in every foreign jurisdiction in which you file a patent application or mark registration. Most U.S. patent attorneys and agents maintain working relationships with IP professionals in industrialized foreign countries.

In all cases, you need to pay the foreign IP professionals' fees and government charges. Usually, neither you nor your attorney have any control over these costs, but you should always ask for a rough estimate when you file overseas. Because foreign costs tend to be substantially higher than in the United States, don't forget to take those expenses into account when preparing your IP budget and laying out your IP protection strategy.

You don't have to worry about searching and selecting agents abroad, but on occasion, your U.S. IP professional may ask you to review their reports.

Coordinating with Other Professionals

Don't forget to keep your other business advisors informed about your IP program.

- ✔ Keep your business or corporate attorney aware of all your IP activities. It's a good idea to give him copies of all your major correspondence with your IP professionals. Your patents and marks may be put to good use in some distributorship and representative agency agreements.

- ✔ Inform your CPA, comptroller, and other bean counters about your IP expenses. Acquiring a patent or developing a trade secret can have important tax implications, and you don't want to miss lucrative amortization or depreciation deductions. Proceeds from the sale of licensing of an invention may benefit from special taxation rules, and your technological acquisitions and research program may qualify for tax credits.

- ✔ Make your PR and advertising agency fully aware of the marks you acquire and register. Those marks can be effectively put to work in your promotional campaigns. As I explain in Chapter 15, your advertising and marketing people can play an important role in selecting your commercial identifiers.

Part II

If You Build It, They Will Come: Patenting Your Product

The 5th Wave   By Rich Tennant

In this part . . .

Getting a patent can be tough; no question about it. But I'm here to guide you through the entire process of preparing and filing the patent application. In this part, I introduce the basics of the patenting process, including the legal and practical definitions you need to get a handle on before you enter the world of patents, and the criteria you and your invention must meet to qualify for a patent. At every step of the way, I illustrate how your hired gun — your IP professional — can clear obstacles from your path.

Acquiring a patent is probably the most complex, expensive, and time-consuming type of IP protection process. Because getting a patent can be so difficult, I help you evaluate whether you should really apply for a patent or use another way to protect your IP.

For similar reasons, making sure that no one else has already come up with your device is the way to go before you start the application process. So I show you how to do an anticipation search to see whether your invention is unique, original, and useful — because these factors determine whether your invention is really patentable.

I then give you tips on preparing your patent application, help you push it through the patent office and deal with the patent examiner, and finally, show you how to get that coveted piece of paper.

Chapter 4

Understanding Patents and How They Work

A patent is the most common, effective, and valuable of all intellectual property (IP) rights, but it also happens to be the most misunderstood. In this chapter, I untangle for you, one step at a time, the knotty complexity of patents so that you have no doubts about what a patent is and whether you can get one. (Chapter 5 gets more into whether you really want a patent as part of your IP strategy.)

Presenting a Patent Explanation

A *patent* is a temporary legal right granted to an inventor by the government to prevent others from manufacturing, selling, or using his invention. I must warn you that this is a loaded definition. Read it again. The most important words are

- ✔ **Temporary:** A patent doesn't last forever, but for a specified number of years.

- ✔ **Right . . . to prevent:** A patent allows its owner to go to court and *ask* a judge to stop someone from doing something. But remember, what's good for the goose is good for the gander. An inventor isn't immune from the *right to prevent* held by another patent owner.

As you can see by this definition, a patent doesn't give its owner the right to do anything — including use, manufacture, sell, license, or otherwise exploit the covered invention — except to prevent others from stepping on your patented toes. That may require a trip to a federal courthouse and paying huge lawyer fees if the infringer isn't deterred by your threat of litigation.

What your patent can do for your country

The United States Patent and Trademark Office (USPTO) is in charge of the United States patent system. This patent system is a bit of an exception to the general free competition and antimonopolistic principles that underline our body of laws because it gives one person sole control of a possibly important technological field. Yet, in a roundabout way, patents still ensure fair competition among all citizens. A patent gives the inventor incentive to disclose and use his precious invention and, to quote the U.S. Constitution, "promote the progress of science and useful arts."

A patent also publishes the nuts and bolts of the invention, giving the public knowledge of the invention very early in the game, even though the inventor gets about a 20-year head start on profiting by the invention.

When the patent expires, anyone can apply the invention or manufacture and sell anything that falls within that previously taboo area of technology — free competition reigns once again and the country is richer for the new technology.

What your patent can do for you

A patent can be a powerful legal tool that affords you, as an inventor, businessperson, or entrepreneur, the sole right to your technology and a competitive edge in the market.

The patent reserves, exclusively for your benefit, an area of technology corresponding roughly to your invention (I explain in Chapter 7 how the scope of a patent is defined). For the life of the patent, you can exclude others from making, selling, or using any machine, device, composition of matter, method, process, plant, or design that falls within the technological area defined by the claims in your patent.

After your patent is granted, you can go into business yourself to practice the invention, free of competition. You can also license your patent to someone else (a lease that allows another party to exploit your invention). If you've invented something really valuable, potential licensees will be lining up for the opportunity to pay you handsome royalties for the right to profit by your invention.

Or you can sell the patent outright for a bundle, giving the new owner the patent's exclusive benefits for the remaining term of the patent.

Dissecting the Beast: The Three Types of Patents

The United States Patent and Trademark Office issues three kinds of patents:

- **Utility patent:** This patent is the type most people think of when they talk about patents — protection for technological advances and innovation. A utility patent applies to the way something is made, how a device operates, or a process for accomplishing some utilitarian purpose. The subject of a utility patent must result from human activity (and not be a product of nature). It can be any one of the following or an improvement on any of them:

  - **A manufactured article:** Such as a corkscrew or a stapler.

  - **A machine:** For example, a photocopier or a computer.

  - **A composition of matter:** Such as a cough medicine or an adhesive.

  - **A process for making or doing something:** For example, a method for refining sugar or a protocol for managing investment accounts.

  The invention can also be a combination of these things. A new use of an old machine can be patented as a process.

- **Design patent:** Covers a new and original ornamental shape or a surface treatment of a manufactured article. The shape or ornamentation can have no functional utility other than an aesthetic one. For example, the cut of a dress or the shape of a table lamp or an automobile body may be protected by a design patent.

- **Plant patent:** Applies to characteristics of a new plant that has been asexually reproduced (by grafting or selective cuttings — without seed manipulation). A new variety of plant, no matter how reproduced, can also be the subject of a utility patent.

You can't patent a law of nature, such as a mathematical theorem, or a physical phenomenon or property, even if you are the first to discover or articulate it.

Claiming your rights as a patent owner

Under your patent, you can sue anyone who manufactures, sells, markets, or even uses your product without your permission. It doesn't matter that you, as the patent owner, might be excluded from all of those activities yourself under someone else's patent — you still can sue, which can lead to the following conundrum.

Say that Jane has a utility patent covering a widget. You've developed a modification to the widget that makes it more efficient and cheaper to produce and have been granted a patent covering the improvement. Jane wants to modify her widget according to your invention, but can't do so without your permission. You, on the other hand, can't make or sell the improved widget without her permission. The solution is to get together and strike a deal. Here are your options:

- ✔ You give her the exclusive right to use your improvement for a fee.
- ✔ She gives you permission, for a fee, to make and sell the improved widgets.
- ✔ Each of you agrees not to sue the other and goes into business using the other's invention.

If you own a design patent, your rights are more restricted. You can't prevent others from using your patented ornamental design on an article unrelated to your original one. However, you can prevent others from making the same or a similar article adorned with a similar styling or decoration. It doesn't matter that the article itself is very common and may be in the public domain.

Say you've patented a new style of silverware that has cylindrical handles with garlands of oak leaves spiraling over their entire lengths. You can prevent others from using the same design on forks, spoons, knives, and serving pieces. If the judge likes you, he may let you convince him that the same style applied to other household items, such as letter openers, hair brushes, and combs, would be an infringement of your patent rights. However, you can't prevent someone else from using your design on columns, fountains, and other things that aren't commonly purchased together with or from the same retail outlets as silverware. But if you flip to Chapter 11, I show you how a copyright on the oak-leaf garland would give you that kind of protection.

A plant patent gives you the right to exclude others from asexually reproducing, selling, or using the plant. It doesn't prevent creation of the plant by fertilization and seeding (sexual reproduction).

Tracing a patent's life span

Each type of patent has a different life span. Here are the details:

✔ **Utility patent:** The life span of a utility patent is determined by the application filing date:

- A utility patent filed before June 8, 1995 will remain in effect until the 17th anniversary of its issue date.

- A utility patent filed on or after June 8, 1995 is good until the 20th anniversary of the earliest priority date claimed by the applicant. The *priority date* can be the filing date of the application or the filing date of a prior domestic or foreign application that disclosed at least part of the same subject matter. A priority date based on a provisional patent application (see Chapter 7) doesn't count.

✔ **Design patent:** Granted for a term of 14 years from its issue date.

✔ **Plant patent:** Determined in the same way as for a utility patent.

A patent can expire before its term if it's declared invalid by a court, recalled by the Patent Office, surrendered or dedicated to the public by its owner, or cancelled for failure to pay one of the periodical maintenance fees discussed in Chapter 10.

The term of a patent may be extended beyond the timeframes just listed under specific circumstances, usually to compensate the owner if the government significantly delayed the application process while, for instance, reviewing a decision of the patent examiner or getting the invention approved for sale by the Food and Drug Administration.

Checking Out the Mechanics: Specifications and Claims

A patent doesn't define any particular device, machine, composition, or process, but sets aside an area of technology just for you. You may compare it to the deed to your house. The deed doesn't spell out the layout of your house and how many bedrooms and bathrooms it has; it describes only the limits of your property by reference to certain landmarks, geographic orientations, and topographic coordinates.

But enough theory — it's time to take a look at how a patent works. Two primary parts of a patent get most of the job done:

✔ **Specification:** A description of what the inventor considers to be the best way to practice the invention, accompanied by drawings if necessary. It must be detailed enough to allow a skilled person to practice the invention itself without undue experimentation.

> ✔ **Claims:** Constitute the legal component that defines the area of technology, based on the specification, that is reserved to the patent owner. Each claim defines a different scope of coverage.

In the following sections, I introduce you to some actual patents, pointing out these two important components in each one. In Chapter 7, I take an in-depth look at how the specifications and claims are drafted, and in Chapter 20, how they are interpreted.

Lining up a utility patent

Check out the appendix's first full patent. This is a very basic U.S. utility patent issued on December 11, 2001, under No. 6,329,033, for a very simple invention, namely, an imitation wax seal. Each section of the patent has a specific purpose:

✔ The *Abstract* gives a general idea of what the invention is all about.

✔ The *Field of the Invention* tells you the areas of technology involved.

✔ The *Background of the Invention* gives you the reasons and purpose of the invention.

✔ The *Description of the Preferred Embodiment of the Invention* provides an example of the best way to practice the invention.

✔ The *Claims* define the legal boundaries of the patent coverage.

In Chapter 7, I explain how the patent application drafter uses each section to make a case for patentability.

Everything from the Field of the Invention through the Description of the Preferred Embodiment of the Invention and the drawing figures is called the *specification.* But the specification doesn't tell you exactly what this patent covers or, more specifically, what the owner of the patent can prevent others from doing. For that you have to look at the claims, which are on the third page of the application in column 2.

This patent has eight claims, but 1 and 8 are the most important. Claims 2 through 7 just add more details to Claim 1. Notice that Claim 1 is more concise and recites fewer components (no mention of a document) than Claim 8, which gives it a broader scope than Claim 8. You might say that with claims, less is more.

The shorter the claim, the broader the coverage. Wait a minute, you say. But think for a minute. A claim defines what the other guys can't do. If your claim lists many elements, you can only sue someone who makes, promotes, sells, or uses a gizmo containing every one of those elements. If you reduce the number of elements recited in the claims, then there are more gizmos out there that include those fewer parts, and more bad guys to sue! Don't go any further until you have fully grasped this claim concept. It is the foundation of most of what follows. Please, repeat after me: Short claim — more coverage. Long claim — narrow patent. You got it.

In many patents, the actual coverage is broader than the structure described in the specification, but this isn't always the case. In some patents, the coverage is extremely narrow, as you can gather from the long list of items recited in the claims. Determining what a patent covers requires a complex, expert analysis, as you'll discover in Chapter 20. Let me warn you for now that a patent seldom is what, at first glance, it appears to be.

Sketching out a design patent

The second patent in the appendix is a design patent issued on January 2, 2001, under No. D435,884, for a paintball gun barrel muzzle.

Note the simplicity of a design patent. It doesn't have an elaborate specification, only the front page and a drawing (a patent drawing usually comprises several figures). In a design patent, the disclosure consists of a line drawing and a brief description of each view. Only one claim is allowed in a design patent, written in a mandatory formal manner.

In a design patent infringement action, the judge or jury compares the accused device to what is shown in the drawing. The infringement test doesn't require an exact sameness, but only a similarity that could confuse an unsuspecting buyer.

Grafting a plant patent

The third patent in the appendix is a plant patent issued on April 29, 2003, under No. PP13,741, for a lily plant.

This is a hybrid patent with elements from both a utility and design patent. The specification, including the drawing, discloses the main characteristic of the new plant in substantially the same manner as in a utility patent, except that a photograph may be substituted for the line drawing. You must word the claim formally, as in a design patent. This patent would be infringed by the production and sale of a plant having the same general characteristics illustrated in the document.

Playing by the Rules: The Three-Part Patentability Test

First things first. To qualify as patentable, the invention must fall under one of the three patent types I outline in the "Dissecting the Beast: The Three Types of Patents" section, earlier in this chapter. U.S. law then requires the invention to pass through a series of elaborate tests in order to meet the three-pronged *patentability test:*

- ✓ **Utility** (practical usefulness)
- ✓ **Novelty** (innovativeness)
- ✓ **Non-obviousness** (something that isn't immediately apparent)

The reason for these laws is to guarantee consistency when granting patents. However, the tests are rather complex, with many accommodations for special cases.

In the following sections, I explore each of the hurdles the invention must clear and then provide you with a checklist that you can use to make sure that your invention meets the requirements necessary to receive a patent.

Making yourself useful

The *utility test* determines whether your invention has any use in the real world. This is an easy one. As long as you can dream up some kind of application for your invention, you won't have any problem passing the utility test. You don't even have to prove that the invention actually works, *except* in the case of some medical inventions. (If you claim a therapeutic treatment or drug that gets rid of bunions, you must prove its effectiveness by producing laboratory or clinical test results.)

Developing a novel approach

The *novelty test* requires that you've developed an original way to solve a problem. Your invention will be compared to everything that has been created in the past, which is called the *prior art.* Contrary to what you may think, the newness test is rarely insurmountable. Your patent can't be denied unless a prior art device, machine, or process includes *all* the basic components of your invention. For example, if you invent a watercraft with a hull made of plastic sheets heat-welded together, it would be considered new even though you found a similar craft in a prior patent, but with glued components. However, you may have some problem with the next test.

Avoiding the obvious

The *non-obviousness test* is the crux of the matter and also the tough one. To pass, the difference between your invention and the prior art must not be obvious to a person with ordinary skill in the relevant field. The problem with the obviousness test is defining that mythical person with ordinary skill in the field. For example, he wouldn't be your typical weekend do-it-yourselfer or a design engineer, but a good technician who knows or has access to all prior art information in the field of the invention.

Another way to look at it is to say that your invention is not obvious if it provides a solution to a long-standing problem in an off-beat way or, as the courts like to put it, by *teaching away* from the prior art. The two tests are illustrated in the following examples.

Stating the obvious

Say you are an artist who molds statues and other artifacts out of polyester or other types of *thermosetting resin* (the resin hardens with increased temperature, instead of melting). You also sprinkle flakes of aluminum and other metals into your resin in order to create decorative patterns. This type of resin is commonly used to cast countertops and bathroom vanities, so to an ordinary bathroom fixture builder, there's nothing new or non-obvious in your process.

However, while experimenting with different types and sizes of metal flakes, you realize that by reducing the size and increasing the number of metal particles, you can color the entire material in various hues, for example, red with copper dust, silvery gray with aluminum, and so on. If you conduct an anticipation search, you won't find your invention in the prior art, but you'd be dead wrong to think that you can get a patent. Even though you've come up with a new product and fabrication process, a patent examiner will probably reject your application for being obvious because a "person with ordinary skill" would expect a change of color when large quantities of small metal particles are scattered in the resin.

Making the best of a non-obvious situation

I'll take our example a little further. Being a curious inventor, you notice that the resin reacts with the metal particles, coating each one with a thin layer of oxidation. You now mix the resin with a metal powder made of extremely fine particles. When the metal particles are almost completely oxidized by reaction with the resin, you discover that you've created a new composite material whose physical properties are substantially different from those of past composites. You also observe that your compound conducts heat more like a metal than a plastic substance, but doesn't conduct electricity.

Can you get a patent on that baby? You bet you can! Your results wouldn't be obvious to anyone with ordinary skill in the fields of plastics and electrical insulators. For years, electrical engineers have been looking for a material that insulates electronic components from one another and effectively dissipates the heat the components generate. They've even mixed resins and metal particles to create electrical contact pads. Congratulations! You found an unexpected solution to a longstanding problem in electrical assemblies.

Making a list and checking it twice

I've got to warn you that the following rules (if you will allow me some lawyer-style wording as a warm-up) are arcane, recondite, and abstruse. Translation: mysterious, obscure, and foggy. Sorry, but they are important, and you'll have to refer to them on several occasions. So, turn the TV off, finish your chicken nuggets, and concentrate.

If you're still a little fuzzy after reviewing this list, don't worry. If you *fully* grasp these concepts, you'll be able to pass the patent bar exam — and no one is asking you to do that. If you decide to go after a patent, your attorney will investigate these matters with you. So for now, just be aware of these rules and make an initial analysis of how your invention would score.

✔ **The invention must be useful.** The utility test can be satisfied if you can show that the invention is practical.

A method for growing parsley in your nose may appear totally crazy and useless. Who would want to grow an herb in his nasal cavities? But who is to forbid such an innocent activity? Certainly not the USPTO. After all, I might relish the fragrance of fresh parsley. What better way to satisfy my olfactory fetish than to keep a sprig of it in my nose at all times? This argument, as silly it may sound, is enough to establish utility.

✔ **The invention must have some credibility.** If you apply for a patent on a product or process that runs contrary to the laws of physics, you'll be asked to provide persuasive evidence that it actually works. Applications for perpetual motion machines are routinely rejected because of the inventors' failure to convincingly demonstrate that their contraptions work.

✔ **The invention must be practicable.** You must be able to practice the invention with existing components and materials. For example, if your invention requires milling a component down to a micron range, and no equipment is available to do so, your invention is indeed useless.

The USPTO demands laboratory or clinical proof that pharmaceuticals are effective. If you claim a new formula to treat hair loss, don't waste your time and money filing a patent application unless you have solid test results or the means to conduct appropriate clinical trials.

✔ **The invention can't have been previously known or used by others in the United States before your date of invention.** If someone else had possession or knowledge of the invention before you did and didn't willfully conceal it from the public, you're out of luck. It doesn't matter that you came up with the invention on your own and didn't know about the other dude.

✔ **The invention can't be patented or described in a printed publication before your date of invention anywhere in the world.** The fact that your invention was known or used for a long time in a foreign country doesn't prevent you from obtaining a patent under the previous entry. But if a printed description of it is readily available to the public before your date of invention, anywhere or in any language, you're out.

✔ **The invention can't be patented or described anywhere in a printed publication more than one year before you file your application.** If someone prints or tries to patent an invention that you had first, you'd better hurry up and file. If you wait more than a year, it won't matter that your date of invention came first. The critical date is not the date of invention but one year prior to the filing date of the application.

✔ **The invention can't be in public use or on sale in the United States more than one year before you file the application.** This clause relates to your own prior activities as well as those of others. However, an experimental use isn't considered to be a public use, so your research and development activities are exempt.

✔ **The inventor can't abandon the invention.** *Abandonment* means you don't intend to pursue the invention by using or patenting it. This intent may be proved by an unjustified long period of inactivity before filing a patent application or putting the invention on the market. Your prior knowledge of the abandoned invention won't prevent a later inventor from getting the patent.

✔ **The inventor can't get a foreign patent before filing an application in the United States, unless the foreign application was filed less than one year before the U.S. application.** Almost all countries impose this one-year deadline from the filing in a foreign jurisdiction.

✔ **The invention must not be described in someone else's patent or published patent application filed in the United States prior to the date of invention by the applicant.** This rule doesn't require that some other guy knew about or used the thing prior to your date of invention, only that the other guy's patent or published application discloses it. However, knowledge and use of the invention abroad (without description in a publication) doesn't, by itself, prevent a later U.S. inventor from obtaining a patent. Chapter 8 explains that most patent applications are published (open to the public) about 18 months after the filing date.

✔ **The applicant must be the inventor.** The applicant must have come up with the invention on his own and not learned about it on his last vacation to Europe.

✔ **The inventor must be the first applicant in the United States.** The rule of priority of invention brings up many thorny issues about who got there first and offers lots of good fodder for attorneys. Inventors should carefully document the development of their inventions and file the application promptly.

✔ **The invention must not be obvious to a person with ordinary skill in the field at the time of the invention.** This is the last and toughest of the rules. Countless court decisions have struggled with this requirement of non-obviousness. Review my comments and examples in "Avoiding the obvious," above. I go over this matter also in Chapter 9.

Chapter 5

Testing the Water Before You File for a Patent

....

....

*P*rotecting a technological breakthrough with one or more patents isn't a trivial undertaking. The complexity, costs, and long delays that accompany such a project necessitate a clear understanding of the process and a thorough exploration of alternative, more practical, and less expensive approaches.

But don't let me scare you — I've no intention of discouraging you from applying for a patent. Far from it. A patent can be an effective protection tool that provides you with a lucrative source of income. However, I've seen many inventors jump into the patent-application fray with no reasonable prospect of seeing it through to a successful completion. If you think you have a patentable invention after reading Chapter 4, take a deep breath and follow me through the prepatent exercises I describe in this chapter.

Assessing What You Have

The first step in attempting to protect an invention or other technological breakthrough is formulating a clear vision of your idea and determining what rights you have to it. Be prepared for some surprises.

Defining the invention in writing

At first glance, preparing a written description of your invention may seem like a childish exercise, but that's what patent attorneys do to narrow down the invention before actually drafting an application. So, follow their lead. Go over your notes, drawings, and models and write down an accurate description of your new device, process, or composition. You need to be as concise as possible — 15 lines at the most — without missing any key features that make your invention new and unique. Help yourself by drawing a little sketch of your invention with cross-reference numbers that refer back to the text.

Focus on the nuts and bolts of the invention in your description — how it's made and how it operates, rather than its advantages and commercial applications. Such a description will become the cornerstone of the patent application, so make sure that it's technically accurate and complete.

Qualifying the invention

Now, you must determine whether your invention qualifies for a patent. You don't need to do the detailed analysis of a patent examiner, but I want you to be sure that your invention exceeds the basic patentability threshold. Don't waste your time pursuing a patent process that's already doomed to failure because of an inherent flaw in your invention or idea.

Surpassing the *basic patentability threshold* first means finding out whether your invention fits into one of the three categories of patents — utility, design, or plant patents. Then, pit your invention against the important patentability factors — novelty, utility, and nonobvious nature — that make up the three-part patentability test I describe in Chapter 4. If your invention still looks good, you can double-check your findings against the patentability checklist, which is a bunch of hoops you must jump through to get a patent, as I discuss in the last part of Chapter 4.

When you get to the last part of the patentability test — the one about whether your invention is something that would be obvious to someone of ordinary related skills, don't waste too much time haggling: That happens to be the $64,000 question that patent examiners or judges ultimately answer.

Coming up with an inventor

Be brutally honest in assessing whether you alone conceived the invention or whether someone else made suggestions or contributed to the concept. You also need to know whether anyone else refined or improved the device when you built the prototype or model. Maybe a co-worker or your 10-year-old whiz kid helped you out. Regardless of the circumstance, make sure that you acknowledge any helpful outside contribution now. Any contributor may have rights that are equal to yours and therefore must (by law) be listed as a co-inventor on the patent application.

Determining exactly who came up with your invention is an extremely tricky but critical legal issue that requires the advice of a competent intellectual property (IP) professional.

Figuring out ownership

Ownership of an invention and patent is related to but still a separate issue from inventorship. I look at it from two perspectives: securing ownership of contributions to the invention by others and ensuring ownership of your own creations.

Acquiring contributions

Taking care of your invention's ownership issues early in the game lessens the likelihood that you'll run into problems later. It's not unusual for a former associate, employee, neighbor, or relative to claim a role in a commercially successful invention, so watch out for that cousin Ernie who's always giving you advice you don't need! Troublesome people always seem to crawl out of the woodwork at the most difficult times in an entrepreneurial venture.

If anyone contributed to your invention, secure your exclusive ownership through agreements with that contributor, regardless of who's named as inventor on the patent application. You can use the same type of agreement discussed in Chapter 12 in connection with copyrights. Ask your IP attorney to draft an invention and patent transfer agreement that fits your circumstances and complies with your state codes and local restrictions on invention assignments (transfers), which I mention in the next section.

Claiming your own creation

If you invent something in your role as an employee, chances are you have no right to that invention, even if you invented it entirely on your own. You need to establish that you own your invention, so check through these sticky points before proceeding with a patent:

- ✔ Employment intake forms often include invention-assignment clauses that folks sign without much thought. Unless state law restricts such an agreement, even an invention made entirely at home and using your own resources in any technological field may actually belong to your boss.

- ✔ An employer may have a *shop right* (a right to freely use an invention) if any part of its facilities was used in developing that invention.

- ✔ Even an unwritten agreement to work together on a project or an advance of funds can trigger the establishment of a legal partnership where everything belongs to everybody.

> ✔ Federal law provides that if the invention was developed as part of a governmental project or under a government grant, Uncle Sam gets a piece of the action.

Don't waste time and money on something that may not be yours. If you have any concerns in this area, consult an IP professional.

Identifying the filing entity

In the United States, an inventor must sign and file the patent application (except for a provisional application, discussed in Chapter 7), even if the inventor doesn't own the invention. However, in most foreign countries, the application can be signed and filed by the inventor or the owner of the invention. If the inventor is dead or incapacitated, a legal representative, such as an executor, administrator, guardian, or conservator can sign and file the application with documentary evidence of his or her authority.

Identifying the filing entity gets a little trickier when inventors can't be found or refuse to cooperate and sign the application. I've seen it happen. Employee-inventors become frustrated after realizing they don't own their inventions and quit their jobs or refuse to help their employers get a patent. When that's the case, anyone who can show a documented right to the invention, including a co-inventor or employer, can file on behalf of an absent or unwilling inventor. The procedure requires an earnest attempt to notify and offer the missing party the opportunity to join in the application.

Making Sure a Patent Is Right for You

So you think you have a patentable invention. It's all yours, and you have the right to file a patent application. Now that all your ducks are in a row, you get to play doctor and diagnose whether a patent is the right medicine for you.

Comparing the pros with the cons of the patent game

Applying for a patent is a lengthy, expensive, and uncertain endeavor. Therefore, you should understand all the alternative, less-taxing approaches for protecting your invention. You may want to use one or more of those approaches instead of or in addition to the patent application.

First, though, look at the advantages and disadvantages of applying for a patent. The advantages:

✔ **Broad scope of protection:** Can extend to a broad field of technology beyond your own creation.

✔ **Powerful anti-competition tool:** Business people are weary of infringing patents because of high litigation costs and damages awards.

✔ **Increase in the value of your business:** A patent portfolio is a must if you want to raise capital.

Not to be ignored, the disadvantages:

✔ **High costs:** The costs are extremely high and unpredictable. Patenting is a continuous process requiring multiple applications to cover all aspects of the invention and eventual improvements.

✔ **Your secret is out:** You must bare it all in your application, making it easy for others to use your invention as soon as the patent expires.

✔ **Long wait for (relatively) short-lived protection:** The protection lasts 20 years at the most from your earliest application filing date.

Exploring alternative routes

If you decide that the advantages aren't worth the disadvantages of applying for a patent, you can still protect your invention. These following approaches are easier, less expensive, and can usually be completed in less time.

Looking at trade secrets

If you're dealing with a chemical or process invention or other improvement that you don't have to expose to the general public and can keep under close wraps, a patent application may not be the best approach.

Check out what Chapters 1 and 2 have to say about using a trade-secret strategy. The most serious risk is that someone else will independently discover the invention you're keeping secret, file a patent application, get a patent, and cause you considerable grief.

In general, keeping an invention a trade secret is a great idea when the useful life of the invention is relatively short — less than seven years. The odds that someone else will discover the same invention and obtain a patent during that period are in your favor.

Backing up your trade secret with a covert patent application

If you think your invention will give you a strong competitive edge for seven or more years, it may be prudent to keep the invention a secret, and also back up your trade secret by filing a patent application within the first year of putting it into general use. If somebody spills the beans, you can let your application turn into a patent whose priority right goes back to your original filing date. Taking advantage of the fact that patent applications are held in secrecy, you begin by filing a provisional application (see Chapter 7). This provisional application is relatively inexpensive and is good for 12 months. This gives you 24 months of back-up protection. If at that time, your trade secret looks like it's holding up and not likely to be broken in the future, you can abandon the patenting process. But if you're still concerned, you can file a scaled down formal patent application with only one or two claims at a relatively low cost. Your technology won't be made public until you allow the formal application to turn into a patent, no earlier than two or three years down the line. You can even extend the covert application process time to several more years by stringing up a line of continuation patent applications and making sure none of them is published (see Chapter 8).

Getting protection under a copyright

As I explain in Chapter 2, copyrights are so simple and inexpensive to secure that they always need to be part of your IP protection strategy.

Copyright doesn't cover facts, concepts, or processes the way a patent does. It does, however, cover the way that a concept or process is expressed. I apologize for this legal nicety, but it's nothing trivial (see Chapter 1). Making the copyright-for-patent substitution may be particularly applicable for protecting:

✔ **An invention that uses a computer program:** Relying on copyright protection is particularly effective if you've invented a type of process or method that's implemented with a computer program. But remember, the copyright covers only the written part of the program and not the actual process.

Say you've developed a complex process for shredding recyclable rubber, melting it, and turning it into a paste that can be molded at room temperature for 24 hours before it cures into a resilient body. The method consists of multiple steps involving precise temperature and timing controls which must be automatically managed by computer.

A copyright on the computer program prevents others from copying your specific application but doesn't prevent anyone who's familiar with your process from independently devising essentially the same process and writing an original computer program to achieve the same results. But you can charge anyone who reproduces any part of *your* software while trying to devise such a process with copyright infringement. Along with copyright protection, you need to keep *your process* confidential as a trade secret. (See Chapter 12 for info about registering a software copyright without revealing your trade secret.)

✔ **Style and ornamentation:** Instead of seeking a design patent to protect the style or ornamentation of your product, a simple copyright may do the trick. The styling or ornamentation must stand separately from the product, meaning they must be detachable from the product for copyright to protect them. Using a table lamp made from a statue as an example, the statue itself, independent of the base, stem, and shade, is protected by copyright.

Although clothing style and fashion can only be protected with a design patent, you can copyright surface embroidery and other decoration that can stand separately from the garment.

✔ **Peripheral material:** Manuals, promotional material, packaging, presentations, lectures, and handouts qualify for copyright protection. Making sure that peripheral materials are properly copyrighted goes a long way toward substantially stifling your competitors.

Because of its inability to cover concepts and processes, a copyright won't extend to some parts of a manual, mode of operation, or game rules because of their essentially functional aspects (see Chapter 11).

Going design rather than utility

A design patent is intended to cover purely decorative and nonfunctional aspects of a product. However, I've seen cases where a design patent turned out to be a more effective tool than a utility patent in quashing an infringer.

In one case, the product was a wallet designed for law enforcement officers. A section of the wallet featured a fabric pad onto which a badge could be pinned and a flap that covered the badge so that the wallet could be used without revealing the owner's profession. The wallet was protected by both utility and design patents, but a competitor, as most copycats do, simply duplicated the whole thing down to the shape of the flap. While presenting the case to a judge, the patent-holder's attorney relied exclusively on the design patent when asking for a restraining order pending a trial. The similarity of the accused's article to the patented wallet was enough to persuade the judge to grant the order. Had the attorney relied on the utility patent, the judge would've required expert testimony about prior art and other complex, costly procedures. The defendant gave up and settled the case the next day.

The protected appearance of your device may be so striking that a copycat would find marketing a competitive product difficult without using the same look. For instance, look at the distinctive shape and ornamentation of the AJAX scouring powder canister. Can you imagine yourself picking up a similar product presented in a totally different container? You automatically rely on the look of the product and don't have to read the brand name to know what you're buying.

Appreciating trade dress

Although it may perform the same function — creating a good first impression — I'm not talking about how to dress for success when I refer to trade dress. *Trade dress,* or the way a product or service is presented to the public, can be protected by a configuration mark. In effect, a *configuration mark* acts pretty much like a design patent by protecting the look of a product or service establishment. Furthermore, a configuration mark, contrary to a design patent, can be established quickly and inexpensively and lasts as long as the configuration is used in commerce. Notice that a configuration mark does not need to meet the novelty requirement the way a patent does.

Trade dress, independent of the product or package, must be distinctive and nonfunctional. To be distinctive, it must be different than anything else on the market. To be nonfunctional, the styling or ornamentation must not present any advantages other than aesthetic ones.

However, the nonfunctionality rule does have a hair-splitting exception: An *arbitrary* combination of functional characteristics can qualify for protection as a configuration mark. Say, for example, you want to open a taco shop with a little character, a nonlegal term for trade dress. At the entrance, you mount a tilting garage door. You serve drinks from coiled hoses hanging from the ceiling like grease guns. The seats are steel benches covered with wire mesh and the table feet are made of chrome car wheels. The door, drink dispensers, benches, and wheels are all functional elements, yet the entire combination is arbitrary. This combination is protected as trade dress.

You may ask: Why, with all the advantages of a configuration mark, would anyone ever bother filing a design patent application? That's easy . . . design patents have their own merits. First and foremost, a design patent carries all the prestige of a patent. Second, it can be acquired and enforced independently of any commercial activity. A configuration mark, by contrast, exists only as a product or business identifier. (In Chapter 14, I show you how to select and protect a configuration mark.)

Recognizing the role of commercial identifiers

All this protection stuff I've been talking about serves only one purpose. It gives you an edge over the competition. The same can be said of good *commercial identifiers,* so don't overlook the marketing power of a good trademark, servicemark, or a company name.

Look at all the products around you. Almost every one of them has a trademark prominently displayed on it. Now see how many patent numbers you can find. Two, one, or none at all? In most cases, the market position of a product or service is enhanced more by a good name than it is by a patent.

Tell me, would you consider buying fabric fastener strips under any other brand than VELCRO? Do you see much advertising for this product on TV or in magazines? Nope. The name does the marketing. You want another motivating brand name? How about COVER GIRL brand of cosmetics? After all, what do many young ladies aspire to be or look like? A glamorous cover girl. Check out Chapter 15 to discover how to create powerful names.

Starting Things Off on the Right Foot

The wild blue yonder of patents and patent applications is no place for a rookie pilot's first solo flight. Even though explosive legal issues lurk behind every cloud, you can do some of the work without waiting for professional advice or assistance. You can also use the guidelines that I provide in Chapter 6 and conduct a preliminary search to find out exactly what has previously been done in the area of your invention. A little preliminary digging can't hurt if you don't waste too much time on it.

Making a record of your invention

As you develop your product or process, take copious notes that include plenty of illustrative sketches, preferably in a bound notebook with numbered pages. Use a pen, not a pencil, and don't erase but cross out your mistakes. Once in a while, ask a trusted relative or friend to review your notes, date, and sign the last written page, stating that on the specified date, she or he read the notes and understood the invention.

If you keep your notes on a computer, print them out and have your witness sign and date every page. *Note:* Even though this method of recordkeeping is easy and convenient, I don't recommend it because of problems exist with the admissibility of loose sheets of paper in patent proceedings.

These precautions are necessary because you need to know how to create a legally admissible document. Don't waste your time sending a description of your invention through the mail to someone else or to yourself. The time stamp on the postmark won't hold up in court as proof that you owned the invention at that particular point in time.

Your well-kept notebook, however, has many uses. It can

- ✔ Provide your IP professional with a complete history and disclosure of the invention. He or she, in turn, may see something in some of your earlier and now discarded designs that deserves a patent.

- ✔ Provide convincing evidence of the date that you first conceived the invention and reduced it to practice, which is especially important when you're trying to resolve an issue of priority against another inventor.

- ✔ Help you organize your thoughts, providing an easy review of your progress and helping you avoid reinventing the wheel.

Using the disclosure document program

Under the *disclosure document program,* the USPTO allows you to file an informal description of your invention that isn't examined but is kept secret for two years. If you file a patent application within two years and mention the earlier filing, the informal description becomes part of your application file although you don't get the same statutory priority as a provisional application. If you go past the deadline, your description is destroyed.

This program is obsolete and is mainly used by unscrupulous invention development companies to make you believe they've "filed" your invention in the USPTO. You're better off keeping well-organized, witnessed records or filing a provisional application.

Chapter 6

The Quest for the Unholy Grail: The Patent Search

In This Chapter

▶ Deciding to conduct a preliminary patent search

▶ Looking for anything related (and not Aunt Agnes)

▶ Developing a search strategy

▶ Understanding search results

▶ Doing other types of patent searches

*I*magine you're looking all over the house for your car keys so that you and your spouse can drive to your mother-in-law's for your mandatory monthly visit. If you go, you'll miss watching your favorite team playing the last four innings of a World Series game. Do you really want to find those keys? In the topsy-turvy world of patents, you may find yourself in a similar situation — searching for something you hope you won't find. The last thing you want to find in a patent search is your cherished brainchild plainly described in someone else's patent or in some publication. But you must keep looking.

Preparing and filing a patent application takes a lot of time and a good chunk of change. Pushing that application through the U.S. Patent and Trademark Office (USPTO) may take even more. After shelling out all that cash, how would you feel, some 15 months down the line, when the patent examiner says that a complete description of your invention can be found in patent number so and so, granted some 30 years ago to a nice fellow in Peoria? See Chapters 7 through 10 for a trip down the long and winding road to a patent.

You can find out whether your invention is old hat or is innovative enough to deserve its own patent by conducting an *anticipation search,* also called a *patentability search* — a careful study of published patents and other documents relevant to your invention. It's also the most common type of search. For info on other types of searches, see the section called (duh!) "Looking at Other Patent Searches," at the end of this chapter.

No law says that you have to do an anticipation search before filing your patent application. But you can save yourself a lot of money and avoid a great deal of embarrassment by first looking at prior patents, as well as technical books and other publications in the area of your invention.

Most inventors don't understand what they can gain or lose by conducting a preliminary patent search, or whether one is even indicated. In this chapter, I talk about the pros and cons of doing a search, how to conduct a search, and how to interpret what you find.

To Search or Not to Search

Before plunking down your credit card for an expensive vacation trip, you probably get lots of information about the places you want to visit. You may study maps, read some guidebooks, talk to someone else who's been there, and even consult a travel agent. If you think of a patent search as a journey to parts unknown, you can see why you want to know a little bit more about where you're headed before you embark on a long voyage.

Deciding to search or not to search is a tough question, but it may be the most important one to answer. Probably the best reason to do a search is because you want to know the odds of your patent application being approved. A search can tell you whether someone else has invented the same machine or process before you. However, because a search delays the filing of your patent application, isn't cheap, and is no guarantee that you'll get a patent, you shouldn't jump into it without weighing the pros and cons.

Compelling reasons to do a search

If your search uncovers something very close to your invention, you save yourself the cost and aggravation of filing a patent application only to have it rejected after two or three years of futile pursuit. But don't despair — you can possibly use this information to improve and refine your invention or to help you draft a more focused and convincing patent application.

Perhaps the best reason to do a search: It gives you some peace of mind and confirms that you and your invention are starting down the right road.

Some valid reasons for skipping the search

One downside of doing a thorough patent search is that while you're waiting for the results before filing your application, someone else may file for a similar invention. And he'll end up with the patent — not you.

As I explain in the "Analyzing your search results" section, later in this chapter, *no one* can ever safely rely on a search to positively conclude that your gadget is new and deserves a patent, or that there's absolutely nothing patentable in its design.

The high cost of a professional search and interpretation, which could set you back by six or seven hundred dollars, is another reason some people avoid doing one. And extending a search to technical publications may end up costing more than the preparation and filing of the application itself.

Deciding whether a search is right for you

Why would anyone trouble with such a time-consuming and costly procedure instead of just filing the patent application? It's all a matter of balance — weighing the peace of mind that a successful search can give you against the high cost in time and money. I can only help you by suggesting a simple, reliable, cost-effective approach — do a preliminary anticipation search only if you suspect that your invention may not be new.

A search may be a good idea if your invention meets two or more of these criteria:

- ✔ The invention is relatively simple.
- ✔ The invention belongs to a high-tech field.
- ✔ The invention isn't fully developed.
- ✔ The invention is marginally useful or practical.
- ✔ The invention uses very old or obsolete technology.
- ✔ The invention is just another version of a very common device.
- ✔ The invention closely resembles something that already exists.

Getting a second opinion

Like every inventor, you may tend to overestimate the importance and novelty of your creation. Before you get carried away, get a second opinion from an expert in the field. Let your technical expert (or a patent attorney) review the previous section and give you an educated guess as to whether your invention is unique before you do a long and expensive search. Check out Chapter 3 about dealing with patent agents and attorneys.

Finding someone who's willing to stick his neck out and give an opinion without the benefit of a search may be hard to do. You may have to agree, in writing, not to hold it against him if he guesses wrong.

Conducting an Anticipation Search

In the classic film *All About Eve,* Bette Davis's character says, "Fasten your seat belts — it's going to be a bumpy night." I can say the same of patent searches, so buckle up and bear with me on a trip through some arcane, Byzantine, convoluted, disorienting, eccentric, foggy, and goofy (I'll spare you the rest of my alphabetical litany of epithets) legal concepts.

When you perform a preliminary patent search, you're trying to anticipate how the patent examiner will deal with your application. Therefore, your search shouldn't be limited to looking through documents for something resembling your invention. You also need to analyze what you find under the rules of patentability to decide if your invention qualifies for a patent. To do this, you must step into the shoes of a patent examiner and

- ✔ Look for legally admissible information about existing technology in the area of your invention, commonly called the *relevant prior art* (see the "Looking for relevant prior art" section, later in this chapter).

- ✔ Apply the patentability test to the invention (the whole utility, novelty, and non-obviousness thing described in Chapter 4), considering the relevant prior art to draw a legal conclusion that your invention is or isn't patentable.

The most you can get from an anticipation search is to find out that some other dude has already made your doohickey. In other words, you may obtain a clear indication that your invention is not new, but you can never be sure that it is new, no matter how long and how deep you search.

Looking for relevant prior art

When rejecting patent applications, examiners have been known to rely upon prior publications as diverse as the writings of Homer, the ninth-century B.C. Greek poet; rare doctoral literature of all types and languages; and, of course, domestic and foreign patents.

I've seen a patent application for a wetsuit rejected because of a drawing of a medieval suit of armor published in an encyclopedia circa 1900!

Accordingly, prior patents are not the only source of prior art. Any other document can be used against your application. However, not all prior technology related to your invention is legally admissible against your patent application. Drawn from patentability tests in Chapter 4, the following prior patents and publications don't qualify as relevant prior art:

✔ Anything done in a foreign country that wasn't described in a printed publication and not generally known in this country.

✔ Anything that wasn't disclosed, published, patented, or generally available in this country more than one year ago.

✔ Anything that falls outside the *analogous field* of your invention, which includes anything that you, as an inventor, would look into while developing your invention and is directly pertinent to your invention. In a landmark decision, a court ruled that paper stapler technology is outside the analogous field of surgical staplers used to repair digestive organs.

Selecting related patents

Believe it or not, by the end of 2002, the United States had issued about 6,500,000 patents (and that's just the U.S.). A patent examiner could use any of these millions of documents (including expired, cancelled and abandoned patents) as proof that your doodad is neither new nor non-obvious. It's almost impossible to sift through such a mountain of documents when doing your anticipation search, but you can make it easier by taking advantage of patent classifications.

Patents are grouped into a number of technological classes, allowing you to limit your search to the fields of technology most related to your invention. You can find the appropriate classifications in the *Manual of Classifications* published by the USPTO. This manual covers all fields of technology, organized according to international standards. After you find the class or classes that relate to your invention, you can use them to retrieve both U.S. and foreign prior patents. If you're lucky, your invention is simple and well defined, and you can limit the search to just one relevant class.

You can find the *Manual of Classifications* by logging on to www.uspto.gov. A shortcut (but not foolproof) method that avoids looking through the entire manual is at www.uspto.gov/patft/index.html.

Examining patent documents

Searching patent documents to see whether someone has already come up with your invention can be as difficult and frustrating as looking for a wayward golf ball in a thorny thicket alongside the fairway. You have to interpret legalese while looking in lots of out-of-the-way places for your idea. Just like you may miss a ball caught in the bushes if you look only at the ground, you have to look at all sections of the patent document, which is not easy to read or understand.

But don't fret — here's a short course in navigating patent documents. Any patent document, whether an issued patent or a published patent application, can be divided into five sections:

✔ The *reference section,* shown on the front pages of the utility patents in the appendix, gives information that identifies the patent. Besides the patent number, title of the invention, names of the inventors, name of the assignee (owner), if any, filing date, and identification of related applications by the same inventor, the section also includes international and U.S. class numbers and a list of related documents under the legend *References Cited.*

The class numbers refer to the standard technological classes where the subject invention falls. The related documents are prior publications that were cited during the patent application examination because they contain material related to the invention. Check out the "Organizing and conducting the search" section, later in this chapter, to see how to use this during your search. For now, just remember that although you didn't see your idea in the patent document, it could be disclosed in one of those related prior publications.

✔ The *abstract* gives you a very concise, but often very narrow, description of the invention, which is usually illustrated by a representative figure of the drawing, as shown on the patent first pages of the appendix. By the way, in the realm of patents, you only talk about drawing in the singular form. A patent has only one drawing even if it consists of 20 figures spread over 10 pages.

Don't conclude that the patent isn't relevant to your invention just because you don't recognize your baby in the abstract or the illustration on the cover page. Don't stop now — this info can be very misleading as to the true contents of the document. Look at the whole enchilada.

✔ The next page carries the drawing figures with reference numbers that identify the components of the depicted devices. Note that some chemical and process patents that can be described with molecular diagrams alone don't have a drawing.

✔ The following pages of typed text, arranged in two columns, under appropriate section headers, give you:

• The field and background of the invention.

• A summary meatier than the abstract.

• A brief description of each drawing figure.

• A detailed description of the inventor's preferred embodiment of the invention with numerous references to the drawing figures. This description is the meat of the document — go over this section with a fine-tooth comb.

✔ After an opening phrase, such as "What is claimed," you find a numbered list of one-sentence definitions (technically called the *claims*) of what the inventor considers to be his contribution to the art — in other words, his invention. Don't let the formal and circuitous wording of these documents confuse you. (Refer to Chapter 4 to get an idea how claims must be read.) If necessary, grab a pencil and a sheet of paper, draw a diagram of the described structure, and add some notes in your own words. Understanding this section is important because it provides you with a very precise picture of what the invention is all about.

Organizing and conducting the search

You must map out a search strategy by deciding where and how to search. The following are your options.

Searching manually or electronically

You can conduct preliminary anticipation searches in two basic ways: manually and electronically.

✔ You can search manually in the library of the USPTO in Arlington, Virginia, or in one of the USPTO depository public libraries in major U.S. cities. Begin by thumbing through reference manuals, such as the *Manual of Classifications,* for a list of patents to look at (see the "Selecting related patents" section, earlier in this chapter). Then, you need to get paper copies of those patents, kept by class in so called "shoe boxes." In a depository library, you must look through microfilm copies of the patents.

To find a USPTO depository library near you (commonly called a Patent and Trademark Depository Library or PTDL), log on to `www.uspto.gov/go/ptdl/ptdlib_1.html`.

✔ You can run electronic searches on the Internet. You can access the full text of published U.S. patent applications on the USPTO databases by logging on to `www.uspto.gov` and heading to the patent section. Also, most PTDLs provide computer access to the USPTO databases. But, you can't do a keyword search for the actual patent images. You can only do a visual review just like you'd do in a manual.

Electronic searches aren't very practical if the field of technology is more than 25 years old. The USPTO databases hold the texts of patents granted after December 31, 1975, but only the images of patents granted since 1790 up to that date.

Considering that your patent application can be rejected because of a prior description in any domestic or foreign published document, you also need to review available foreign patent applications. You can access European patents and published applications, published international *Patent Cooperation Treaty* (PCT) applications, and Japanese patent abstracts by paying for a subscription to Delphion at `www.delphion.com`. (See Chapters 7 and 18 for more information about the PCT.)

Searching strategies

Many professional searchers have their own approaches and connections for conducting an anticipation search, which they keep very close to their vests, much like trade secrets. But here are two effective searching strategies, one based on my own experience and the other straight from a Patent Office publication. If these approaches look too complicated, hire a professional.

Do-it-yourself (and it's not home improvement)

If you're willing and able (and have plenty of strength and fortitude), you can try to do the search yourself. There are two ways to do this.

Because the best searching strategy is one that's thorough and also saves time and money, here's my own shortcut approach that you should try first:

1. **Locate the latest patent that's most closely related to your invention by conducting an electronic keyword search in the most pertinent class.**

   For example, if you invented a new formula for an epoxy glue, you may want to try searching resin adhesives.

2. **If that patent doesn't completely describe the invention, find the *References Cited* listing on the first page of the patent.**

3. **Check out two or three of the most recent U.S. patents on that list.**

4. **Repeat the last two steps, going back in time through the cited references on each newly found patent until you have reviewed at least 15 patents.**

Promptly abandon branches that deviate from the invention and concentrate on the ones that look most promising.

Remember, it's not over 'til it's over. An anticipation search isn't complete until you find what you don't want to find — an exact description of the gismo that you invented. By definition, you could search forever, so it's up to you to decide when to stop searching.

A more elaborate approach is the multi-step search strategy recommended by the USPTO that you can find at `www.uspto.gov/go/ptdl/step7.htm`. Here are the steps, in a nutshell:

1. **Look at the classification definitions in the *Manual of Classifications* to identify all the classes your invention fits into.**

   You can also get this info by logging on to `www.uspto.gov`.

2. **Browse through the titles of patents listed to help narrow down the class list.**

   Look for keywords related to your invention and then note the corresponding classes.

3. **Retrieve the list of all patents in those corresponding classes.**

4. **Check the weekly *Patent Official Gazette* and add to that list all patents issued during the current week.**

5. **Repeat these steps for all the patents remaining on your list.**

   Review the abstract of each patent, and eliminate those that don't relate to your invention. Note that the *Gazette* is also posted on the USPTO Web site at `www.uspto.gov`.

Be sure to have plenty of coffee handy: This job takes a few hours!

Don't forget to look at published patent applications as well as issued patents. Some of these applications may have been filed before your invention or been published more than a year ago, thus making them a part of the relevant prior art.

An anticipation search shouldn't only examine what a patent covers in the claims, which describe what the owner can prevent others from doing. You must look at everything the document discloses, teaches, and even suggests. For example, don't overlook a design patent document just because it deals only with the ornamental aspect of an object. Check out any design patents in the same class as your contraption because a drawing in a design patent may depict a something that anticipates your invention.

Getting professional help

At some point in your search, you may feel like you're in way over your head. But you don't need to drown — just call in the lifeguards (in this case, a professional searcher) to help you navigate the patent maze.

The most valuable professional assistance you can get for an anticipation search is from a reputable searcher, preferably in the Washington, D.C. area, who can conduct searches in the USPTO library. A professional searcher routinely consults an examiner assigned to the department where your application will be processed. Because a patent examiner reviews applications in a limited field of technology, he can provide invaluable information about the closest prior art. The professional searcher doesn't have to be registered to practice before the USPTO. Someone with a technical background may be all you need.

You can find professional searchers in the Internet's Yellow Pages under Patents, Patent Attorneys, Patent Lawyers, or Patent Searches.

Analyzing your search results

You have found a stack of patents and documents related to your invention. Now what? It's time to act like a patent examiner and apply the novelty and non-obviousness tests, outlined in Chapter 4, to your invention in view of the relevant prior art found during the search.

Would a patent examiner reject your application based on this material? As with all legal concepts, many nuances and exceptions blur the rules about novelty and non-obviousness. The prosecution of a patent application is like a court battle. Patent attorneys and patent examiners often fight like cats and dogs and seldom find common ground.

Only in a clear and blatant case of exact duplication can a layman safely conclude that the invention is not patentable. Usually, only a competent patent attorney, after a careful analysis of the search results, can provide a reliable opinion of non-patentability.

Beware! Search results are always full of holes

Patentability standards are extremely subjective. After you find out what's been done in the past, you must make an educated guess about how a patent examiner will apply those findings in assessing the patentability of your invention. The more you know about patent law, the more accurate that guess will be. Unfortunately, there's no black-and-white answer. You may want to refer to Chapter 1 to find out what types of things are more patentable.

Most anticipation searches only look at U.S. patents and published patent applications and overlook a vast volume of prior material, such as technical books, foreign patents, and scientific articles. Ignoring this material puts you at a big disadvantage compared to the legal eagles and can make for some unpleasant surprises if potential competitors come to light later in the process. Whoops — your educated guess just became a wild goose chase!

Compounding the problem is the fact that patent applications are held in secrecy until they're published, some 18 months after their filing date. The file of a patent application, commonly referred to as the *file wrapper,* is open only to the inventor or owner. Therefore, the hundreds of thousands of patent applications filed over the last year and a half won't show up during a search. By the time your application reaches an examiner's desk, many of those pending applications may be published or turned into patents. If one of those pending applications, lurking like a shark underwater, discloses your invention, the patent examiner will cite that document in rejecting your application. You can see now that your wild guess looks more like a shot in the dark. The moral of the story — no matter how thorough your search, the results are always full of holes.

To locate a patent attorney or agent, log on to www.uspto.gov/web/offices/ dcom/olia/oed/roster/index.html.

Don't forget to keep all the prior art you found during the search and send it to the USPTO with your patent application or shortly thereafter. As the inventor and applicant, you must be completely candid with the USPTO and disclose anything that may be pertinent to your application. Failure to do so could be considered a fraudulent act and cause your patent to be voided.

Looking at Other Patent Searches

An anticipation search is the most common type of patent search, but some-day, you may need one of these three other types of patent searches.

Stepping on someone's toes

An infringement search is a totally different kettle of crabs from an anticipa-tion search. The most common reason for doing an *infringement search* is if your anticipation search reveals an unexpired patent that seems to cover your invention. This information is disappointing, but not fatal. If you've already manufactured and sold your thingamajigs, you may worry that some-one will get you for patent infringement. Before you panic, find out from an attorney whether you're really infringing on an existing patent. What you see in a patent isn't always what's legally covered. That patent may be very easy to get around.

An infringement search is extremely complex and requires a thorough study and analysis of currently active patents and published patent applications in your field. My best advice? Consult an experienced patent attorney who has studied zillions of patent infringement cases. Check Chapter 20 to find out more about patent infringement.

Searching for state-of-the-art

A *state-of-the-art search* is often conducted as part of a program of research and development or to gain expertise in a technical field. It requires looking at the latest patents in a particular field, but has very little to do with getting a patent. In most state-of-the-art searches, inventors review the most recent advances in that field, not just patents — it's a very detailed and technical search of electronic databases and Internet sites. You probably wouldn't do a state-of-the-art search by yourself — it's usually a job for engineers, scien-tists, and other research and development types.

Finding the owner: A patent title search

A *patent title search* finds out the current owner of a patent. To be fully effective, the sale of an ownership interest in a patent (legally called an *assignment*) must be recorded in the USPTO, which keeps a chronological record of all assignments and other recorded transactions related to a patent. Log on www.uspto.gov, and you can find the current owner of any patent.

Chapter 7

Preparing Your Patent Application

*I*f you take my advice, you'll let your patent attorney or agent prepare your utility patent application for you. But he or she can't do a good job without your supportive participation. You're the one who came up with the invention after all. In this chapter, I give you a basic understanding of the purpose, structure, and function of the patent application, so that you can efficiently and effectively assist your IP professional.

If you're after a design or plant patent, you might be able to prepare and file the application yourself, following the guidelines in Chapter 8 and using the information you download from the USPTO Web site (www.uspto.gov). These patent applications don't require the highly legalistic claim drafting of a utility patent application. With a little common sense, basic writing skills, and a willingness to follow directions, you can write a complete disclosure of your new plant characteristics or a sound and convincing description of each figure in your design application drawing. This chapter, therefore, deals almost exclusively with preparing a utility patent application.

Understanding the Patent Application

A patent application is a request that the United States Government grant you the exclusive legal right to a certain area of technology. Your primary goal when preparing your patent application is to make that area of technology as broad as possible — within the scope of your invention. Your patent may eventually cover inventions that are inconceivable today but that fall within the exclusive area covered by your patent.

The strength of your patent depends as much upon the skills of your attorney or agent to persuade the patent examiner to grant legal rights to the broadest area of technology as on the value of your invention. However, the patent examiner's duty is to make certain that your patent doesn't carry more rights than your invention deserves.

Patents aren't granted for the asking. The complex application process often takes unexpected turns into long appellate detours, procedural sidetracks, and disappointing dead-ends. The process breaks down into three major phases:

1. **Preparing the application:** For patents, preparation is definitely the key to success, and that's what this chapter is all about.

2. **Filing the application:** It's not just tossing forms in the mail. I cover the nuts and bolts of filing in Chapter 8 — which you definitely want to check out if you're flying solo with a design or plant patent application.

3. **Pushing the application through the USPTO:** Technically, this phase is called the *prosecution*. At this point, your attorney may have to answer communications from the patent examiner or state your case before one or more appeal tribunals.

Choosing between Formal and Provisional Applications

One of the first choices you and your legal eagle have to make is whether to file a formal, non-amendable application or a provisional application.

- ✔ A *formal application* (a *non-provisional* application in USPTO speak) is the most common type of utility patent application upon which a patent can be granted. It's subject to examination as soon as it's filed. But, given the enormous backlogs, few applications are examined during the first six months from their filing dates.

- ✔ A *provisional application* isn't really an application because no patent can issue from it. It's never examined and must be followed by a formal application within one year of its filing date. A provisional application essentially contains a complete disclosure of the invention and therefore establishes a *priority date* over any subsequent disclosure of the invention and a *priority right* against the subsequent application of another person anywhere in the world. A provisional application is kept secret until a patent resulting from a formal application is issued. If no formal application follows within a year, the provisional application is destroyed and never made public.

  A provisional application is a gimmick instituted to level the playing field for foreign applications among nations. See Chapter 18 for more on that. Just remember that because it's not examined, it doesn't need a lot of legal massaging.

Making things formal

A formal application is the most direct, and thus the quickest, route to a patent. I recommend starting with a formal patent application if:

✔ You want to get a U.S. patent as soon as possible. Your invention is already on or about to hit the market, and it's likely to be copied by your competitors. You're gonna need that patent to stop them in their tracks.

✔ You expect your invention to have a relatively short life, like four to seven years. Electronic and software inventions often fall into that category. Although the law allows you to sue an infringer up to six years after the infringing act, you want to stop those copycats ASAP.

This is the quickest, most prestigious route, but it's also the most expensive at the onset, and it can't be amended to include any new improvement.

Starting with a provisional application

A provisional application offers a convenient way to file a complete disclosure of your invention and establish an early priority date without the high cost of drafting a formal application. The filing fee for a provisional application is about one-fourth of the fee for filing a formal application.

You can also file additional provisional applications to add improvements to the invention for up to a year, at which point you *must* file a formal application. Mark your calendar — you don't want to miss your formal application's filing date.

Going international from the get go

Under the Patent Cooperation Treaty (PCT), you can also opt to file an international application first, designating the United States as one of the countries you want patent protection in. The whole procedure is outlined in Chapter 18. Filing internationally first may work for you if

✔ **You're in a big hurry to obtain patents abroad.** Most inventors like to wait until the last minute to file patent applications in foreign lands, which is 12 months after the filing of their provisional or formal applications. They want to wait and see whether the invention is going to be commercially successful in this country before applying abroad. However, because it takes three or four years to obtain a foreign patent, you can chop off 12 months by filing an international application first.

✔ **You've got plenty of money to spare.** Foreign filings are more expensive than a domestic one, but you've got enough money and the quicker coverage is worth it to you.

In general, filing a provisional application is a good idea, especially if any of these circumstances apply to you:

- Your invention isn't fully developed and you expect to make significant improvements within the next few months. After you file a formal application, you can't modify the description of the invention.

- You're in no hurry to get your patent, but want to establish early priority rights. Because your invention won't hit the market for three or four years, you can postpone the expenses associated with a formal application for a year (including those incurred in dealing with the patent examiner). In the meantime, your provisional application establishes a record of the invention that trumps applications by subsequent inventors.

- You want to keep your invention confidential as long as possible. If you request it, you can delay the publication of your formal application 18 months from its filing date. Your invention will become known only when the patent is granted, some three to four years after you file the provisional application (one year of provisional status and two or three years of formal prosecution). For more on deciding whether to publish your application, see Chapter 8.

- You want to add an extra year to the life of your patent. A provisional application isn't taken into account when calculating the earliest filing date — so you get 21 years instead of the usual 20 (see Chapter 4 for more information on the life span of a patent).

The disclosure in a provisional application must be sufficient for a person skilled in the field to implement all aspects of the invention you want to cover later in the formal application. Because patent professionals usually are more adept at appreciating all the patentable features of an invention than the inventors, having a qualified professional review or prepare your provisional application may be wise. (Inventors tend to focus more on technical features that they think are valuable and overlook vast areas of technology they could have controlled.) The improved quality and breadth of the provisional application can be worth the added expense of a professional review.

However, most patent attorneys will probably refuse to review your work because of rapidly rising malpractice insurance rates. They prefer to start from scratch, analyze all the facts, and draft their own applications. You can join the doctors and blame the trial attorneys for this one.

Note that you can petition to change the provisional or formal status of an application from either one to the other within one year of its filing date, subject to the payment of all applicable fees. It's unlikely that you'd change the status of a provisional application into a formal application because it wouldn't contain a disclosure of any interim improvement and good legal patentability arguments. But, changing a formal application into a provisional one is common in order to avoid examination and delay publication.

Deconstructing the Patent Application

A well-drafted utility patent application should contain:

- ✔ A complete description of the invention, called the *disclosure*.

- ✔ A well-organized argument about the worth and patentability of the invention.

- ✔ Legal definitions of all aspects of the invention and corresponding areas of technology over which you want to gain control.

The disclosure and the argument are grouped in what is called the *specification*, which for a utility patent application usually includes:

- ✔ **Abstract of the invention:** A concise description of the invention. In one paragraph of 150 words or less, the abstract gives a general overview of the invention. As shown in the appendix, it's printed on the front page of the patent to give a rough idea of what the invention is all about.

- ✔ **Drawing:** An illustration, in as many sheets and figures as needed to support the disclosure.

- ✔ **Reference to any prior application:** A short statement that ties the application to any provisional or other previously filed application by the same inventing entity that discloses the whole or part of the invention. (This part isn't allowed in a provisional application.)

- ✔ **General field of the invention:** A one- or two-sentence summary of the area of technology affected by the invention.

- ✔ **Background and circumstances of the invention:** A good argument for the need for the invention and the problems it resolves.

- ✔ **Summary of the invention:** A condensed explanation of the nuts and bolts of the invention, its utility, and its advantages.

- ✔ **Description of each figure of the drawing:** A short sentence explaining each figure.

- ✔ **Description of the preferred embodiment of the invention:** A description of what the inventor considers the best implementation of the invention. It's not necessarily what was built and sold, but what would be built and sold under the best practical circumstances. This part refers to the figures in the drawing.

The legal definitions are called the *claims* and define the area of technology covered by the patent as well as your rights to the invention.

It takes a well-rounded IP practitioner to draft a good patent application, even a provisional one. The strength of the eventual patent depends upon the completeness of the specification and the claims. If you have some technical savvy and basic writing abilities, you can write an acceptable description of your invention. However, the specification isn't the most important part of a patent application. What legally defines the rights of the patent owner and the area of technology covered by the patent are the claims — and you really need your patent attorney to write the claims.

IP professionals spend years honing their claim-writing skills. In spite of all those "how to" books about patent applications, I've never seen a non-professional draft a decent claim, no matter how smart the individual. I would make a tiny exception in the field of chemical inventions, where a good scientist can learn how to write viable claims with a minimum of training.

Disclosing Your Invention in the Specification

Writing a good patent specification requires your active participation and candid communication with your attorney or agent. You're the only one who knows all the ins and outs of your invention and can point her in the right direction when its various embodiments, applications, functions, and great advantages have to be explained. The specification must meet two basic requirements:

- ✔ **The enabling rule:** The specification must clearly and concisely disclose enough for a person skilled in the field of the invention to practice the invention without a lot of experimentation.

- ✔ **The best mode rule:** The disclosure must state what you consider to be the best manner of carrying out the invention.

Complying with one rule but missing the other can make your patent invalid. For example, you may clearly explain how to practice your invention, but this may not be your best mode. On the other hand, your description of the best way to apply your invention may be too sketchy to meet the enabling requirement. The following guidelines should keep you on the straight and narrow path to compliance:

- ✔ **Select the best mode:** In the *Description of the Preferred Embodiment of the Invention* section of the specification, you must reveal what you believe is the most efficient way to practice your invention, which may not necessarily be the manner you build your own prototype. If you've thought of other ways to exploit the invention, you can add them as alternate embodiments. Don't be shy about mentioning various ways to construct a particular structure or perform a specific process step.

✓ **Teach enough but no more than required:** When you try to meet the enabling requirement, you're writing for a person skilled in your field. So you can use technical jargon and skip obvious details. Don't waste time explaining how to use every little component or tool. Your skilled readers can figure out which tasks are necessary on their own. Just make sure that they don't need to do a great deal of experimentation before they can use your invention. You can require time of them, but no head scratching. For instance, if you're disclosing a computer program, draw a flow chart and briefly describe the step represented by each box on the chart. However, you don't need to provide a program code listing.

Remember that after your patent expires, others can use the disclosure of your invention to compete against you. Also, revealing too much may help someone figure out how to avoid your claims by designing around the patent — something that's perfectly legal.

Don't treat the specification like a promotional device or a marketing tool for your new business. It's not the place for puffery about your product or for disparaging comments about your competitors. Allow your attorney or agent to stick to the legal requirements. Don't insist on adding material that's not necessary to support the claims. In infringement litigation, the defendants' attorneys can use this extra material to attack the validity of your patent.

Arguing Your Case for Patentability

According to the law, your patent application only has to include a description of the preferred embodiment of the invention and one claim. But, you need a lot more to make a case for the patentability of your invention. Convincing the examiner or the appeal judges (if you have to appeal a rejection by the examiner) that you deserve a patent usually requires a little extra. You need to provide your IP professional with as much information as he needs to establish the utility, novelty, and non-obviousness of your invention (for the basic conditions of patentability, see Chapter 4).

How do you convince a patent examiner that your invention is the greatest thing since the corkscrew? You must persuasively demonstrate that

✓ Your invention solves a technological problem that has existed for some time.

✓ Others have tried to resolve this problem with questionable success.

✓ You have taken a fresh and different approach.

✓ Your invention provides a fantabulous solution to the problem.

And the places to demonstrate these things are the *background of the invention* and *summary of the invention* sections of the patent application.

Defining the problem

Here's a simple approach to the background section:

1. **Define the general application of the invention.**

   Strap-tightening ratchet mechanisms, commonly called strap ratchets, are used in connection with cargo-securing harnesses . . .

2. **Note the shortcomings of the current devices.**

   The ratchet mechanisms are usually provided with short tightening levers that yield very little torque force. Accordingly, the harness cannot be tightened to the full extent possible . . .

3. **Describe the prior approaches for resolving the problem, including their shortcomings.** You can refer to prior patents, publications, or well-known devices already on the market.

   Some mechanisms of the prior arts have been provided with extended levers as disclosed in U.S. Patent No . . .

   . . . The length and bulk of these extended levers often interfere with the placement of the ratcheting device near a corner of the cargo . . .

4. **Close the section by stating that your invention is an attempt to resolve the outlined deficiencies in the prior mechanism.**

Stating the solution

The summary section shows how your invention solves the technological problem at hand. You usually begin by stating all the objectives of the invention:

   The principal and secondary objects of the invention are to . . .

You must be very careful not to overstate you case or give the impression that this is all there is to your invention. Your statements will be carefully scrutinized by the defendant's attorney in an infringement case and used to limit the scope of your creation. Just state what you need to justify the worth of the invention, but no more.

Then you add a condensed definition of the invention:

   These and other valuable objects are achieved by means of a tool . . .

This last statement should closely follow the wording of your broadest claim. Because you want your claims to be as vague, and therefore as broad, as possible, you want to use very general terms — and this is the place to introduce them.

This example doesn't have to be rigidly followed. Each IP professional tends to have a preferred format, which she adapts to the specific circumstances of each case. Look at the appendix for another example of how to demonstrate the patentability of an invention.

Staking Your Claims

Your patent claims define the area of technology covered by the patent, and in the end, are the only part of the patent that really counts because they legally define your rights to the invention. The specification has only one purpose — to support the wording of the claims.

Notice that the claims don't define your new device or process, which is a tangible or concrete thing, but an area of technology represented by that device or process. Your actual invention is an abstract construct that can't be easily or precisely defined; the specific device or process is only one of many possible applications of the invention. Your patent attorney needs to take care of the claims, but here's a crash course on what he'll be doing.

Less is more: Mastering the mechanics of claims

The wording of a claim has a lot in common with the description of a piece of property in a deed. Just as a deed description defines only the limits of the lot and not anything that may be on it, a claim recites only the minimum elements that must be present for a device or process to be covered by the patent. Of course, anything that falls within these limits belongs to the title owner — the landlord or the patent owner.

A claim usually covers a lot more than the limits it spells out. And the shorter the claim, the broader its coverage.

For an example of this less-is-more rule, take a look at Figure 7-1, which shows the first horseless carriage, invented by Nicolas Cugnot around 1769. If Cugnot had asked me to draft a patent application for his invention, I would have worded my first claim as follows:

> *A vehicle comprising:*
>
> *a cargo-carrying member,*
>
> *at least two wheels supporting said member, and*
>
> *an engine driving at least one of said wheels.*

Cugnot's carriage had a back axle supporting a pair of wheels. The steam engine was coupled to a front wheel. But being a very astute (and extremely modest) patent attorney, I could also imagine motored vehicles riding with only two wheels because 80 years earlier, another Frenchman, Mede de Sivrac, had developed a crude bicycle. I therefore listed the minimum components necessary for a workable device. And it's a good thing I did. If the patent were still in effect today, it'd cover locomotives, cars, trucks, and motorcycles.

Figure 7-1:
Nicolas
Cugnot's
horseless
wagon.

But someone could get around this claim by using only one wheel (possibly a long roller) or by detaching the engine from the wheels (by using a jet engine). You can plug these loopholes by rewriting the claim as follows:

> *A vehicle comprising:*
>
> *a cargo-carrying member,*
>
> *at least one wheel supporting said member; and*
>
> *an engine positioned to propel said vehicle.*

Because the second claim lists only three elements instead of four like the first, more devices out there are likely to fall within its limits. So the more concise second claim has a broader scope than the first and can catch more infringers.

Just for fun, try to redraft this claim to cover a boat or an aircraft.

Checking the various types of claims

Not all inventions can be described by a concise list of components, also called *limitations,* as in the Cugnot example in the previous section. That's why the law provides more than one way to pet a cat.

Listing elements in a claim

The kind of component-listing claims I illustrate in the Cugnot example are commonly used with machine, device, and composition of matter inventions. Here are some variations on the same theme that lend themselves to other types of inventions:

- ✔ **Using functional limitations:** If you have to list a component that has many equivalents capable of performing the same job, you can describe that component in a *means-plus-function* form. For instance, a wheel can be attached to a vehicle frame by means of an axle or a pin or with a complex articulated structure, like the one used on the front wheel of a car. You can effectively describe the component or limitation like this:

  . . . means for rotatively securing the wheel to the vehicle frame . . .

  Can't find *rotatively* in your dictionary? It doesn't matter. When you write claims, you can create your own vocabulary, as long as you clearly define the new term in the specification section of the application.

  In an infringement action, the judge will interpret the scope of a means-plus-function claim to cover the component described in the specification, plus any equivalent structure. An *equivalent structure* is one that achieves the same results (with insubstantial differences) as the one described in the specification, if the equivalent structure is available when the patent is granted. Therefore, enhance your patent by describing as many equivalent structures as possible in the specification. For example, in the wheel attachment component described above, the axle, pin, and complex car front wheel mounting structure should be described in the specification.

- ✔ **Grouping similarly effective components:** Another way to cover a large gamut of similar components in a single claim is to list a group of applicable elements. This style of claim, called the *Markush claim,* is often used to define chemical inventions. The only requirement is that the group of alternate components must be introduced by the all-inclusive phrase *to consist essentially of.* Elements not listed as part of the group are excluded from coverage. For example:

  . . . a dry lubricant taken from a group to consist essentially of graphite, molybdenum sulphide, and boron nitride . . .

The specification must mention the utility and effectiveness of all the listed components. For example, you may explain that tests have been conducted with each type of lubricant with the same effective results.

Claiming a method or process

An invention component can also be defined in a claim by its unique manufacturing method:

. . . a spacer made by bending a length of steel wire into a closed loop . . .

If your invention consists of a method or process, you can describe it as a series of steps:

> *An online method for confirming receipt of an electronic purchase order contained in an e-mail message, said method comprising the steps of:*
>
> *assigning to said order an account number and a job number;*
>
> *clicking a reply button on a toolbar of said e-mail message;*
>
> *typing said account and job number; and*
>
> *clicking a send button on said toolbar.*

Note: This is just a claim-drafting example. I wouldn't wager that you could actually get a patent on that method.

Focusing on an improvement

When the invention consists of a refinement to an existing structure, you can use a *Jepson claim.* First recite the basic structure in the opening phrase, called the *preamble.* Then follow the preamble with a linking term such as *an improvement comprising,* and finally, list the limitations of the invention:

> *In the manufacture of a body armor in which metal plates are piled into a plurality of stacks and each of said stacks is spread in a substantially flat pattern of overlapping plates on the bed of a riveting machine, an improvement for facilitating said spreading, said improvement comprising the steps of:*
>
> *sprinkling a light coat of a dry lubricant over each metal plate before piling into one of said stacks;*
>
> *after riveting, placing said metal plates into a vertical position; and*
>
> *shaking said vertically positioned plates to slough off said coat of dry lubricant.*

Combining structures

A claim can recite a combination of two or more objects. This method is particularly handy when the inventive gadget's utility and novelty are only evident when applied to an existing device. However, to patent combined structures, they must have some interaction between them. For example, a phone mounted on a washing machine for the convenience of the housekeeper isn't a patentable combination because the two devices don't work together, but are only located in the same place. However, the combination of a cylindrical eraser mounted at the end of a pencil might be patentable because the pencil acts as a handle for the eraser.

Playing a medley

An astute IP professional may cleverly use a cocktail of various claiming styles in a single claim in order to obtain the broadest coverage possible. He or she can also claim the same invention in a series of differently phrased claims. Take a look at the claims in the utility patent for an imitation wax seal in the appendix. Notice that Claim 1 lists a component and a means-plus-function limitation. Claim 8 has the same elements as Claim 1 but is phrased as a combination.

Building a claim pyramid

Your name may not be Rameses or Nefertiti, but you can erect a mighty monument for posterity — by building one claim upon another. A claim may be *dependent* upon one or more earlier *parent* claims that it incorporates. For example, if a Claim 2 begins with *The method of Claim 1 which further comprises . . .* or *The device of Claim 1 wherein . . .*, Claim 2 includes all the limitations recited in Claim 1, plus some. In the utility patent in the appendix, Claims 1 and 8 are independent, but Claims 2, 3, 4, 5, and 7 are dependant on Claim 1, which is a parent claim. Claim 6 is dependant upon its parent, Claim 4, and its grandparent, Claim 1. Accordingly, Claim 6 incorporates all the limitations listed in Claims 1 and 4.

Claims can be spread in a radial pattern as Figure 7-2 shows, where all dependant claims are directly connected to a single parent claim. This technique allows you to add just one more element to the basic and most concise independent claim.

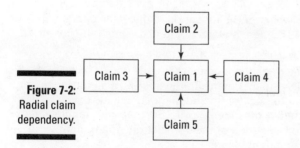

Figure 7-2: Radial claim dependency.

Claims can also be lined up in a cascading or daisy-chain pattern where a claim can be both parent and child — see Figure 7-3. It's used to avoid having to continuously repeat the same element in a series where you keep adding one more element in each additional claim while keeping the elements entered in the previous one.

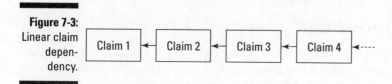

Figure 7-3: Linear claim dependency.

Finally, claims can be scattered in a mixed pattern of radial and linear single and multiple dependency, as Figure 7-4 shows. This may be the most common way to cover an invention with many complex variations.

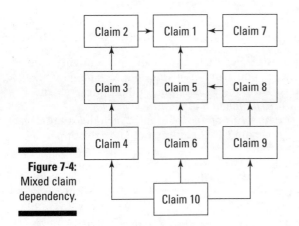

Figure 7-4:
Mixed claim
dependency.

How the claim drafter phrases and organizes the claims depends on the number and types of invention variations to be covered. Her skill and experience are critical. Here's the basic claim-drafting strategy:

✔ Cover the fundamental aspect of the invention in one or two independent claims that recite just enough elements to distinguish the invention from the prior art.

✔ Cover each variation in a dependent claim that adds one or more elements to one of the independent claims. In the course of an infringement action, it's very common to declare the independent claims overbroad and invalid because of newly discovered prior art that the examiner overlooked during the prosecution of the application. You then have to rely on the narrower dependent claims.

✔ Start the whole process again with a new family of claims based on a different style, such as means-plus-function, Markush, combination, or Jepson types, instead of a simple recitation of components.

This shotgun approach to claiming is the only way to cover all potentially infringing technology, including future developments that you can't predict.

Following the grammatical rules

Claim drafting is more than a science — it's an art at which any patent attorney worth his "whereas" should excel and which requires every semantic and legal trick possible. Don't feel bad if you can't comprehend the full scope of each claim in your application. Rules for interpreting claims are even more complex than those that control claim drafting. In a patent infringement proceeding, only the judge can interpret the claims of the patent. It's assumed that jurors can't competently make these types of determinations themselves.

Claims must comply with very peculiar grammatical rules. With apologies to your grade school English teachers, get used to the following oddities, which are just a few of the crazy grammatical twists and turns you'll run into:

- A claim must be written in a single sentence, even if that sentence extends over three or more pages. So run-on sentences are okay.

- A claim must begin with a preamble that briefly states the framework of the invention, followed by a linking phrase such as *which comprise(s), including,* or *which essentially consist(s) of,* followed by the limitations (elements) of the invention. If necessary, you can tack on a *whereby* clause after a limitation in order to clear up any potential confusion as to the nature, application, or function of the invention. The whereby clause doesn't define a necessary limitation of the invention and is often discarded by the judge interpreting the claim. See the "Focusing on an improvement" section, earlier in the chapter, for a preamble example.

- You can't use a definite article in front of an element unless you've already introduced that element in the body of the current claim or in a parent claim. For example, you can't start a claim like this:

  A video camera which comprises a shutter behind the lens . . .

  The word lens hasn't been defined yet, so you have to write:

  A video camera which comprises a lens and a shutter behind the lens . . .

- You can use the terms *which comprise(s), comprising, including, having,* and so on, without excluding other elements in the claimed invention. However, the phrase *essentially consisting of* or *which essentially consists of* excludes any other element. So a claim that recites *a table which comprises a flat top and three legs* also covers tables with four or five legs. However, a claim stating *a table consisting essentially of a flat top and three legs* wouldn't cover a four-legged table.

- You can reference previously introduced elements with the term *said* without repeating the qualifying terms, for example:

  A camera comprising a zoom lens;

  a shutter positioned behind said lens

- Don't use the conjunctions *or* and *nor* or the phrase *such as* if they make the definition vague or ambiguous. For example, the statement *a camera having a lens made of a material such as glass or plastic . . .* won't cut the mustard. Instead, use multiple claims, each reciting one type of lens or, better yet, use a Markush claim (see the previous section), which covers a number of substitutable components: *A camera having a lens made of a material taken from a group consisting essentially of glass, plastic, and silicone.*

✔ Words have the meanings that you give them in the specification, even if these meanings are different from the ones commonly found in dictionaries. Of course, you can't go so far as calling a cat a dog.

✔ You can't list voids, holes, and cavities in structures as primary elements, but can use them to qualify an element. For example, *a wooden beam and a transversal hole in a mid-section thereof* is a no-no. Instead, you must write *a wooden beam having a transversal hole in a mid-section thereof.*

✔ Any descriptive words you use in a claim must first be defined in the specification.

Here's a claim for the structure in Figure 7-5, with all the language rules applied. Can you pick them out for extra credit?

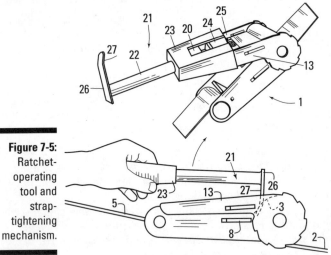

Figure 7-5:
Ratchet-operating tool and strap-tightening mechanism.

The combination of a ratcheted, strap-tightening mechanism having a hand-operable cranking lever and a resiliently biased ratchet-locking member, and

a manipulating tool, said tool comprising:

a rod;

a socket having a proximal end attached at a first end of said rod and a distal end opposite said proximal end, said socket comprising four flat joined sides defining a channel shaped and dimensioned to axially engage over said lever; and a tongue projecting from a second end of said rod opposite said first end, said tongue being shaped and dimensioned to leveredly bear against said resiliently biased member and pry it away from a locking position to release said mechanism;

wherein at least two opposing ones of said sides taper inwardly down axially from an opening at said distal end toward said first end of the rod,

whereby said socket can be securely engaged over a plurality of levers of different sizes.

Actively Participating in Application Preparation

The best thing you can do to ensure that you get your patent is to give your attorney as much information as possible. Your attorney may be the best on the planet (even if you didn't hire me), but he can't do the best job without having all the data.

Compiling the record

So what information do you need to scrounge up to help your legal eagle draft your patent application?

If you kept a good notebook while you were developing your invention, as I mention doing in Chapter 5, dig it out now — it contains a lot of what your IP professional needs. Otherwise, here's a helpful list:

- ✔ Short definition of the general fields of technology to which the invention relates. Include any device or process to which your invention applies.

- ✔ Reasons that led you to develop the invention.

- ✔ Explanation of how the invention came about (unexpected discovery, trial and error approach, a flash of genius, in a dream . . .).

- ✔ Where you developed the invention (for example, as part of your employment, within the scope of a contracted job, or using someone else's resources or facilities).

- ✔ Outline of the existing problems the invention resolves.

- ✔ Account of how these problems were handled in the past.

- ✔ Your opinion about what the invention does that couldn't be done before, or why it's an improvement over past devices or methods.

✔ Depiction of the closest thing to your invention.

✔ Documents or references that best describe the most recent advances in the field of the invention.

✔ Lists and copies of all patents, publications, treatises, articles, and other written material at your disposal that may be relevant to your invention. You are not required to conduct any particular research. If you've done a search (described in Chapter 6), you'll have all this information at your fingertips.

✔ Copies of anticipation search results and any professional patentability opinion.

✔ All records of your development efforts.

✔ Dates of conception of the invention, first sketch or written description, first prototype construction, first public showing, first published description, first public use, first offer to sell, first advertisement, and first sale.

✔ Explanation of the circumstances if the invention was first implemented in a foreign country.

✔ Identification of all persons (including children) who may have contributed to the conception and a brief description of each party's contribution. Include the full names, mailing addresses, residences, and citizenships of any co-inventors.

✔ Copies of any prior filings, such as a Disclosure Document (see Chapter 5) or prior patent applications, whether still active or abandoned.

✔ Copies of any assignment, license, or business agreement related to the invention. Chapter 19 talks about assignments and licenses.

✔ Copies of identifying documents, such as Articles of Incorporation, Partnership Certificates, and fictitious name registrations, for any business that is (or may become) owner of the patent or the invention.

✔ Complete description of the invention, including drawings, photographs, prototypes, test results, newspaper accounts, testimonials, and anything else that could help your IP professional understand and appreciate the invention.

✔ Concise description (a single paragraph of 10–15 lines) of the basic structure of your invention that can serve as a model for the *abstract* portion of the application. You don't need to get into the invention's advantages here. (See "Deconstructing the Patent Application" section, earlier in the chapter.)

✔ Brief account of how you plan to exploit your invention, either through your own manufacturing, by licensing others, or by outright sale.

Looking over the pro's shoulder

You just received the first draft of your patent application and are about to review it alone or in a tête-à-tête with your attorney. Here's what you should be looking for.

Your IP attorney or agent is working for you, so don't be afraid to ask her to clarify anything you don't understand or to change anything that doesn't adequately describe your invention.

Scrutinizing the claims

Because the claims are the most important part of the application, you should go over them with a fine-tooth comb. Be sure that you and the claim-drafter are on the same wavelength. Verify that the part of the technology that's recited is exactly the one that needs to be protected.

You may discover that the most critical aspect of your invention is recited in a dependant claim. Because you can claim only one invention in a patent, ask your attorney to reverse the organization of the claims to recite the most important portion of the invention in an independent claim.

If a claim lists every detail of the structure, down to the kitchen sink, stove, and oven, talk with your attorney about eliminating or rewriting it. A narrow claim doesn't provide much of a net to catch an infringer, it takes up too much space, and it adds to the filing fee (see the section "Paying the piper").

Do make sure that every inventive feature is listed in one or more claims. Don't worry too much yet about whether you're claiming more than one invention in a single application. Later, you can answer the patent examiner's objection by reshuffling the claim pyramid or by withdrawing some claims to be resubmitted in a continuation application (see Chapter 8).

Focusing the abstract

Verify that the abstract describes the gist of your invention. It must be a single paragraph of no more than 12 lines (150 words) and written in plain language, without using legalistic terms such as *means for* and *whereas*. Typically, the abstract reflects the principal claim (usually Claim 1).

Checking the drawing

The drawing must be done in accordance with USPTO guidelines. Patent attorneys and agents use professional patent draftspersons, who work from sketches prepared by the professional based on your description. The drawing must illustrate every item that's recited in the claims. It can be as simple as a block diagram or a flowchart. Don't include more figures than are absolutely necessary to describe the preferred embodiment of the invention. You don't need to draw every nut and bolt. A patent drawing is only an illustration, not a manufacturing blueprint.

Reviewing the disclosure

When you look at some patents, you may think that the drafter was paid by the page. There's too much information, including verbiage that's not legally required and doesn't advance the case for patentability.

Brevity gives you a practical advantage. When you file abroad, you'll be charged by the word or page for the translation and filing. Therefore, you can save hundreds of dollars with a little literary restraint. For example, the *background of the invention* section is no place for a lengthy listing and discussion of prior patents and publications. You can do this when you file the *Disclosure Statement by Applicant* (Form PTO/SB08A) — see Chapter 8.

To make your application short and effective, cross out anything that doesn't support the language of the claims or demonstrate that your invention is useful, new, and above the skill of other people in the field.

Paying the piper

Now is the time to painfully reach for your wallet. Most IP professionals insist that you pay their fees before they file the application. After an IP professional enters the papers in the USPTO under her Joan Hancock, she is obligated (whether or not she's been paid) to do everything reasonably necessary to advance your case (unless she is relieved of her duty by petitioning the Commissioner of Patents).

You also have to pay the application filing fee, which is based, in part, on the number and types of claims you present. Check out the *Fee Computation Sheet* (Form PTO/SB17) in Chapter 8 to see you how much you owe.

Chapter 8

Filing Your Patent Application

*Y*ou probably think that the hardest part is over after the patent application is prepared. It's true that a lot of the detail work is done, but you still have a lot of things to keep in mind when getting ready to file your application, and even more things to keep track of after your application hits the United States Patent and Trademark Office (USPTO). Your patent attorney takes care of most of these details, but you should have a clear view of the filing process, so I describe it here in as much detail as you need. I refer you to more extensive source material in case you want to find out more on the subject.

The contents of this chapter apply to the filing of utility, design, and plant patent applications, including provisional applications. I add some additional special comments about provisional applications and applications for design and plant patents.

Packaging the Application

If you plan to file and prosecute your patent application yourself (which I don't recommend, unless you're dealing with a provisional or a design patent application), you need to obtain a *customer number,* which acts as a password in accessing your application file. Because it's linked to your name and address, the customer number also acts as a mailing code for all correspondence from the USPTO. Instructions about applying for and using a customer number can be downloaded from www.gov/ebc/digitalcert.htm.

Whether you're using a patent attorney or agent or going it alone, get one of the following pamphlets by downloading it from the USPTO Web site at www.uspto.gov/web/patents/guides.htm. You can also order a pamphlet by calling the USPTO General Information Service at 800-786-9199.

- ✔ *Provisional Application for Patent* brochure
- ✔ *Guide to Filing a Utility Patent Application*
- ✔ *Guide to Filing a Design Patent Application*
- ✔ *General Information about 35 U.S.C. 161 Plant Patents*

In this section, I supplement the information in these pamphlets with a handy checklist of all the documents that accompany the application, I discuss additional material you may want to submit, and I tell you how to get a discount on the filing fee and other charges during the application process.

Application checklist

In addition to the patent application specification and claims (see Chapter 7 for preparing the application itself), you must fill out and send the following forms. You can download the forms from the USPTO Web site, www.uspto.gov, by clicking on **Patents** and then on **Forms.** The USPTO is forever adding, splitting, or canceling forms. Make sure you pick up the latest ones for your particular needs and type of patent application.

- ✔ An application transmittal form (there is one for each type of application).
- ✔ A declaration form (for all formal applications).
- ✔ A fee transmittal form (for formal utility patent applications only).
- ✔ A Non-publication Request form when applicable (see "Keeping Your Application under Wraps," later in the chapter).
- ✔ An Information Disclosure Statement by Applicant form. This form is optional at this time (see "Showing all your cards," later in the chapter).
- ✔ And don't forget the filing fee, itself, by check or money order.

Include a self-addressed, stamped postcard (like the one in Figure 8-1) identifying your application if you want to get an early confirmation that the USPTO received your application. The USPTO takes weeks to issue an official receipt. With early confirmation, you won't have to wonder if your application ended up in the dead letter office.

```
PATENT APPLICATION          Case No.

Applicant:

Title:

Design: ( )  Dwg Sheets _____
Utility ( )  Pages: _____   # of Claims
Declaration ( )  Small Entity ( )
Check enclosed in the amount of $_____

Please acknowledge receipt of the enclosed PATENT APPLICATION
by returning this card stamped with the date received and the
Serial Number to the addressee on the reverse side.

THANK YOU
```

Figure 8-1:
Early return
card format.

Showing all your cards

The law requires that you submit copies of documents disclosing information related to your invention that you found during your patent search and any other matter that may be relevant to the examination of your application. You need to reveal every document you're aware of that relates to your invention, and isn't generally known by the public, before your application is examined. So you may as well do this now — when you file the application. List all the documents on the Information Disclosure Statement by Applicant form.

You may (don't feel obligated) also attach a statement explaining what distinguishes your invention from each piece of *prior art* (everything relating to your invention that's already been created) disclosed in the submitted material. (I discuss prior art in Chapters 4 through 7.) This statement necessitates some legal conclusions about the patentability of your invention over the disclosed material. Don't try to do it yourself or you may put your foot in your mouth by overstating the relevance of a piece of prior art. If you can't get a patent attorney to draft it, you'd better skip the thing all altogether.

If you're not sure that a particular piece of information is relevant, send it anyway. If you don't disclose known prior art, your patent is doomed to be invalidated sooner or later.

Asking for a break

If you're an individual or a small business, you may get a 50 percent reduction of the patent application filing fee and most other USPTO charges you have to pay before and after the grant of your patent. Indicate your *small entity* status by checking the appropriate box on the application transmittal form. To qualify for the small entity break, no part of your invention can be owned, licensed to, or assigned to an entity that's not a small business.

Letting Go: Sending Your Application to the USPTO

Mail your patent application to the Commissioner of Patents, P.O. Box 1450, Alexandria, VA 22313-1450. If you send it by an overnight delivery service or some other non-governmental system, you must use a special mail stop. Check the USPTO Web site for the appropriate current mail-stop address. But there's no reason to use an overnight service.

The USPTO considers your mailing date as the official filing date, no matter when it actually receives your application, providing you use the following Express mail procedure — something that's highly recommended. An application sent via any other delivery service is given the date of receipt as its filing date. Send your application via U.S. Express Mail service and paste the Express Mail label in the box provided on the Transmittal Form.

You can also file your utility patent application electronically. In a few years, electronic filing will be the norm for all applications, if not the only accepted method. But for now, the procedure is still being adjusted. You first need to download and install a processing program on your computer. Check the USPTO Web site for the latest scoop on the subject. Click on **Patents** and then on **Apply For Patent Online (EFS).** Applications filed electronically are immediately dated and the receipt is generated on the spot.

You can also hand deliver your application during business hours. Check the Web site for the right Alexandria, Virginia, address.

Meeting Your Filing Deadlines

Dates are everything, and I'm not talking about what you're doing this weekend. In the United States, a patent application, whether formal or provisional, must meet all the following time frames:

- ✔ A reasonable time from the date of invention. Any unjustified delay may be legally construed as an abandonment of your invention, which can allow a later inventor to get the patent.
- ✔ One year after:
  - Your offer to sell the invention.
  - A public use or showing of the invention.

- A description of the invention in a publication.

- The filing date of a foreign application upon which you want to claim priority (this period is only six months for a design patent application).

✔ At least three months before the filing date of another inventor's application for the same invention. This head start lessens the chance that you will be drawn into an *interference* (a lengthy and expensive piddling contest, conducted in the USPTO, between claimants to the same invention) (see Chapter 9). Of course, you don't know whether somebody else has come up with the same invention and is about to file a patent application. That's why I added the last entry to this list.

✔ As soon as possible after you've developed a viable invention. If you know you're going to apply for a patent, why wait?

Most foreign countries require that you file your first domestic patent application before any public disclosure of the invention and that you file your application abroad within one year of the first filing (six months for a design application). Early filing of a provisional patent application can satisfy this requirement, providing that the application fully discloses the invention.

Keeping Your Application Under Wraps

Utility and plant patent applications are automatically published about 18 months after the filing date (or from any earlier priority date you may have claimed based on a prior domestic or foreign application). Until an application is published on the USPTO Web site, only you and your patent attorney can access the application file, commonly called the *file wrapper.* (For even more info than I provide here on the subject of publication, download or request the pamphlet entitled "Published Patent Application Access and Status Information Sheet for Members of the Public."

To avoid publication of your application, you must request it when you initially file your patent application by filling out and enclosing a Non-publication Request form. There's no extra fee for that request, and it can't be denied. It's now or never: You can't stop publication later. If you request non-publication, the file wrapper remains confidential until the patent is granted (and it remains hidden away forever if the patent isn't granted).

If you previously filed a provisional patent application and are filing your formal application just short of one year later (see Chapter 7 for a discussion on provisional and formal applications), your application could be published within seven months. If you're filing a continuation application (see "Filing Again: Entering a Continuation Application," later in the chapter) on an application filed more than 18 months earlier, your new application may be up for publication within a few weeks.

Whatever you do, make an active decision. Don't let your application be published by default, especially if you're concerned about loss of your trade secret. If you're confused, talk to your IP professional and let her help you make the right decision.

Advantages of publication

Before you decide whether to have your application published, consider the advantages and disadvantages. First, the advantages:

- Anyone who infringes on any published claim of your patent application is liable from the publication date, providing that the claim is part of the patent when it's granted. You can't sue the infringer until you get the patent. But, after you do, you can request compensation for all losses resulting from the infringer's activities since the date of publication. Your patent may not be granted for more than a year after publication, so these losses may translate into a lot of moolah in damages.

- The publication of your application acts as a public notice of your impending patent, which is particularly important if you have practiced your invention publicly or sold items manufactured according to your invention before you get your patent. The law gives immunity to anyone who copies a product without a patent number, unless that person is duly notified of the existence of the patent. Because the items you sold before getting your patent can't carry a patent number, the chance of one of these items being copied is fairly high. Your right to compensation for infringement doesn't apply until the infringer is notified, either personally or by the publication of your application.

The presence of the patent number (see Chapter 10 for the appropriate notice) on all items ever sold constitutes proper notice to the entire world. The legend "Patent Pending" on a product has no legal value. If you sold patented items before the patent was issued, the infringer may not be liable for copying those items until you notify him by letter or otherwise.

- You can file an application abroad claiming the priority date, based on the filing date of the U.S. application, providing you do so within one year of that filing date.

The request for non-publication bars you from filing abroad with claim of priority. There is a way out though. If you initially requested no publication and decide, within one year, to file a foreign application claiming priority based on your U.S. application, you must petition that the application be published no later than 45 days from the foreign filing date, and pay a petition fee of about $120.

Back in the good old days

In the '60s and '70s, the federal government subsidized the USPTO, and applicants' fees were negligible. However, these days, inventors and patent owners pay hefty sums to the USPTO almost every time they file a document or ask for special treatment. At the end of every budget year, the USPTO kicks back millions of unspent dollars into the "General Fund." Yet fees increase every year, sometimes by huge percentages — with no relief in sight.

These increases exist because a few years ago, Congress, as part of legislation deceptively called the Budget Reconciliation Act, decided that inventors and patent owners were sheep that could be mercilessly shorn. Now individuals and companies like you have to finance the whole USPTO operation and also pay for unspecified federal expenditures. When you get tired of being shorn and milked dry, as I predict you'll soon be, don't complain to your IP professionals. It's not their fault. Instead, write your congressperson and asked why you are being unfairly taxed.

To get the most benefit from publication, request that your application be published anytime prior to the statutory 18-month scheduled date. You can also change your mind and request early publication even if you initially petitioned for no publication. The petition fee applies to both a request for early publication and a rescission of a previous non-publication request. Get the appropriate forms from the USPTO.

Disadvantages of publication

Don't forget to factor in the disadvantages:

- ✔ Publication may punch a big hole in your trade-secret protection strategy. As I point out in Chapters 1, 2, and 5, you may want to keep your invention confidential for as long as you can. This is particularly true if you intend to rely on your trade-secret strategy to protect your invention and are just filing a patent application as back-up protection (I talk about this strategy in Chapter 5).

- ✔ If your invention isn't quite ready for the market, the publication gives an early opportunity to some wise gals to start working around your patent claims, and beat you in the race to the market place.

- ✔ You must pay a fee of about $300 in addition to the regular issue charges to get your patent issued if the application was published either automatically or at your specific request.

Asking for Special Status

In general, patent applications are examined in the order of their *effective filing dates,* typically their actual filing dates or their priority dates (see Chapter 7), whichever came first. I have to qualify my statement with words such as "in general" and "typically" because this rule is subject to many exceptions. So, what else is new? I won't get into irritating details, but because of the lack of proper staffing and other such excuses, your application may not rise to the top of the pile for one to two years.

But you can ask that your application get special status and go to the top of the pile for an expedited examination if you meet certain qualifications. If your petition qualifies, it's moved ahead of all the non-special applications, but still sits behind the special applications that qualified before yours.

Depending on how many applications are ahead of yours, the benefit to special status could be minimal, saving you only a few months. If you're lucky, you may gain six months to a year. Unfortunately, you can't predict the effect of the petition. Considering that most applicants petition to have their applications made special, your application will definitely be pushed to the bottom of the barrel if you can't or won't petition as well.

A petition to make your application special should be filed with the application or shortly after. Because the USPTO takes two or six months, depending upon your supporting reason, to review and approve the petition, filing the petition months after your application filing date may delay your application instead of expediting it.

You can claim 1 of 12 grounds to support your application's special status, as I outline in the following sections. I also discuss a backdoor approach for those who have friends in high places.

You must present your petition on a paper separate from the specification and claims, together with the applicable fee.

The fee-less quartet

If you base your petition for special status on one of the following four situations, you don't have to pay a petitioning fee.

- ✔ **Alleging old age:** If you're 65 years or older and can provide supporting documentation such as a birth certificate, you're in the pink, even if you have only a few gray hairs.

- ✔ **Standing on your last leg:** No matter how young you are, if you're critically sick and may not be around long enough to assist in the examination of your patent application, you have my deep sympathy. I can cheer you up a bit by assuring you that attaching a statement from your attending physician to your petition will get you that special status.

✔ **Joining the green crowd:** If your invention benefits the environment by contributing to the restoration of basic life-sustaining natural elements, such as air, water, and soil, you land on the green, your application qualifies for special treatment.

✔ **Conserving energy:** If your invention leads to a new source of power or to a more efficient use of energy, such as a more efficient appliance, you get a gold star that moves your application to that coveted special status.

The costly group of eight

If you base your petition on one of the eight grounds listed here, you must pay a petition fee, which is about $130. (Check for any change by logging on the USPTO Web site at www.uspto.gov. Click on **Fees and Payments,** then on **Fee Schedule,** and look under code 1460-1.17h.)

Searching required

A petition based on one of the following two grounds must be accompanied by the results of an anticipation search and analysis (see Chapter 6). The search and analysis should be done by an IP professional and must report the classes and sub-classes of prior patents searched.

✔ **Going into manufacture:** If you can demonstrate, through credible documentary evidence, that you can't begin manufacturing your inventive gizmo until a patent is granted, your application deserves special status. Investors and lenders sometimes refuse to advance funds till they see the patent. A declaration by your investors, banker, or other lending institution is a good example of supporting evidence. The search analysis must demonstrate that your patent is likely to be granted in view of the prior art that has been discovered.

✔ **Facing infringement:** If you discover that your invention is already being practiced by someone else, you may petition for special status, presenting documentary evidence that at least one claim in the application is being infringed.

Going high-tech

If your application relates to any one of the following high-tech fields, it qualifies for special status:

✔ **Safety of research on recombinant DNA:** Because of serious potential health and environmental hazards associated with manipulating recombinant DNA, the USPTO will grant special status to applications for inventions relating to the safety of research in that field.

- ✔ **Electrical superconductivity:** The electrical superconductivity of certain materials may have great energy-saving potential and strategic advantages. Patent applications for inventions related to superconductivity materials, their fabrication, and application will be given special status on request.

- ✔ **Detection and treatment of HIV/AIDS or cancer:** AIDS and cancer are the major scourges of our era. Patent applications relating to the treatment or prevention of HIV/AIDS or cancer merit prompt handling, which they will receive upon request.

- ✔ **Counter-terrorism:** Countering international terrorism has become a national priority. The USPTO will grant special status to patent applications related to technology for countering terrorism. These inventions include, but aren't limited to, systems for detecting or identifying explosives, aircraft sensor or security devices, vehicular barricades, and vehicle-disabling systems.

Struggling in a field of giants

If you are a small business involved in biotechnology, you may ask that your application be made special. However, you must demonstrate that the development of your technology will be significantly impaired if examination of your patent application is delayed.

Doing part of the examiner's work

Even if you don't qualify under any of the previous grounds, you can petition for special status under the *Special Examination Procedure* program. To qualify, have your patent attorney conduct a preliminary examination of your application in the same manner as a patent examiner's. You must supply a complete report of the examination, including the results and analysis of an anticipation search, a list of classes and sub-classes searched, copies of all the prior art documents uncovered, and a professional analysis of their impact upon the patentability of the invention. If the USPTO is satisfied with the competence and thoroughness of the search and the soundness of the analysis, it'll put your application on the fast track.

A special examination has some drawbacks, in addition to the high cost of the preliminary examination. It takes a bit of time for your IP professional to conduct the preliminary examination, and more time for the USPTO to assess the value of that examination. The amount of time saved doesn't always justify the cost (in both time and money) of the procedure.

Coming through the back door

The law provides that if your invention is important to some branch of public service, your application can be given priority at the request of the head of a governmental department. Of course, to get your invention noticed, you'll need some friends in high places, a lot of chutzpah, and a dose of good luck.

Preparing and Filing Some Simplified Patent Applications

Chapter 7 dealt primarily with the preparation of formal utility patent applications. Preparing a provisional, design, or plant patent application is a little less complicated. Due to their relative simplicity and lack of specific claims, they don't require legal expertise. With the help of one of the pamphlets listed above and the following guidelines, you should be able to prepare and file one of these applications on your own, although the assistance of an IP professional is recommended.

Provisional applications

A provisional application is never examined and doesn't need to be laid out in any particular format. It only needs to fully describe the invention to support the following formal patent application. A patent attorney usually writes the specification in the same manner with the same list of topics as in a formal application (see Chapter 7 for utility applications, and the following sections for design and plant patent applications) because that's the best and the most common way to describe an invention. You may try to do the same or create your own format, as long as you don't leave out any substantial aspect of the invention that could be separately claimed in the following application. Needless to say, a patent attorney may do a better job because of her training and ability to quickly identify all patentable aspects of your invention.

The filing of a provisional application doesn't require the declaration and fee transmittal forms, just a Provisional Application for Patent cover sheet, and a modest fee of about $80.

Design patent applications

A design patent application, which is relatively simple and inexpensive, addresses the ornamental aspect of an article of manufacture (see Chapters 4 and 5 for more info). In most aspects, the process of filing an application for design patent are the same as for a utility patent, except that the filing fee is only about $170 for a small entity. However, the specification and claim are a lot simpler than for a utility patent. Here's where design patents differ:

✔ The description of the invention is limited to a drawing or set of photographs that illustrate the article from all angles and a brief description of each view (see Page 3 of the design patent in the appendix).

✔ The description must start with a formal preamble giving the name of the applicant, the title of the design, and a brief description of the nature and intended use of the article in which the design is embodied as follows:

> *Be It Known That I, Jane Dee, a citizen of the United States of America, resident of Dade County, State of Florida, have invented a new and ornamental design for a TEA KETTLE of which the following is a specification.*

✔ You only need one formally written claim (see the last page of the design patent in the appendix).

✔ The drawing must be in accordance with the rules spelled out in Section 1503 of the *Manual of Patent Examining Procedure* (MPEP) (see Chapter 24).

Plant patent applications

An application for a plant patent, which I describe in Chapter 4, follows the same format as a utility patent application, except that the illustration is usually one or more photographs. Only one formal claim is allowed (see the last page of the plant patent in the appendix). Use a plant patent application transmittal form, and pay a standard fee of about $260 for a small entity.

Making Money and Taking Precautions While You Wait for Your Patent

You don't need to wait for your patent to be granted before you do something with your invention. Years may pass before a patent is issued and that's never a certainty. I've seen utility patents issued within 6 months from their application date (extremely rare), and others that required up to 10 years. The average pending time is about 32 months, but don't count on that estimate for any serious business planning.

While you're waiting, you can exploit your invention by the same methods you'll use to make some cash after you get your patent. I discuss these avenues in detail in Chapter 19:

✔ Manufacturing and selling products embodying the invention

✔ Licensing your invention and eventual patent to others for royalties

✔ Selling the invention and patent rights

The one thing you must not do is disclose the contents, serial number, or filing date of your patent application to anyone, except under strict conditions of confidentiality. Even if the receiving party has signed a confidentiality agreement, you shouldn't disclose the wording of the pending claims.

While your patent is pending, someone who's filed an application for the same invention may challenge your application. This process, called an *interference,* determines which of two inventors claiming the same invention deserves the patent (see Chapter 9). Someone privy to your patent application can file his own application, copying some of your claims and triggering an interference proceeding. If the person knows the date of your patent application filing, he can claim a date of invention that precedes yours. Just the expenses and delay associated with the interference are enough to give you nightmares. But what should really worry you is the risk that the usurper might walk away with the patent.

Of course, after your application has been published, you don't need to keep it confidential because the USPTO has taken care of making it public.

Don't forget to mark your products with a *Patent Pending* notice and make your licensees do the same. The notice acts as a good deterrent to potential copycats. They'll hesitate to invest in manufacturing your product, for fear they may be shut down within a few months. But if you let it be known that you just filed your patent application, a copycat may speculate that he has two or three years to compete with you without consequences.

Filing Again: Entering a Continuation Application

Quite often, something comes up after you file your formal patent application and you need to file a *continuation application.* Here's what a continuation application allows you to do:

✔ File a more complete application that includes some recent improvements to the invention in place of the original application.

✔ File a new application disclosing the same device or process as the original application, but claiming a second invention embodied in that original device or process. For example, a filtering mechanism for a new coffee maker might be the invention claimed in the original application, but a continuation application could claim an improvement in the coffee maker's heating element. You can't claim them together in one application because a patent can only cover one invention. An inventor usually finds it necessary to file a series of applications in order to fully cover his or her creations.

If you go the continuation route, remember these peculiarities:

- A continuation application must have at least one inventor in common with its parent application.

- If the continuation application contains *new matter* (anything not described in the original application), the new application is called a *continuation-in-part application.*

- If the continuation application doesn't disclose anything new, but simply claims something previously disclosed but not currently claimed in the pending original application, the new application is called a *divisional continuation application* or simply a *divisional application.*

  A divisional application often results from an examiner's request that certain claims in an original application be withdrawn because they refer to a separate invention. In such a case, claims cancelled in the original application and now presented in the continuation application are immune to certain grounds for rejection. Divisional applications are like teachers' pets — they get preferential treatment by the patent examiner because they're mere extensions of their parent applications.

- After a continuation application has been filed, you can formally abandon the original application, let it expire, or keep it alive until the first patent is issued (see tactical considerations in Chapter 10).

In order to claim priority on an application filed earlier, the previous application must be in good standing when you file a continuation application. Don't let the original application expire because you forgot to answer a communication from the examiner.

Chapter 9

Wrestling with the Patent Examiner

*Y*ou've just sent your patent application to the U.S. Patent and Trademark Office (USPTO). So what can you expect now? I could be cynical and answer: Lots of heartburn. But the process of pushing your application through the USPTO (called *the prosecution*) isn't that bad if you're patient. Like the wheel of justice, the gears and cogs of the USPTO turn very slowly — and all at your expense because the 20-year life of your patent is computed from the date you file the application. Only the time you spend successfully appealing adverse decisions of the patent examiner isn't held against you. Even if your application benefits from a *special* status (see Chapter 8), you can expect to wait 12 to 36 months. So, it pays to move your patent application through the USPTO as diligently as possible. Because utility patents are the most complex, I focus on their examination in this chapter.

No matter how ambitious you are, you probably won't be able to single-handedly answer the examiner's requests, objections, or rejections after reading this chapter. I know this book is good, but it isn't law school. You have to rely on your IP attorney and trust his or her judgment. All communications from the patent examiner are written in a formal style and are often accompanied by citations of statutes, rules, or controlling court decisions. They should be answered the same way, point by point, with contrary citations supporting your position when appropriate.

Also, in the narrow confines of this chapter, I can only give you a basic outline of the rules and regulations that govern the prosecution of patent applications. There are many nuances, exceptions, and special provisions that are too numerous to address.

Touring the USPTO

Before tackling the substantive issues that the patent examiner will raise after looking at your application, you really should get more intimately acquainted with the USPTO first. The USPTO is an administrative agency of the U.S. Government that manages these patent-related tasks:

- ✔ Accepting and examining patent applications
- ✔ Granting patents
- ✔ Resolving conflicts between applicants claiming the same invention
- ✔ Maintaining a library of issued patents
- ✔ Correcting defective patents
- ✔ Registering and keeping copies of documents related to patents and patent applications
- ✔ Qualifying and disciplining patent attorneys and agents
- ✔ Collecting hefty fees from applicants and patent owners

Notably absent from this list is helping applicants obtain their patents. In fact, the USPTO examiners act contrary to your best interests. One of their duties is to prevent you from getting a patent that goes beyond the merits of your invention. Don't expect much help from a patent examiner except to guide you through some minor administrative procedures.

You'll also notice that the USPTO has absolutely nothing to do with patent infringement matters — the exclusive domain of federal courts.

Consulting the golden book

All the USPTO's activities related to patents and patent applications are governed by the rules and legislations in the *Manual of Patent Examining Procedure* (MPEP). This manual lists the patent laws, the federal regulations applicable to patents, patent applications, and all related administrative procedures, and very detailed instructions and guidelines for use by patent examiners and USPTO personnel. To order the manual or consult the MPEP, see Chapter 24.

Meeting your examiner and the art unit

The patent examining section of the USPTO is divided into art units. Each *art unit* specializes in a specific field of technology identified by reference to one or more groups. A *group* is a subdivision of the patent classification system that includes several technological classes and subclasses (see Chapter 6).

And within each art unit are the patent examiners who work their legal voodoo on your application. The *patent examiner* performs the down-in-the-trenches work of reviewing hundreds of patent applications a week, conducting anticipation searches, and drafting examination reports. Over many years of personal dealings with the USPTO, I've found that the examiners are well-trained, dedicated professionals.

Whenever you communicate with the USPTO about a pending application, include the number of the relevant art unit in the top right corner of your first page. You can find that number on the original application receipt and on all papers from the examiner. If you know the name of the examiner assigned to the case, you must add it to the art unit number.

Crying to the commissioner and other appeal routes

The big kahuna at the USPTO is the *Commissioner of Patents,* who oversees the entire organization. You may have to kiss his knickers occasionally while applying for your patent, if you know what I mean. If you get a decision you don't want by the USPTO, your appeal options are illustrated in Figure 9-1.

- ✔ **Regulatory matters:** Petition the commissioner directly to reverse a decision by the examiner of a procedural rather than legal nature, such as a refusal to accept a filed document on technical grounds or an objection to the contents of your patent application. (See the "Getting In on the Action —The Office Action" section, later in the chapter.)

- ✔ **Legal decisions:** Rulings of a legal nature, such as a rejection of claims in your application for lack of novelty or obviousness, must be taken to the Board of Patent Appeals and Interferences (BPAI), on which the commissioner sits. All proceedings before the Board are conducted in accordance with the *Federal Rules of Civil Procedure* (see Chapter 24) — the kind of stuff that gives law students nightmares.

  If your appeal to the commissioner or to the BPAI is unsuccessful, your attorney can take your case to the Court of Appeals for the Federal Circuit and, if necessary, all the way to the U.S. Supreme Court. Instead of appealing to the BPAI, you can also sue the commissioner in the U.S. District Court for the District of Columbia to force him to grant you a patent. Talk with your attorney about which is the best route to follow.

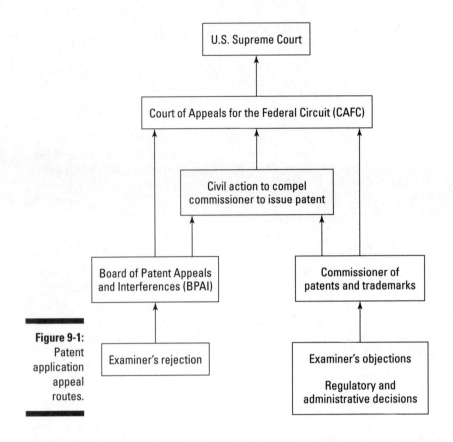

Figure 9-1:
Patent
application
appeal
routes.

Clearing Initial Administrative Hurdles

The USPTO only corresponds with one person. If you're flying solo, that's you. However, if you take my advice and hire a professional, that person is your patent attorney or agent.

Meeting the minimum requirements

After you drop your patent application in the mail or hand deliver it to the USPTO (see Chapter 8 for filing info), it's forwarded by the mailroom to the *Office of Initial Patent Examination* (OIPE). The OIPE immediately mails you back the early return card (that I suggest you submit with your application in Chapter 8) stamped with a temporary and conditional application filing date and serial number.

If you don't get the return card within a week of mailing your application, you may assume that something went awry in the mailing of the application.

Don't disclose the filing date or serial number to anyone, except under strict conditions of confidentiality. Why give a potential competitor a free ride by letting him know that you just filed and can't sue infringers until you get your patent in another two or three years? Plus, somebody armed with your serial number has the ammo to file a protest against your application in the USPTO (see "Avoiding a Third-Party Protest," later in this chapter).

The OIPE then checks your application to see whether it meets the minimum filing requirements— just a specification and one claim. If so, the application's temporary and conditional filing date and serial number are confirmed for the record of the USPTO. Meeting these minimum requirements only puts your application in the USPTO's hopper. It doesn't guarantee you'll get a patent. Your application needs a lot more, as I explain in Chapters 7 and 8, to survive the examination.

If the application doesn't include a complying specification and at least one claim, the OIPE sends you a *notice of incomplete application,* asking for the missing part, and cancels your temporary filing date and serial number. You're given two months to complete the application before it's returned to you. When you mail in the complying part, you must include a declaration that identifies the supplied material, indicating that it accurately describes, illustrates, or claims your invention. Use the supplemental declaration form.

Dealing with additional issues

When your application meets the minimum requirements, it takes about six weeks before you receive an official *notice of receipt* of your application, and sometimes a *notice of defective application.* You get the latter if, for instance, you didn't enclose the filing fee or a signed declaration form. In such a case, you have a few weeks to send the missing part and pay a fine of about $70.

The OIPE may also object to some components of your application. For example, if you printed your specifications on both sides of a sheet, used the wrong size of paper, or sent a drawing of such a poor quality that it can't be clearly reproduced, the OIPE will request that you submit acceptable substitute material within two months.

The OIPE, or later on the examiner, sometimes wants a little more information about the invention. They may request information about the field of technology to which the application pertains or ask for existing documentation or reference material about the general area of the invention. This information helps them determine the application's relevant art unit. A reply is usually required within two months of the request.

Receiving a foreign filing license and secrecy order

For most applications, a foreign filing license accompanies the official notice of receipt. You can't file in a foreign patent office until you get this *foreign filing license* from the USPTO.

Disclosing your invention or filing for a patent in a foreign country before filing in the United States or before receiving the foreign filing license may prevent you from getting a U.S. patent. Depending on the subject of your application, you could be prosecuted for violating export regulations, which means that your next communication to the USPTO could be on federal penitentiary letterhead. The main purpose of the foreign license requirement is to prevent U.S. residents from disclosing to other countries critical inventions that have military applications. See Chapter 18 for more on filing for foreign patents, and Section 140 of the MPEP if you want to know more about this license business.

If your invention relates to atomic energy or space, you must certify that it wasn't developed under a government-sponsored program or grant, which includes acting as a subcontractor to a company working under a government contract. You can find a sample of the required certification under Section 150 of the MPEP.

More significantly, all patent applications that have military applications are subject to review by the U.S. Department of Defense or a law enforcement agency. Depending upon the sensitivity of the technology, a foreign filing license may be denied and your application placed under a *secrecy order.*

A secrecy order forbids you and anybody else from disclosing your invention to anyone and prevents the USPTO from publishing your application or allowing it to mature into a patent. You can petition to have the order rescinded by proving that secrecy is fruitless — for example someone has already let the cat out of the bag. But, if the secrecy order is maintained, you can request monetary compensation from the agency that issued the order.

Failure to comply with a secrecy order makes you criminally liable, subject to a fine of up to $10,000 and two years in the federal big house.

Splitting Up Is Hard to Do: Restricting the Application

A few months later, when your patent application makes its way to the top of the pile on the examiner's desk, she may issue a request for restriction. A *request for restriction* demands that you limit the scope of your application. Request for restrictions occur only if you claim more than one invention — or several *species* (variations) of a single invention — that could be patented independently from one another.

Say you invented an electric toothbrush with bristles that have different directions and ranges of motion. You claim several species of the brush — one with a straight handle, one with a curved handle, one with a metal handle, and one with a plastic handle. The metal and plastic handle species aren't patentably distinguishable from each other because substituting a plastic handle for a metal one would be obvious and not deserve a separate patent. But using a curved handle instead of a straight one may provide some significant and not necessarily non-obvious advantages (making it easier to reach some back teeth) that could be the object of a separate patent. You'd have to restrict your application to one of these last two species of brushes.

If a claim applies to all species of the invention, that claim is said to be *generic*. A generic claim defines the *genus* that has the basic characteristic of all claimed inventions. In the toothbrush example, a claim that recites the bristle arrangement and simply "a handle" would be generic because it covers all the various handle species.

The examiner expresses the restriction request by singling out one or more generic claims, and listing all the independently patentable species she can identify. She then asks you to elect claims addressed to a single species and withdraw the claims that recite non-elected species.

If you comply with the request, the claims you withdraw are set aside. If, at the end of the examination process, one of the generic claims is allowed, all the withdrawn species claims covered by that allowed generic one are automatically brought back and allowed. If no generic claim is allowed, you end up with the group of claims addressed to a single species that you've elected. In that case, in order to cover the inventions recited in the claims you have withdrawn, you must include them in one or more divisional continuation applications (see Chapter 8) that you must file before the issue or abandonment of your original application.

You have to respond to a request for restriction by electing one of the inventions. You can't refuse to restrict the invention and elect a species. But, you have options: You can choose the one invention with or without a protest.

If you make your claim election without filing an objection to the request for restriction (called filing *without traverse*), the restriction is final and can't be contested later. If you *traverse* (contest) the request, the examiner will probably find your argument unconvincing, reject it, and fire back a final request that can be appealed. You can then petition the commissioner to reverse the examiner's decision, and wait about four to eight months for a ruling. In the meantime, you have to make an election, and it better be the right one because you may have to live with it if your petition is denied. So deciding which aspect of the invention to patent first is very important.

The best choice is the aspect of the invention that gives you the most legal rights against your eventual competitors, not necessarily the one that you think is the most clever or innovative. When in doubt, let your IP counselor help you make the most sensible decision.

The main reason for contesting a request for restriction is to force the examiner to reconsider her decision. Another reason is to reserve the right to appeal the examiner's decision to the commissioner, or later, the BPAI if you're not satisfied with the final outcome of your application. But there's a problem with that approach.

When you try to argue that the request for restriction isn't warranted, you may have to point out that the various embodiments and species claimed aren't patently distinguishable. This could be dangerous, if not fatal, for your application. If you maintain that all embodiments and species are patentably equivalent, and later the examiner finds that one embodiment is anticipated by the prior art, your entire invention is in jeopardy. Most patent attorneys prefer not to take the risk and file a restriction without traverse.

Before answering a request for restriction, take a good look at the way your claims are drafted. You may want to amend them to eliminate some of the grounds for restrictions. For example, you may enter one or more means-plus-function claims that cover several or all of the embodiments of your invention. You could also reshuffle the claim hierarchy to place the most valuable invention in the generic claim, or at least in an elected one. I explain the various kinds of claims in Chapter 7.

You can modify the claims in a *preliminary amendment* to your application. The amendment must be submitted before any substantive examination by the examiner, but no later than your response to the request for restriction. In addition, if you file a preliminary amendment after you receive a request for restriction, you must elect the embodiment and species in relation to the amended claims and not the claims as originally filed.

Getting In on the Action — The Office Action

After you have the whole request for restriction thing straightened out (see the "Splitting Up Is Hard to Do: Restricting the Application" section, earlier in this chapter), you're ready for the next test. If you avoided that fun because the claims of your application address a single invention (or through some other stroke of good fortune), your story continues here as well.

The examiner conducts an anticipation search (see Chapter 6) and issues an *office action* (OA) — the first report on the merits of your claims. If you're the exception, all is well. You receive a *notice of allowance* of all your claims, and you can go straight to Chapter 10. However, if the OA contains an adverse ruling, you have to attempt to refute it. Most likely, you'll amend (change) the specification or claims to make them more acceptable. Then the examiner fires back with another, but final, OA, giving you a last opportunity to argue or amend. Additional procedures allow the exchanges to continue until you and the examiner reach a meeting of the minds as I explain later. Unfortunately, these procedures also include additional fee payments.

The OA may contain two types of decisions:

- ✔ **Objections:** Objections usually mean you didn't comply with the *definiteness requirement* in drafting the specifications or claims. Typographic and grammatical errors (including the peculiar grammatical rules of claim drafting in Chapter 7), vague or long-winded descriptions, discrepancies between the written description and the drawing, and otherwise defective drawings are examples of indefiniteness.

   These mistakes are fairly easy to correct and should be addressed in the first portion of the amendment filed in response to the OA. An objection is subject to review by the commissioner. (See Figure 9-1 for a refresher course on the appeals routes.)

- ✔ **Rejection:** If the examiner rejects some or all of your claims, you have a more troublesome matter that may require vigorous arguments on your part. You may also need to make extensive amendments to a claim or cancel it altogether. A rejection applies to a claim and more specifically to the invention recited in that claim. It doesn't relate to any particular component, element, or other limitation listed in that claim. A rejection can only be appealed, preferably by a competent lawyer, to a qualified federal court (see Figure 9-1).

   The examiner can reject claims on a number of grounds. In the sections that follow, I cover each kind of rejection and how you can overcome it.

Overcoming a rejection for indefiniteness

A rejection of one or more claims for indefiniteness usually parallels an objection on the same ground. Or it can state that your wording is incomprehensible or too vague. This last ground can present a serious problem for you. As I cover in Chapter 7, having claims that are as broad as possible is to your advantage, and broadness can be achieved by not being too precise. Here lies a tug of war between you and the examiner. You want a claim that can cover as many machines or processes as possible even at the risk of being ambiguous. But the examiner wants to make sure that one can readily assess the coverage of the claim from its wording.

You can overcome the rejection of a claim for indefiniteness by cleaning up the informalities and tightening its wording. But you have to be very careful not to unduly narrow its coverage. That's when your patent attorney's experience and expertise become invaluable.

Fighting a lack-of-utility rejection

Being rejected because of a lack of utility basically means the invention has no demonstrable practical use. (Utility, along with novelty and obviousness, is one of the tests of patentability, as I discuss in Chapter 4.) See section 101 of the patent law for a complete explanation of the utility requirement.

The courts have interpreted this requirement to mean that a person with some skill in the area can immediately appreciate that the invention is useful, and that its utility is specific, substantial, and credible. The following list contains examples of questionable claims content and the statements you'd see in the first OA:

- **Compound for softening fingernails:** *The claimed invention lacks patentable utility. There is no conceivable application for a nail-softening compound. The role of a nail is to strengthen a fingertip. Softening a nail would be counter-productive.*

- **Perpetual motion machine:** *The claimed invention is inoperative and therefore lacks utility. The invention is a perpetual motion machine that defies the laws of physics and cannot be credible.*

- **Method for growing hair by exposure to a magnetic field:** *The claimed invention has no demonstrable utility. The effect of a magnetic field on the physiology of hair growth is neither demonstrated in the specification nor credible in view of current knowledge in the medical arts.*

If you get a rejection for lack of utility because the invention is absolutely nutty, you can't do much about it, so I won't waste time trying to show you how to salvage a claim to an absurd invention. But an invention with merit can be rejected if you didn't do your homework when preparing the application. Your application should've mentioned any actual or potential utility of your invention in the specification. But you can easily counter a lack-of-utility rejection with a reasonable answer that demonstrates whichever one of the following attributes the examiner says your invention lacks:

- ✔ **Substantial utility:** You must demonstrate a use or application of the invention that's reasonably related to the invention itself and isn't insubstantial or frivolous. For instance, you can't argue that a nail-softening solution can also be used to fill the capsule of a bubble level because any liquid can do that. However, arguing that fingernails softened with your solution can be reshaped for a more aesthetic appearance would be sufficient to overcome the rejection.

- ✔ **Specific utility:** You must indicate at least one plausible, specific application for the invention. Claims rejected for lack of specific utility are usually for chemical products and therapeutic preparations or treatments because the specification doesn't include examples and test results that sufficiently support the invention. For example, indicating that a compound may be useful in the treatment of unspecified disorders isn't specific enough to overcome a rejection, without also submitting clinical test results that prove that the compound works as claimed.

- ✔ **Credible utility:** An invention, such as a perpetual motion machine, that's deemed totally incapable of achieving a useful result will be rejected for lack of credible utility. However, even a minimum of utility can salvage the invention. Just because an invention lacks sophistication, performs poorly, or operates only under very specific conditions doesn't mean it should be rejected. Demonstrating partial success in achieving a useful result is enough to avoid the rejection.

Contesting a lack-of-novelty rejection

Lack-of-novelty rejections happen when the invention is already known or is disclosed in a prior document. Ah, but if it were only that easy. Section 35 U.S.C. 102 of the patent law contains several subsections that outline the circumstances for rejecting a patent. Any lack-of-novelty rejection that you get will cite one or more of these subsections as the grounds for the rejection. For a plain-English explanation of these circumstances, see the patentability checklist in Chapter 4.

It may help you to follow me through the next section to take a look at the seven subsections — (a) through (g) — of Section 35 U.S.C. 102 in all their glory; simply choose the Patent link at www.uspto.gov and then select the USC patent laws link.

Like any other legal concept, lack of novelty isn't easy to delineate. A piece of prior art cited against one of your claims may look black or white, but there's always a large gray area that leaves room for argument and interpretation. Enter the skill, experience, and advice of an IP pro. But you're here for some answers. So in the sections that follow, I outline the two most common paths for rebutting lack-of-novelty rejections.

Using the different invention defense

A claimed invention can be rejected for lack of novelty if the examiner believes that it's *anticipated* by the prior art because every element in the claim is explicitly or implicitly described in an alleged prior art reference. In other words, the earlier device or process must be *exactly* identical in *all* details. This rule gives you two options:

- ✔ Demonstrate that your claimed invention is different from the disclosures in the prior art reference.

- ✔ Amend your claim to show a difference between your invention and the cited prior art. (See "Presenting a timely and professional answer," later in this chapter, about how to amend a claim and present an argument.)

In most cases, differentiating your invention from prior art is relatively easy, although examiners have a few tricks up their sleeves to counter your defense. Be on the lookout for these common examiner comebacks:

- ✔ If you argue that the prior art reference, although it may be similar to your invention, doesn't disclose a characteristic listed in your claim, the examiner may cite another earlier or contemporary patent or reference. Inevitably, that citation will mention that the characteristic in question was well known, and thus inherently disclosed in the first cited prior art reference.

- ✔ If you claim a generic compound, the examiner can use a reference disclosing a single species of that generic compound, even if the earlier species is only a partial example of the broad generic compound (see "Splitting Up Is Hard to Do: Restricting the Application," earlier, for the difference between generic and species).

- ✔ If you claim a species, the examiner can use a previously known genus as well as other evidence to show that a person with ordinary skill in the art would envision your species.

- ✔ If your claim specifies a range or a list of equivalent elements, the examiner need only find a prior reference partially within that range or list to make a case of anticipation.

Setting the date: Swearing back of reference

A patent usually doesn't give any clue about the date that the invention came about. So, lacking any other evidence, the law presumes that the invention took place just around the application-filing date or the publication date.

Depending on the specific subsection [namely the second paragraph of 102 (a) or 102 (b)], if your claim is rejected for lack of novelty, you can take advantage of this presumption. You can use the *swearing back defense* — demonstrating that you developed your invention before the filing date of the patent or the publication date of the document cited against your claim. You have to declare, under penalty of perjury, that you were the first to develop the invention. The declaration must:

- ✔ Establish that you developed your invention before the effective filing date (see Chapter 8) of the patent or the publication date of the document used against your claim.

- ✔ State the dates of your invention conception, its first written description, first construction, and other pertinent acts.

You must also support the declaration with evidence, such as copies of an engineering notebook, correspondence, photographs, and whatever else is available to prove your case. I recommend in Chapter 5 that you keep detailed notes about your invention development in a bound notebook, periodically witnessed by someone you trust. Such a record can provide convincing evidence of your date of invention.

I realize this is complicated stuff, but I've tried to condense and simplify the convoluted rules that govern the swearing back defense. First, the swearing-back-of-reference defense can only be used if the rejection falls under one of two subsections:

- ✔ Under subsection 102 (a), you can't get a patent if the invention was known or used in this country before you came up with it (what was done abroad doesn't count). You also face rejection if your invention was patented or described in a printed publication anywhere (yes, even the writings of Confucius, printed on woodblocks circa A.D. 750 in China, are printed publications).

- ✔ Under subsection 102 (e), you're out of the game if your invention was described (it doesn't have to be claimed) in a published U.S. patent application or in a U.S patent before you developed your invention.

Also, keep in mind that you can't use the swearing back defense if:

- ✔ Your invention was already known or used by someone in this country when you developed it as stated in the first part of subsection 102 (a).

- ✔ You abandoned your invention, expressly or by prolonged inactivity.

- ✔ You goofed — you applied for and obtained a foreign patent more than 12 months before filing in the United States.

✔ Someone else published a U.S. patent application or obtained a U.S. patent claiming the same invention as yours.

✔ The document cited against your claim came out more than one year before you filed your patent application.

Nabbing the invention thief

What can you do if the person responsible for the reference cited against your claim actually stole your invention? What if Cousin Ernie, who was always milling around your garage, asked too many questions, got too many answers, whipped off a quick application, and beat you to the patent office?

In a magnanimous display of fairness, patent law allows you to use the swearing back defense to prove that Ernie copied your invention. You need to file a declaration, with supporting evidence, showing that you're the real McCoy. In your declaration, you also have to explain how that sneaky Ernie found out about your invention.

Be totally honest in your statements — you're under penalty of perjury. You'll go to jail or pay a heavy fine if you're caught lying.

Applying the defenses

I'll try to bring all these defense tactics into focus with a hypothetical example that describes the sequence of inventing something, filing a patent application, getting rejected, and forming your responses.

You've noticed that the circular pads on your rotating polishing machine wear out more quickly around the edge than in the center. This happens because with each rotation, the bristles on the outer edges of the pad travel a longer distance in contact with the work surface than the bristles in the center.

So, you've developed a new buffing pad with a graduated thickness of pile. The tufting gets tighter as it moves away from the center, even though the length or height of the pile is the same on the entire pad. You've filed a patent application including the following claim:

Claim 1. A rotary polishing pad which comprises an arrangement of strands of equal length and thickness, tufted in a gradually increasing number of strands per square centimeter from a central region to a peripheral region of said pad.

You can't believe your eyes when you read the following statement in the first OA:

Claim 1 is rejected under 35 U.S.C. 102(a) as being anticipated by Abbott Publication of U.S. Application No.0,000.

> *Abbott discloses a rotary polishing pad comprising strands of equal length but gradually increasing thickness from a central region to a peripheral region of said pad.*
>
> *It is well known in the art and therefore inherent in the disclosure of Abbott that increase in density of a pile can be achieved by either increasing the thickness of the strands or tufting the strands in a tighter pattern.*

Looking at Abbott, you notice that the application was filed just six months before yours and has just been published. You could try the "different invention defense," but you'll have to overcome the examiner's opinion that thicker strands are inherently equivalent to more strands and are therefore a substitutable method for increasing pile density. Your best bet is to apply the "swearing-back-of-the-reference" defense by filing a declaration, supported by a copy of your development notebook, showing that you conceived and tested your invention before Mr. Abbott filed his patent application.

Challenging an obviousness rejection

Basically, this rejection states that the invention doesn't rise beyond ordinary skill in the field. But if you thought that rejections for lack of utility or novelty were tough nuts to crack, you ain't seen nothing until you wrestle with a rejection of a claim for obviousness. So put on your thinking cap and send the kids to Grandma. This is going to require your undivided attention.

Subsection 35 U.S.C. 103 (a) of the patent law provides that:

> *A patent may not be granted though the invention is not identically disclosed or described as set forth in section 102 . . ., if the differences between the subject matter sought to be patented and the prior art are such that the subject matter as a whole would have been obvious at the time the invention was made to a person having ordinary skill in the art to which said subject matter pertains.*

This short paragraph has inspired shelves full of books and thousands of court battles. If you review the patentability criteria sections in Chapter 4, you know as much technical info as you need to know about obviousness. So here I explain the strategy you and your IP counselor must follow to challenge a rejection of a claim for obviousness.

The examiner may cite one or more prior art references in his rejection. A reference may be a patent, a published patent application, or a document published anywhere in the world — how's that for all-encompassing? The examiner may also refer to "well-known" facts, practices, or information without providing any documentary evidence. Each reference must have already existed at the time of the invention.

You can overcome a rejection for obviousness with a gamut of defensive approaches, including:

- Contesting the applicability of the references on the grounds that either they're disqualified as prior art or they don't meet the conditions necessary to support a lack of novelty rejection under one of the 102 subsections.

- Arguing that the references belong to a *non-analogous* (unrelated) *art* into which an inventor would never look to resolve the problem addressed by your patent, and don't teach anything relevant to your invention.

- Challenging the examiner's combining two or more references to support her rejection, on the grounds that there is no basis for the combination, either in the references themselves or in the common knowledge.

- Specifying that the differences between the claimed invention and the prior art are beyond the capability of a person with ordinary skill in the art.

- Demonstrating secondary factors of non-obviousness, such as wide or enthusiastic acceptance of the invention in the field, commercial success, or unexpected advantages.

For convenience, I'll stick to your handy-dandy buffing pad from the previous section in which the tufting gets tighter as it moves away from the center, even though the length or height of the pile is the same on the entire pad.

To your great disappointment, you also read the following statement in the first OA:

> *Claim 1 is rejected under 35 U.S.C. 103(a) over Abbott Publication of Application No.0,000, and also over Abel British Patent No. 11,111,111, in view of Babele Italian Patent No. 22,222,222 or Chizu Japanese Patent No. 33,333,333.*
>
> *Abbott discloses a rotary polishing pad comprising strands of equal length but gradually increasing thickness from a central region to a peripheral region of said pad.*
>
> *Abel discloses a rotary polishing pad having strands arranged in gradually greater length from the center to the periphery.*
>
> *Babele discloses a car floor mat having a more densely tufted area in the center where the heels of the driver are resting.*
>
> *It would have been obvious to a person with ordinary skill in the art to use the variable tufting of Babele in the manufacture of the Abbott pad instead of using thicker strands, or in the manufacture of the Abel pad instead of using strands of different lengths.*

Chizu discloses a sanding belt having a coarser grade along the center of the belt than along its longitudinal edges. It would have been obvious to a person with ordinary skill in the art to use a coarser (thicker) tufting on the Abbott or Abel pad in areas subject to greatest friction than in other areas as taught by Chizu.

The diagrams in Figure 9-2 illustrate the various pile configurations.

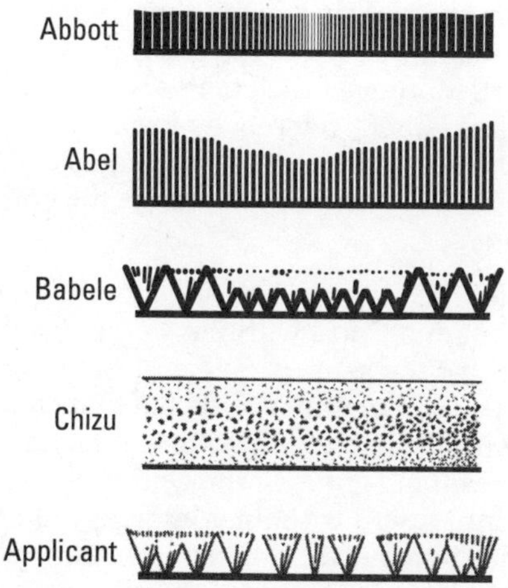

Figure 9-2:
Claimed
inventions.

When you examine these references, you discover that Abbott and Abel address the same problem you noticed, but with progressively thicker or longer strands. You also observe that the different sanding grades of Chizu are intended to create contrasting finishes on polished metal surfaces for purely aesthetic reasons. Abel, Babele, and Chizu were filed several years before your application. To overcome the obviousness rejection, you could try these defensive approaches, in this order:

1. **Not part of prior art:** Get rid of Abbott by showing that this reference isn't applicable: It was already disqualified as prior art because it wasn't patented or published before your application. But, the other references are too old to be polished off (pun absolutely intended) that way.

2. **Non-analogous art:** Try to disqualify Babele and Chizu on the grounds that they belong to non-analogous arts by arguing that your buffing pads are in different and unrelated fields from automobile floor mats or sanding. Citing Babele's mat is a good point. But the Chizu argument is very weak because buffing pads and sanding belts are commonly found in wood and metal shops and often used on the same work piece.

Even if you win the argument, you still have to meet the second part of the test by demonstrating that the non-analogous art reference doesn't teach anything about the invention. Babele does teach a very relevant technique of using a tighter tufting of the pile in areas of maximum wear. One could point out that Chizu suggests the use of different grades of grinding, sanding, or polishing agents on the same tool. So, non-analogous art isn't a very strong defense. Look at the other defenses.

3. **Improper combination of references:** You may have better luck here. To combine one reference with another, that combination must be suggested in the references themselves, or be part of the general knowledge of one with ordinary skill in the art. Moreover, the combination can't change the principle of operation of the primary reference or render the primary reference inoperable for its intended purpose. For example, if the sanding belt of Chizu was mounted on Abel's rotary machine, the combination wouldn't function as a buffer.

The remaining primary reference is Abel. The secondary references are Babele with the floor mat and Chizu with the sanding belt. Abel and Babele are designed to resolve the same problem of excessive wear in the most worked areas of the pad or mat. It'd be difficult to convince the examiner that the Babele approach couldn't be practically used on Abel's pad. However, the coarser sanding grade in the center portion of Chizu's belt can't be carried over into Abel's without completely changing the operation of the buffing pad, so you can eliminate Chizu. You'll win that round, and get rid of the last ground for rejection.

4. **Non-obvious differences:** You're left now with Abel and Babele. You can try to discredit the examiner's application of the obviousness test spelled out in the statute.

The difference between the teachings of the combined references (what you can learn from them) and the invention is extremely small. Abel recognized the problem of excessive peripheral wear in the pad and Babele teaches how to minimize that type of wear in a floor mat. The issue remaining is whether a person with ordinary skill in the field of buffing pads who is fully aware of the two references would be inclined to combine their teachings and develop your invention.

You could argue that Abel's use of longer strands to solve the wear problem was a poor solution because the pad now has an uneven working surface that puts more pressure on the edges than in the center. The shorter strands in the center of the pad won't wear out until the peripheral strands wear down to the same length as those in the center. At which point the initial problem reappears. So Abel's invention is a nice try but is an unsuccessful way to solve the problem. I can predict the examiner answering: "Yeah, Abel didn't know about Babele, but a person with ordinary skill in the art would have." You still have a chance to win the argument by pointing out the following. Buffing pad design isn't rocket science and the "level of ordinary skill" in the field is relatively low. Abel is a good representative of the person with ordinary skill. So if Abel didn't know about Babele, neither would that person. That last argument might just carry enough water to win the case.

5. **Secondary factors:** Another opportunity to salvage the claim is to demonstrate some unexpected advantages of your invention called *secondary factors,* such as great commercial success or its important contribution to the industry, by presenting sales records, testimonials from qualified people in the field, and copies of professional magazine articles praising your achievements.

Proving that your invention is patentable subject matter

Section 35 U.S.C. 101 of the patent law provides the granting of a patent to *whoever invents or discovers any new and useful process, machine, manufacture, or composition of matter or any new and useful improvement thereof.* Those things are called *statutory subject matters.*

You may have a hard time imagining an invention that doesn't fit into one of these categories. Yet there's always someone who tries to patent (and therefore monopolize) a law of nature, a natural phenomenon, a mathematical algorithm, an abstract idea, a simple manipulation of abstract ideas, or some purely descriptive material. These subject matters are patently non-patentable. Albert Einstein couldn't have patented his famous formula $E = mc^2$ because it's an algorithm expressing a law of nature.

The rejection of a claim on the ground that it recites *non-statutory* (non-patentable) subject matter is rather unusual, except in the area of computer programs and software inventions that involve a method of doing business. Such a rejection is often tacked on to a rejection for lack of utility. Indeed, if the invention is useless, it is a non-statutory invention.

To answer a lack of statutory subject matter rejection, you must convince the examiner that your claim recites a physical structure, composition, or process that produces a tangible result. For example, a database or compilation of information, even in an electronic form, fulfills neither of these requirements. However, the structure of a computer database that is organized and indexed to facilitate access to specific information constitutes statutory subject matter.

A pure manipulation of data to obtain a final dimension or other parameter is not statutory subject matter. However, when this calculation is done by a computer coupled to an industrial process machine, such as a computer that drives a machine to regulate rubber vulcanization, the regulation method, including the algorithm used by the computer program, becomes patentable.

Showing that your disclosure is enabling

A rejection for lack of enabling disclosure claims the specification doesn't teach how to make and use the invention. It is based on the first paragraph of section 35 U.S.C. 112 of the statute that states:

> *The specification shall contain a written description of the invention, and the manner and process of making and using it, in such clear, concise, and exact terms as to enable any person skilled in the art to which it pertains, or with which it is most nearly connected, to make and use the same...*

In Chapter 7, I discuss how to meet this requirement. If you try to claim something that isn't adequately disclosed in the specification, you'll get a rejection that's hard to overcome. Basically, if you don't spell out the enabling material somewhere in the specification, you must either:

- ✔ Convince the examiner that what is missing is common knowledge to people skilled in the art, using supporting documents such as treatises, encyclopedia excerpts, or magazine articles. If possible, also provide declarations by experts in your field to support your argument.

- ✔ Cancel the rejected claim and file a continuation-in-part application (see Chapter 8) that fully supports the claim to the invention. This solution is foolproof, but costly and time consuming. Therefore, use it only as a last resort, after the first approach has failed.

Dodging a double-patenting decision

Section 35 U.S.C. 101 of the patent law specifies that *whoever invents . . . may obtain a patent* — that's one patent for each invention, not two or more. This rejection can come in one of two flavors:

- ✔ **Same invention double patenting:** If you already have a patent or an application pending that claims the same invention in similar language, your claim will be rejected on the ground of *same invention double patenting*.

  You can overcome this type of rejection by slightly rewording your claim so that the two claimed inventions aren't identical. The objective is to make sure that a structure or process can't infringe on both the original patent and the one you're applying for.

  After you overcome a same-invention-double-patenting rejection, the examiner will probably fire another rejection for non-statutory *obviousness double patenting*. And the game goes on.

✔ **Obviousness double patenting:** If you claim an invention that's not identical to one claimed in your earlier patent or other pending application, but is not distinct from it either, your claim will be rejected not because the statute says so but because of a judge-made rule of *obviousness double patenting.* Courts have decided that it would be wrong to let you obtain multiple patents for inventions that are obvious modifications of one another.

You can overcome a rejection for obviousness double patenting by filing a *terminal disclaimer,* in which you dedicate any portion of the pending patent beyond the life of your earlier patent to the public. Even if both patent applications have the same effective filing date (thus the same expiration date), you should still file that disclaimer. The USPTO provides a handy form to do that.

A double-patenting rejection can't be issued in a divisional application that's filed after a request for restriction in the parent application (see "Splitting Up Is Hard to Do: Restricting the Application," earlier in this chapter).

Presenting a timely and professional answer

You have to answer an OA in a format specified by the commissioner. This format is subject to periodical changes as published in the *Gazette of the Patent Office* and the MPEP. You can consult either one online at www.uspto.gov.

Amendments to the specification, claims, drawings, or remarks (including any arguments) must each begin on a new page. Like all communications with the Patent Office, there are specific ways to present each amendment:

✔ **Specification:** Type a replacement paragraph or a marked-up one that shows all the additions underlined and the deleted words crossed out. You can conveniently show deletions and insertions using the track changes feature of your word processing software.

✔ **Claims:** Use the same deletion and insertion method as for the specification.

If you're deleting less than six characters, you may frame the deleted part between double brackets instead of crossing it out. That's the only way you can delete the numeral 4 standing alone.

Also, you must list the claims with one of seven status indications — (original), (currently amended), (canceled), (withdrawn), (new), (previously presented), and (not entered) — after the claim number as shown in the following example. (*Note:* The cancelled and not entered claims need not be typed out.)

> *Claim 1 (currently amended) A rotary polishing pad which comprises . . .*
>
> *Claims 2-5 (canceled)*
>
> *Claims 6 (original) The polishing pad of Claim 1 wherein . . .*
>
> *Claim 7 (currently amended) The polishing pad of Claim [[4]] 6 wherein . . .*
>
> *Claim 8 (previously presented) The polishing pad . . .*
>
> *Claim 9 (withdrawn) The polishing pad . . .*
>
> *Claim 10 (previously added) The polishing pad of Claim 6 . . .*
>
> *Claim 11 (not entered)*
>
> *Claim 12 (new) The polishing pad of Claim 10 which further comprises.*

✔ **Drawings:** Submit each drawing on a replacement sheet, explaining the change in the Arguments section of the amendment.

✔ **Arguments:** Under the title REMARKS, answer point by point every statement in the OA, following the same format and paragraph sequence. Make sure you point out every correction or addition you made in answer to each examiner's objection and rejection.

If the amendment introduces a new word or phrase in the specification, make sure that it doesn't introduce *new matter* — something that wasn't present or obviously implied in the original text. If you add a new word or phrase to a claim, you must point out where support for the added material can be found in the original specification text or drawing.

The argument must be based on the law with appropriate citations of statutes and precedent legal decision. A faulty argument may not support a subsequent appeal. Trust your attorney to draft that part in a professional style.

You have one or two months to answer a notice or request, such as a notice of defective application or a request for restriction, and three months to answer an examination report on the merit of your invention. In most cases, this period can be extended by up to three months by filing a *request for extension,* accompanied by the applicable late fee. The OA will specify the period to answer. There's no need to file the request for extension before or on the deadline; just include it with your delayed answer.

Reviving an abandoned application

If you don't answer an OA or pay a fee within the initial time allocated or during the extension period, your application will be declared abandoned. If your application is declared abandoned, you can petition the commissioner at any time to revive an abandoned application on one of two grounds:

✔ **Unavoidable abandonment:** This is very hard to prove, but has a low filing fee of about $60 for a small entity. An anthrax attack on the U.S. Postal Service or a destructive fire at your local post office may constitute good cause, but the fact that you moved without leaving a forwarding address or notifying your attorney isn't enough.

You can petition to revive an application on grounds of unavoidable abandonment if you provide the following:

- A reply to the last OA or requested fee unless previously filed or paid.

- An explanation, with supporting evidence, showing that the delay in filing an answer or paying a fee was totally beyond your control.

- A *terminal disclaimer,* which states that you agree to forfeit any time that the delay could add to the life of your patent. Use form PTO/SB/63 to file the disclaimer.

- The applicable fee payment with form PTO/SB/61.

✔ **Unintentional abandonment:** This is easier to establish, but has a high filing fee of about $650 for a small entity. On a petition for revival because of involuntary abandonment, you just need to state that the delay was unintentional (and it must in fact be), without stating the reasons for the delay. Use form PTO/SB/64.

Don't miss a filing date or intentionally abandon your application and rely on these petitions to save your hide. The undue delay may cast some doubt on your credibility. The commissioner may ask you to explain the cause of the unintentional abandonment. Any misstatement can be used against you later on when you try to enforce your patent against an infringer.

Reacting to a Final Rejection

You've replied to the first OA with a clever amendment and what you thought was an ironclad argument proving that all your claims are allowable. Yet you get another rejection of some claims or maybe an objection to the specification. Furthermore, the examiner declares that this last decision is final. Don't panic — the fat lady really hasn't sung yet.

A final OA is as definitive as a stand-up comic's retirement. It simply means that you're given a last chance to save your hide. You still have some alternatives:

✔ Try to comply with the examiner's requirement in the final OA.

✔ Make a last ditch effort to change the examiner's mind with a logical and persuasive argument.

✔ Amend your claims one more time.

✔ Answer as soon as possible to give the examiner an opportunity to review it before the answer deadline. You may get a break if he reviews your application and is persuaded by your brilliant argument to pass all your pending claims. If there are unresolved issues, as a matter of professional courtesy, he may call your attorney and attempt to iron out the remaining problems. Don't count on that if you're flying solo.

Any argument or amendment filed after the final OA should bear the following legend in red ink in the upper right-hand corner of the first page:

AMENDMENT UNDER 37 C.F.R. 1.116 AFTER FINAL REJECTION.

This guarantees that your reply is handled promptly by the USPTO receiving office. However, examiners have no obligation to do anything after the final OA. But being the gentlepersons that they are, I've never been refused the courtesy of an answer to a promptly filed post-final reply.

Asking for an examination rerun

After a final rejection, you may ask to restart the examination by filing a *Continued Prosecution Application* (CPA). Simply fill out and mail form PTO/SB/29 to the USPTO (with the applicable filing fee of course). This is particularly appropriate when the examiner has rejected all your claims or allowed some but rejected the ones you really need or want. If the examiner refuses to consider your last amended claims, it's usually on the grounds that the amended claims require a new search.

The new examination will start where the original left off. You're entitled to two reviews by the examiner. If the examiner refused to enter some claims presented after the final OA, include them in a preliminary amendment filed with or immediately after your CPA.

You can't enter an amendment to a specification that introduces new matter as part of a CPA. Instead, you should file a continuation application (see Chapter 8). Include all the new material. Make sure the original application is still pending when you file your continuation. Your original application will lapse if you don't timely answer or appeal the final OA.

Meeting the examiner face-to-face

At any time during the examination of your application, you can request a face-to-face interview with the examiner to try and resolve pending objections and rejections. Make the request directly to the examiner in writing or by fax, e-mail, or telephone. The request must specify the topics to be discussed.

I can't overemphasize the advantages of a heart-to-heart conversation with the examiner, especially when the outstanding patentability issue or the invention itself is very complex. Occasionally, with a few minutes of live conversation, I've been able to resolve rejection problems that would have consumed months of written communications.

If you request in advance, the USPTO will make audiovisual equipment available to you so that you can play a video showing your invention in action. You can even bring your computer or a small prototype to your meeting to demonstrate the workings of a piece of software.

With at least three days prior notice, you can arrange a long distance interview through the USPTO Video Conference Center. You can also request e-mail communications with the examiner after filing an authorization worded as follows:

> *Recognizing that Internet communications are not secure, I hereby authorize the USPTO to communicate with me concerning any subject matter of this application by electronic mail. I understand that a copy of these communications will be made of record in the application file.*

I don't suggest that you personally engage in a live or audio-visual interview with an examiner. Let your patent attorney act on your behalf. Examiners aren't particularly keen on dealing with a nonprofessional who isn't versed in patent law and doesn't speak the language. More significantly, on your own, you're more likely to agree to a concession offered by the examiner even if that concession is detrimental to your case. Your attorney can help you interpret and consider any written concessions.

Getting Flagged for Interference

An *interference* is a USPTO procedure to decide who gets the patent if two or more inventors claim (not just describe) the same invention. It fulfills the mandate of subsection 35 U.S.C. 102 (g) that basically says the first to invent gets the patent.

Interference may be declared:

- When one or more claims in two or more pending applications are addressed to substantially the same subject matter.

- When an application contains a claim that's been copied from, or is almost identical to, a claim found in an issued patent.

Because of their complexity and cost, try to avoid interferences. Your best bet is to try to settle the issue of inventorship amicably.

Initiating an interference

You or the examiner may initiate an interference under one of these scenarios:

- ✔ The USPTO asks your examiner to trigger an interference if your application conflicts with another pending application.

- ✔ Another inventor let you read his patent application (bad move). To your amazement, you discover that he claims your invention. Seeking justice, you file an amendment to your own application that includes one or more of John's claims. Then, you ask the examiner to declare an interference, specifically citing the other application's serial number.

- ✔ Your examiner notices that your invention is already covered by an issued patent or claimed in a pending published application. He orders you to copy one or more claims of the issued patent or published application in your own application to remove any issue of dissimilarity between the two applications. Then, he declares an interference.

- ✔ You discover a patent or published application on your own that covers your invention. You copy one or more of its claims into your application, and ask for an interference.

Note that it's none of the USPTO's business if two issued patents address the same invention. This kind of conflict can only be resolved in a federal court where the complexity, time, and lawyers' fees are much higher than in USPTO proceedings.

Still confused? I'll give you some useful information and basic rules about interferences:

- ✔ An interference can't be declared until the claim in your application is found allowable.

- ✔ You can't justify an interference by copying claims from a patent or published application that was issued or published more than one year earlier, unless you've already claimed substantially the same invention in your application before that one-year deadline.

- ✔ An interference can't be declared between applications or patents that have the same owner.

- ✔ An application under a secrecy order can't be part of an interference.

Determining priority of invention

An interference is conducted like a trial, according to standard Federal Rules of Civil Procedures. Therefore, you need the services of a knowledgeable IP attorney. Interferences are held before the Board of Patent Appeals and Interferences (BPAI), which I also mention in the "Crying to the commissioner and other appeal routes" section, earlier in this chapter.

To determine priority of invention, the BPAI looks at two phases of the invention process:

- ✔ **Conception:** The mental process through which you, the inventor, first imagine and devise a clear definition of your invention.

- ✔ **Reduction to practice:** The physical embodiment of the invention into a structure or process that can be shown with a prototype or computer model (actual reduction to practice) or by filing a patent application (constructive reduction to practice).

Here's the legal rule for deciding priority of inventorship in an interference. Like everything legal, it's nowhere near simple. Pay attention. This rule confirms the importance of what I've been preaching all along — diligence and good record-keeping.

The first inventor who reduces the invention to practice gets the patent *unless* another inventor conceived the invention earlier *and* was diligent in doing his or her own reduction to practice. The following example should help:

In January, you get the idea for a turbo-charged, five-cycle stroke, air-cooled engine for a lawn mower. You finish building a working prototype in late September. In June, Johnny conceives the same engine and having access to his brother's machine shop, gets a model running by late August.

Because Johnny was the first to reduce the invention to practice by building a working model, he'd get the patent, except that between June and September you worked diligently to put your prototype together. If you'd waited for a year to build a prototype or file your patent application, Johnny would've won the interference and got the patent. However, you win because you can demonstrate your diligent work before June, when Johnny had his brainstorm.

Keeping detailed records of your entire invention development process so that you can prove your diligence should the need arise is *very* important. If you haven't kept a periodically witnessed notebook, as I suggest in Chapter 5, you may not be able to prove your dates of conception and reduction to practice.

Don't waste time fiddling with your invention for months before filing a patent application. To protect yourself, prepare and file the application as soon as you think you have a valuable invention. It's better to file a provisional application early (see Chapter 7) and supplement it later with a more complete application. Otherwise, if someone files ahead of you, you could lose your right to the patent.

Requesting a Statutory Invention Registration

If you get frustrated with the lack of progress in the prosecution of your formal patent application (or for a variety of other reasons), you may decide to give up and drop your application. But now you have to worry that someone else could get a patent covering your invention and prevent you from practicing your own discovery in the future.

You can avoid this situation by dedicating your invention to the public by requesting a Statutory Invention Registration (SIR) on Form PTO/SB/94. By filing an SIR request, you waive your right to obtain a patent for your invention. You can't claim anything that's disclosed in the SIR in a future or pending application, but you can still manufacture, use, or sell your invention.

If you request a SIR while your application is pending and pay the applicable fee, the specification and drawing (but not the claims) will be published without further examination of the merits of your claims.

Your SIR is treated like any other patent or publication — it becomes prior art that can be cited against any other application. Also, an SIR is treated as a constructive reduction to practice when determining the issue of priority between you and any other inventor who is trying to get a patent. However, the SIR has no effect on the rights of any other inventor who manages to get a patent, even if the subject matter of your SIR and that of another inventor's application are identical.

As you can imagine, the effects of a SIR are quite drastic and final, so you may prefer to have your application published and then, if you still want to waive your rights to the invention, let it lapse for failure to answer an office action or pay the issue fee. This may be a more convenient and less risky way to waive your rights to the invention because you still have the possibility of reviving an abandoned application.

Avoiding a Third-Party Protest

If you made the huge mistake of disclosing your application serial number, you may have given someone the key to your application file. This allows another party to file a protest against the grant of your hoped-for patent in the USPTO. A protest can be based on a number of reasons, including an allegation that you're not the first or only inventor, prior art, public disclosure, or an offer to sell the invention made more than a year before you filed your application.

The USPTO doesn't entertain a protest if it doesn't include your application serial number, or, even when it does, if the USPTO receives the protest after the publication of your application or the issue of a notice of allowance, whichever comes first.

You'll be notified of the protest and be able to contest all its allegations. The protestor won't see your filings or participate in the prosecution of the patent.

Why put yourself through that kind of wringer? Don't tell anyone about your application, except under tight conditions of confidentiality.

Chapter 10

Entering the Home Stretch: Getting Your Patent Issued

*B*elieve it or not, and you may not if you've read Chapters 4 through 9, the day will come when you or your attorney go to the mailbox and find a letter from the United States Patent and Trademark Office (USPTO) telling you that your patent application is squared away, and all you have left to do is pay a few more fees to get your patent.

It's five o'clock somewhere in the world, but it's not quite happy hour for you just yet. You have a few more issues to consider before you get that snazzy patent. In this chapter, I walk you through one last reconsideration of your patent strategy and how to finally secure your patent. But problems can occur and corrections may be necessary even after you get the piece of paper, so I also help you tie up loose ends after a patent is issued. Finally, I take you to the finish line with a few comments on correctly affixing your patent number to your now-patented invention. The topics in this chapter apply to utility, design, and plant patents. Forms I mention that aren't sent to you automatically by the USPTO are available on its Web site (www.uspto.gov).

Getting the Green Light

When you, your attorney, and the patent examiner are finally through slugging it out in the prosecution phase (see Chapter 9), the USPTO issues a notice of allowance. The *notice of allowance* is a letter telling you that all the pending claims in your patent application are allowed. The patent press is warming up and all you have to do is grease the wheels with a bit more cash.

Which brings me to the more somber news: With your notice of allowance, you also get a *fee transmittal form.* Yes, just when you thought you were through shelling out fistfuls of dollars (and I don't mean singles) to the USPTO, here comes the least expected bill of them all. At this time, you have to pay a hefty patent issue fee and a publication fee (if you didn't petition for nonpublication as I explain in Chapter 8). Plus, the USPTO will nickel and dime you to death for extra copies of your patent. By the time you add your attorney's last bill, you'll need more than a thousand bucks to close the deal.

So before you shell out the cash for these last expenses, you may want to take a hard look at how much your upcoming patent really contributes to your intellectual property (IP) protection strategy.

Reviewing your patent strategy one last time

In Chapter 5, I detail alternatives to acquiring a patent for protecting your IP assets. Now, two or three years down the line, you're staring a possible patent in the face. But you're also probably looking at a new set of circumstances, which now may not justify taking the last step of getting the patent issued.

 Thoroughly reevaluating your patent strategy with the help of your IP professional, even at this late date, isn't a bad idea. Take a good look at the allowed claims, the part of the patent that spells out the extent of your protection, and with a cool head, ask yourself:

✔ Do the allowed claims give you the scope of protection you originally expected? If not, is the protection they do give sufficient to enhance your market position? If the answer is negative, you don't need this patent.

✔ Could you reasonably obtain broader coverage by filing a continuation or a continuation-in-part application (which I go over in Chapter 8)? If so, consider abandoning your current application after you file a new one. Not only will you save the issue charges for a patent of questionable value, but also the maintenance fees that are due three and a half years from the date of issue and every four years thereafter (see the "Remembering to Pay Maintenance Fees" section, later in this chapter).

Your money will be better used on the new application. If you think your about-to-issue patent has some value and could be used immediately against some infringer, get it. But don't overlook the possibility of getting a better one by filing a new application.

✔ Can you get the same degree of protection under one or more alternate forms of IP rights? You can still rely on a trade-secret strategy to protect your invention if your application hasn't been published. If it has been published, take another look at copyrights, trade dress, and some effective commercial identifiers. They may offer you as much protection as the upcoming patent.

✔ Could you benefit from adding a few broader claims to those already allowed and asking for a continuing prosecution (see Chapter 8)?

These are tough business and legal decisions that every inventor has to make. You can benefit from some advice from an IP professional.

Signing the check and requesting copies

You're convinced that you need that patent after all. All you need to do is fill out the fee transmittal form and mail it back to the USPTO with your check or money order made out to the Commissioner of Patents. And don't forget to pay your last patent agent or attorney invoice.

Don't miss the payment deadline. If you miss the date or your check bounces on the last day, your application will lapse and need to be revived (see Chapter 9). Don't forget to indicate how many extra copies of the patent (at about $3 a piece) you want. Actually, they aren't copies, but unadorned duplicate originals. Order at least ten for your files. You don't want to send that one-and-only beribboned original to a court when you sue an infringer.

If you've assigned your invention to another person or your company, and you want the assignee's name on the patent, fill out Item 3 on the form.

Put the Champagne Down: Taking Corrective Action

That's right. Don't touch that cork. Slowly back away from the bottle. Even though you've just received that long-awaited, blue-ribboned, fancily-bound patent, don't celebrate until you've carefully gone over every line of the document. If you spot a glitch, you need to get with your IP professional about fixing it up. And to determine if it's a bit more than a glitch, see the "Dealing with Defective Patents" section, later in the chapter.

You can easily fix typographic or grammatical errors and omissions in one of two ways. If your intended meaning is obvious from the context despite minor errors or omissions, you can simply point the errors out in a letter to the commissioner. The letter will be made part of the patent file. And here's a pleasant surprise — there's no filing fee for this service.

If, however, the errors or omissions aren't obvious or require some additional information, you need to file a *certificate of correction* (Form PTO/SB/44). Here's an example of how to word your corrections on the form:

> In column 3, line 33, "the bands of the" should read: --the strands of the--.
>
> In column 4, formula XX, the part of the formula reading "H_2CO_4" should read --H_2SO_4--.
>
> On Figure 2 of the drawing, reference "25" should be --35--.
>
> On Figure 3 of the drawing, reference numeral "40" should be applied to the nut engaged on threaded shaft --39--.

Common practice is to put deleted material between quotation marks and frame added material with double hyphens.

A couple of months later, after the USPTO accepts the certificate of correction, you'll receive a copy, and the certificate becomes an integral part of your patent in the USPTO's library. If you were responsible for the error, you must include a filing fee (currently $100) with the certificate. If the USPTO personnel caused it, filing the certificate of correction is free. But you need to indicate in a cover letter why the error isn't yours.

Note: The two procedures I just described are only available if the corrections don't affect the scope of the patent, don't introduce new material that could affect the nature of the disclosed or claimed invention, and don't require a reexamination. If they do, you've got yourself a defective patent that requires a more drastic and expensive corrective action.

Dealing with Defective Patents

A *defective patent* is one that, through errors or omissions but without deceptive intention, provides you with more or less coverage than your invention deserves. Maybe you failed to claim a prior application as the priority date or you claimed the invention too narrowly. The only way to correct a defective patent is by filing a *reissue application* (your defective patent is cancelled and replaced by a corrected one). Reissues are subject to the following rules:

✔ Only the patent owner, or the inventor with the consent of the patent owners, can file an application for reissue.

✔ An application that seeks to enlarge the coverage of the patent must be filed within two years from the issue date of the original patent and bear the signature of the inventor.

✔ A reissue application filed more than two years after the issue date of the original patent may be rejected for lack of diligence if you can't provide a reasonable excuse for the delay.

With a reissue application, you offer to surrender the patent you just received, alleging that it's wholly or partly inoperative, and ask for a new one. All the claims in the reissue application, including those copied from the original patent, are examined and may be rejected on new grounds. You also risk a third party submitting info that affects the patentability of your claims. In the worst case, you could end up with an extremely weak reissued patent.

The surrender of your original patent doesn't take effect until the grant of the reissue. So if you don't like the way the reissue application is going, you can abandon it and keep your original, uncorrected patent.

Reissue applications tend to be trickier than original applications because of the additional complications of having to admit errors and possibly needing to recapture a previously overlooked patent coverage. Let a good IP professional be your pilot — and navigator.

Combing over common errors

You must allege at least one error of conduct to justify your application for reissue. An *error of conduct* must meet three conditions:

✔ The error occurred during the preparation or prosecution of the original patent application.

✔ The error was made without deceptive intention.

✔ The error directly causes your patent to be wholly or partially ineffective.

The following sections outline the most common errors alleged in applications for reissue.

Correcting the inventors' names

If the inventorship is incorrectly stated (the wrong inventor is named or inventors need to be added or deleted) *and* one of the original inventors doesn't consent to the correction, use a reissue to correct the inventors' names. The disagreement will be disputed and settled as part of the reissue examination. If all inventors agree that changes need to be made, you simply need to petition the commissioner, as I detail in the "Changing the Names of the Inventors or Assignees" section, later in this chapter.

Broadening the claims

The most common reason for a reissue is that the original patent claims less than the invention deserves. Here's a typical scenario:

About 23 months ago, you obtained a patent on a turbo-charged, five-cycle engine for lawn mowers. All of your claims recite a combination of a lawn mower with the improved engine. In a recent issue of the *Garden Gopher* magazine, you discover that the Kopikatt Company has just come out with a leaf blower that uses the same type of engine as your lawn mower. Your attorney says that a leaf-blower engine doesn't infringe on any of the claims in your patent. You must file an application for reissue that amends and broadens at least one of your claims to recite the improved engine independent of the lawn mower.

You have to file the reissue application no later than the second anniversary of your original patent.

Broadening a claim can be complicated stuff. You may have to restrict one of its elements while enlarging another in order to achieve your coverage goal. Such legal maneuvers may make it difficult to determine, at first look, if the amended claim now has a broader coverage than before. You can resolve the ambiguity by applying the following rule:

An amended claim is considered broadened if it can be read upon any conceivable thing that wasn't covered by that claim in its original form. A claim is said to *read on* a device or process if, as you read each element of the claim, you can find a corresponding element in that device or process.

Another way to determine that the claim has been broadened: Check whether you can now sue somebody for infringement that you couldn't sue before.

Don't think for a minute that, in the reissue process, you can reclaim patent coverage that you willingly abandoned during the prosecution of your original application. If, by mistake, you added a limitation to the claim trying to get around some prior art when in fact overcoming that prior art didn't require that particular limitation, you're stuck.

Narrowing the claims

You might wonder why you'd ever want to narrow the scope of your patent — you just got a lucky break, right? Wrong. Your deceptively broad patent can be declared invalid by a judge when you try to sue an infringer.

Allow me to return to the lawn mower example from the last section. This time, I assume that all the claims are addressed to the engine without mentioning its application to lawn mowers. You just discovered that in the past, the same type of engine was used on small handheld power tools, such as leaf blowers and string grass trimmers. However, you were the first to draw enough power from this kind of engine to drive a lawn mower or any other device requiring more than one horsepower. Your invention uses a weighted lawn mower cutting blade as a flywheel to smooth out intermittent power gaps inherent to your five-stroke engine.

Because your current claims read on (recite elements found in) prior art machines, they shouldn't have been allowed (see patentability requirements in Chapter 4). However, because no prior patent or documentation existed for that kind of engine, you couldn't have discovered it through a comprehensive anticipation search. And, of course, you didn't hear about this use of the engine until recently, so the error isn't due to any deception on your part.

You need to promptly file an application for reissue that amends your claims to a narrower scope by reciting the lawn mower or any other tool that requires more than one horsepower. You may also for good measure add some claims that simply mention the flywheel.

Correcting the disclosure

As I explain in Chapter 7, the disclosure consists of the specification supported by a drawing of the invention. If you unintentionally misstated some facts in the specification or inaccurately drew a particular structure, you can set the record straight with a reissue application — as long as the error didn't prevent someone from practicing the invention and your proposed corrections don't introduce *new matter* (information necessary to use the invention that wasn't present in the original application).

For example, you didn't appreciate the regulating effect of the flywheel blade in the new lawn mower engine you've patented, so you gave some other incorrect explanation for the engine's exceptional performance. No sweat. That error didn't prevent someone with skill in the mechanical field from building your lawn mower. You can correct the problem with a reissue.

Another example: A structural detail, such as the distribution of the weight around the blade, may have been adequately described in the specification, but not illustrated in the drawing. Because the rules require that everything recited in a claim be shown in the drawing, your omission may cast doubt on the validity of some of your claims. You can dissipate this cloud of doubt by offering an amended drawing in your application for reissue.

Referencing a previously omitted prior application

Establishing the earliest priority date (see Chapter 7) for your invention is critical to eliminate any interim prior art that could be cited against your claims. To do so, you may need to refer to an earlier filed application in the U.S. or abroad. You can use the reissue process to remedy these situations:

✔ You forgot to claim priority of a prior domestic or foreign application.

✔ You claimed foreign priority, but forgot to submit a certified copy of the foreign application.

✔ You forgot to make reference to a prior co-pending nonprovisional application.

✔ You forgot to claim priority on a provisional application filed before November 29, 2000. If the provisional application was filed after this date, you can't claim priority upon it once the formal application that followed it is no longer pending.

Preparing the reissue application

A reissue application is a bit more complex than a regular formal application. You must comply with strict special rules or the application will be rejected. The contents of the application and the accompanying documents are basically the same as for a formal utility, design, or plant patent application (see Chapters 7 and 8). However, the formatting of the disclosure and claims and the declaration is different. Some additional enclosures are required.

The specification, drawing, and claims

The specification and claims must be a clean, reproducible photocopy of the original patent, mounted in a two-columns-per-page format on a single-sided sheet. The specification and claims must reflect the status of the patent as of the filing date of the reissue application and must include all the changes previously made by certificates of correction. The drawing must also be a clean and reproducible copy of the original.

The proposed amendments

Proposed amendments to the specification and claims can be presented in one of the following two ways:

✔ By cutting and pasting a photocopy of the original patent specification and claims. The amended part must be typed and inserted between pasted sections of the photocopied text, showing the deleted material between brackets and underlining the added material. I don't recommend this method.

✔ By providing a separate amendment paper, formatted in the same manner as a patent application amendment, which I discuss in Chapter 9. This is a more practical and cleaner way to format the reissue application.

You must submit an amendment to the drawing as a sketch on a separate paper, showing the proposed changes in red. When the examiner approves the changes, you file a new formal drawing that incorporates the changes.

The declarations

A reissue application must include a declaration, under penalty of perjury, signed by the inventor. In a reissue application for a patent that's wholly owned by an assignee and doesn't seek to broaden the scope of any claim, only the assignee has to sign the declaration. Because of the precision and completeness required in the reissue declarations, I strongly suggest that you use Form PTO/SB/51 for the inventor and Form PTO/SB/52 for the assignee. The declaration form is pretty straightforward.

You can indicate that the original patent was wholly or partly inoperative or invalid because of a defective specification or drawing or because you claimed more than you had the right to by checking the appropriate box. However, if you're filing for a reissue for any other reason, such as you claimed less than the invention merited in your original application and you want to broaden the patent coverage, you must provide an explanation in the space provided at the bottom of the declaration.

If you're trying to broaden a claim, you may state the following (pulled from the earlier engine example):

> *Applicant seeks to broaden Claims 1, 5, and 6 by removing limitations relative to the type of machinery upon which the engine can be used.*

If you forgot to claim priority on a prior application, you may state:

> *Applicant failed to claim the priority of a parent application, Serial Number XX/X,XXX, that was still pending when the application for the patent in reissue was filed.*

Other documents

Your reissue application must also include the following material:

✔ **Written consent from each assignee (Form PTO/SB53).** If any interest in the patent has been assigned, you must submit a written consent to the reissue from each assignee, accompanied by documentary evidence of the assignee's interest. To establish the assignee's ownership of the invention and patent, you can specify the reel and frame numbers of all the documents recorded in the USPTO regarding the transfer of the invention and patent. For example, if you assigned the invention and patent to your corporation, Big Deal, Inc., and the corporation then assigned the whole thing to the Bunco Bank as security for a loan, you must identify the two recorded assignments, even though only the bank (the current owner) needs to sign a written consent to the reissue.

✔ **Information disclosure statement.** You must submit any information that may be relevant to the patentability of the reissue claims, including prior art. Use Form PTO/SB/08A to list patents and Form PTO/SB/08B to list non-patent documents.

✔ **Copies of any litigation or reexamination documents related to your patent.**

✔ **Offer to surrender patent.** You may include an offer to surrender the original patent, or you can wait until the examiner makes a specific request. If you have lost that original patent document, use Form PTO/SB/55 to report the loss.

✔ **Return receipt postcard.** Suggested when mailing anything to the USPTO.

✔ **Fee transmittal form (PTO/SB/56).** And, of course, a check or money order to cover the filing fee.

✔ **Reissue patent application transmittal form (PTO/SB/50).** Make sure you list on this form all the documents you're submitting.

After you file your application for reissue, the USPTO will publish a notice of your application in the *Official Gazette.* The examiner will wait at least two months after publication before taking your case, which gives any interested party an opportunity to file a protest against your application. Reissue applications are given priority over regular applications. However a hard fought case may take two or three years before the patent is reissued.

Submitting to Reexamination

Your patent is subject to reexamination throughout its life. Reexamination must be based on prior patents or printed publications that the examiner didn't properly consider during the prosecution of your application, if this omission casts doubt on the validity of some or all of your claims. Anyone — you, the guy down the street, or the examiner— can initiate a reexamination.

Distinguishing reexamination from reissue

Although a reissue and a reexamination overlap a bit, a reexamination is usually preferable, as the following list demonstrates:

✔ A reissue application brings the whole patent into question, but you can limit a request for reexamination to one or more claims.

✔ A reissue application must be filed quickly, preferably within two years of the original patent issue date. A request for reexamination can be filed any time during the life of the patent.

✔ An examiner can take an undetermined number of months to review an application for reissue. However, a request for reexamination must be acted upon immediately. The examiner must determine within three months of the filing date whether the prior art submitted raises a question of patentability sufficient to warrant a reexamination.

✔ In an application for reissue, you have to establish why the patent is ineffective yourself, including the materiality of the error. You must sign an affidavit, under oath, or a declaration under penalty of perjury to that effect. That puts you at risk if what you stated is later proven false. In a request for reexamination, you only need to cite the new prior art and point out each substantial new question of patentability. It's the examiner's responsibility to determine the validity and relevance of your allegations.

There are a couple of drawbacks — at the end of a patent reissue process, you may end up with narrower or broader coverage than you had under the original patent. A reexamination never enlarges the scope of a patent but can result in a narrower patent. Moreover, the filing fee for a reexamination request is about seven times more than for a reissue application.

Kicking things off

Anyone can initiate a reexamination, and for a multitude of reasons:

✔ You or someone interested in buying your patent or licensing your technology wants to confirm the validity of all your claims in view of a newly discovered prior art. Call it peace of mind.

✔ A potential or actual infringer of your patent wants to eliminate some of your claims that cover his own activities.

✔ Another inventor who filed a patent application covering the same subject matter as your patent elects the less expensive approach of requesting reexamination to challenge you, instead of asking for a declaration of interference (see Chapter 9 for more on interference).

You can initiate a reexamination of a patent by filing Form PTO/SB/57. Attach copies of the new prior art material and a statement that includes the following information:

✔ A list of claims to be reexamined and the prior art documents that apply to them.

✔ An explanation of how the cited prior art relates to each claim at issue. This is best done in a two-column format. Quote each element of a claim in the first column and place the matching quotation from the relevant prior art next to it in the second column, as shown below using the polishing pad example from Chapter 9.

Applicant's Patent	*Prior Art*
Claim 1: A rotary polishing pad . . .	Abbott and Abel disclose rotary polishing pads.
that comprises an arrangement of strands of equal length and thickness . . .	Abbott's strands are of equal length. Abel's strands are of equal thickness.
tufted in a gradually increasing number of strands per square centimeter from a central region to a peripheral region of said pad.	Babele discloses a car floor mat wherein strands are tufted in a larger number of strands per square centimeter in the center than in the peripheral region.

✔ A statement pointing out the substantial new question of patentability and stating that the cited prior art wasn't considered by the examiner during the prosecution of the patent application.

✔ The required filing fee of about $2,500, of course.

If you file a request for reexamination of your own patent, you may include a proposed amendment of the claims and specification if warranted. However, you can't offer an amendment when filing a request for reexamination of someone else's patent. Instead, you must serve a copy of the request to the patent owner according to standard legal procedure and certify, on the request you file with the USPTO, that you have done so.

Selecting the relevant prior art material

You can't base a reexamination on a prior art patent or printed publication that was used by the examiner in the original examination against the claims at issue.

The rule used to be more restrictive and allowed only prior art material that wasn't considered by the examiner at all. Under some recent and more liberal interpretation by the courts, even a reference listed on the front page (see Chapter 4) of the patent may be the basis of the reexamination if the examiner didn't specifically cite it as grounds for rejecting the claim in question.

The new interpretation has been a bonanza for attorneys filing adverse requests for examination. Indeed, they don't have to look very far to find prior art material. Many references listed on a patent are only cited by the examiner as relevant, without being considered applicable to the claims. But attorneys are very adept in alleging reasons why the cited prior art is directly pertinent to the patentability of the claim.

As a result, owners of some very valuable patents have been dragged into years of reexaminations on very tenuous grounds. Don't be surprised if, in a few years, the pendulum of the law reverts to a more restrictive interpretation of what constitutes prior art in reexamination proceedings.

In requesting reexamination of your own patent, cite only prior art that could reasonably be used to attack your patent's validity in future litigation against an infringer. Don't complicate and prolong the reexamination by bringing up all the potential but tenuous prior art that could be frivolously cited by an adverse party. However, if your patent has already been litigated, make sure that you submit all the prior art that the accused infringer brought up in attacking your patent. If the patent survives the reexamination, it'll prevent other future infringers from presenting the same prior art.

Criticizing the patent: How much is too much?

As the name indicates, a reexamination subjects the claims at issue to the same level of examiner's scrutiny as in the examination of the original patent application. When someone else's patent is on the stand, you may bring up all the patentability issues mentioned in Chapters 4 and 7. However, be careful not to overly criticize or disparage your own claims when you request a reexamination of your patent. Your request for reexamination will be published in the *Official Gazette* of the USPTO, which makes the reexamination file open to the public. You don't want someone using your own statements in the reexamination against you in future litigation.

In either case, you should rely on your patent attorney to prepare the request, draft the statement, and submit the amended claims.

Prosecuting the reexamination

About three months after filing for reexamination, you'll receive the examiner's answer to your request. If reexamination of your patent is denied, you can pop the champagne cork. Your patent has withstood an attack at very little cost to you. If the request for reexamination of your own patent is approved, you're back to square one and must again deal with the examiner, as you did during the prosecution of your original application. Do not pass Go. Do not collect $200. Go directly to Chapter 9.

If you requested reexamination of someone else's patent, all you can do now is monitor the process and file protests. As I describe in Chapter 9, you can present additional prior art you find, along with an appropriate statement of its relevancy to the ongoing procedure. You can obtain the right to actively participate in the reexamination of the other guy's patent by filing for what is called an *inter partes* reexamination, providing you can afford the filing fee of about $9,000.

If your request to reexamine a potential opponent's patent is rejected, you may petition the Commissioner of Patents to review the examiner's decision. If your petition is denied, you can appeal to the Court of Appeals for the Federal Circuit.

Deferring to others' intervening rights

A reexamination has no effect on the rights of anyone who made, purchased, offered to sell, used, or imported anything that's covered by the new or amended claims before the reexamination is complete.

Only activities covered by the original patent can be prohibited. A court may even allow activities that should constitute an infringement when substantial preparation was made prior to the reexamination. It's an issue of fairness and equity, and, of course, a source of costly litigations I wouldn't wish on my worst enemy.

Changing the Names of the Inventors or Assignees

A patent that misstates the names of the inventor may be declared invalid and unenforceable, which is pretty serious, especially when an infringer's attorney discovers the error in the middle of an infringement case. If all parties agree that an inventor was omitted or listed by mistake on your patent, you can use the *petition and certificate of correction* procedure to clear up the issue. (If everyone doesn't agree, I'm sorry, but you have to take the reissue route; see the "Correcting the inventors' names" section, earlier in this chapter.)

You simply petition the commissioner to correct the names of the inventors listed (or omitted) on the patent or to correct the names of the assignees. When the petition is granted, the commissioner issues a certificate of correction, saving you the trouble and expenses of applying for a reissue.

The petition, with the applicable fee, must include statements by the following:

- ✔ Each person whose name is being deleted, stating that he or she has no disagreement regarding the requested change.

- ✔ Each person whose name is to be added, stating that the omission occurred without any deceptive intention on his or her part.

- ✔ Each assignee consenting to the change, accompanied by documentary evidence of that assignee's interest in the patent.

If the patent is involved in an interference, you must also address a motion requesting permission for the change to the *Board of Patent Appeals and Interferences,* the tribunal handling that procedure.

Remembering to Pay Maintenance Fees

Utility patents are subject to periodic maintenance fees during the first 12 years following their issue dates (but not design or plant patents; you got the easier road to hoe in this regard, too).

Failure to pay a maintenance fee on time (or late with penalties) results in the cancellation of the patent. About half of all issued patents are cancelled early because maintenance fees weren't paid. You can revive a cancelled patent, however, if you petition the commissioner within two years.

At the time of this writing, the patent maintenance fees due at the 3½, 7½, and 11½ anniversaries of the issue date are $445, $1,025, and $1,575, respectively, for an individual or small business entity. Double these figures for a large business entity. The surcharge for late payment during the six month grace period is $65 and $130, respectively. Unintentional late payment and revival of the expired patent is $1,640 for a small or large entity. No chicken feed, as you can see.

I strongly recommend that you register your patent with a maintenance and annuity fee service. The service gives you plenty of notice before any forthcoming payment and can even pay the fees on your behalf, for a small charge. You can get information on one of the oldest and most reliable maintenance and annuity fee services by going to www.cpaglobal.com or e-mailing your questions to enquiries@cpaglobal.com.

Most importantly, keep the USPTO and your maintenance fee handler informed of any long-term change of address.

When you look at a patent that's more than four years old, don't automatically assume that it's still effective. It may have been canceled for failure to pay the maintenance fee. You can check its status by e-mailing MaintenanceFeeInquiries@uspto.gov or by calling 703-308-5036 or 5037.

Marking Your Widgets with the Patent Number

The law requires you to put your patent number on all products covered by your patent or made according to your patented process. The requirement applies to all products made under your authority by your associates or licensees.

A person isn't liable for patent infringement unless that person is notified of the existence of the patent. A proper notice may be laid out as follows: *U.S. Patent No. 19,999,999.* If appropriate, you may add: *Other domestic and foreign patents pending.*

Don't place a false patent or patent pending notice on your product. You may be subject to a fine and lose the right to enforce your patent through certain proceedings. Note that a patent pending notice has no recognized legal value. It just acts as a deterrent to potential infringers by warning them that a patent could be issued at any time. It can only be used when, and only as long as, an application is pending.

Part III
Knowing Your Copyrights

The 5th Wave   By Rich Tennant

"I'm sorry, Mr. Garret, a 35-year-old tattoo doesn't qualify as a legal trademark for 'Mother.com'."

In this part . . .

Whether you're writing a novel, creating an architectural drawing, developing new software, or filming an instructional video on the care and feeding of pet ferrets, you own a creative work that may need protection. In this part, I categorize, dissect, and otherwise pick apart the wide variety of creative works that you can protect with a copyright.

But you have to make sure that you actually own the creative work, so I give you some tests, tips, and tricks to help you make sure that it belongs to you and not your employer, employee, or someone else who had a hand in the creation. And even though you have some automatic copyright protection (who said there's no such thing as a free lunch), I explain how to register your copyright and put some teeth into your protection.

Chapter 11

Entering the Whimsical World of Copyrights

*O*f all the types of intellectual property rights, copyrights are probably the easiest to understand. Certainly they're the easiest to acquire. However, for all its apparent simplicity, the concept of copyright resembles a fish under water. It's easy to see, but it's hard to get a good grip on it. You first have to get a handle on what an original work of authorship (OWA) is and what it is not, understand which part of an OWA is covered by the copyright, and finally, appreciate the scope of protection that the copyright law provides. In this chapter, I define the various kinds of works protected by copyright and then analyze the rights held by a copyright owner. I end the chapter by going over some copyright acquisition and ownership issues.

Of course, this chapter covers only the basic nature and limitations of copyrights. In Chapters 12 and 13, I show you how to avoid major problems with copyright acquisition and transfer and also how to bulletproof your rights against copycats. However, there's even more. Check out Chapter 19 to find out how to make money from copyrights, and Chapter 20 to get the scoop on enforcing your copyright through litigation.

Getting to Know the Copyright

A *copyright* is primarily an exclusive right to reproduce an original work. That right falls to the person who created the work or to her employer. But because it's a legal matter, it's somewhat more involved and complicated.

Copyrights and patents spring from the same constitutional clause mandating that Congress *"promote the progress of science and useful arts, by securing for limited times to authors and inventors the exclusive right to their respective writings and discoveries."* And like patents, copyrights are exclusively regulated by federal law. State courts have no jurisdiction over copyright issues.

But, unlike patents, copyrights aren't granted by the government after a complex and expensive application process. Instead, and here comes the good news, a copyright automatically attaches to an original work as soon as it's created. That's right: As soon as you write that next book-club selection or record the next chart-topping song, it's already copyrighted. You can even mark copies of your work with a legal notice including the © symbol, as shown in Chapter 13. And for extra added protection, you can register your copyright with the U. S. Copyright Office, as I also explain in that chapter.

The U.S. Copyright Office, a division of the Library of Congress in Washington, D.C., administers copyright matters under the direction of the *Register of Copyrights*. Title 17 of the U.S. Code (*The Copyright Act*) contains the fundamental laws regulating copyright matters. The Copyright Office Web site, `www.copyright.gov`, is full of well-organized information.

Defining an Original Work of Authorship

So, now that your interest is piqued, here's the official definition: An *original work of authorship* (OWA) is a substantial and fixed creative work of a nontechnical character originated by its author. Clear as mud? Hang on. This definition can be broken down into four basic parts, which I cover in the following sections. Each section outlines one of the requirements that an OWA must meet to be copyrightable.

When courts have to decide whether a specific creation complies with these basic requirements, they narrowly limit their decisions to the special circumstances of the case. These rulings are sometimes inconsistent, depending on when and where they're made. Nevertheless, these decisions provide us with the following general guidelines.

Fixed creation of the mind

An OWA must be the result of creativity, originating in the author's mind and not merely a discovery of something that already exists. Furthermore, the work isn't considered "created" until it's fixed, tangible, permanent, or stable, and reproducible or otherwise communicable. Here are some examples:

✔ Making a natural-looking plaster-cast replica of a tree trunk to serve as a pedestal doesn't require any mental creativity. But, composing a symphony that suggests wildlife sounds of a virgin forest requires many mental steps to select and arrange sounds in a pleasant composition.

✔ Giving an ad-libbed speech or improvising a musical composition doesn't result in a fixed creation and doesn't qualify as an OWA unless it is recorded simultaneously.

✔ Once upon a time, video games were denied copyright protection on the grounds that the moving images only occurred in response to the players' commands and were therefore not fixed and reproducible. Eventually, the courts recognized that coded instructions stored on a computer chip dictate everything on the screen. By manipulating a joystick, the player selects a series of pre-recorded program sequences. Thus, the screen images aren't only recorded, but are also reproducible at will.

For your own protection, you must fix your work as early as possible. If you're developing a teaching method or an aerobic dance routine, have somebody record it as you go. If you created an original knitting design, take pictures of it. Keep track of the date you fixed and distributed your OWA. You'll need that information later, as I explain in Chapter 13.

An OWA must be the result of creativity, originating in the author's mind, and not merely a discovery of something that already exists. Observing something and carefully listing its characteristics isn't an OWA; it's a mere representation of preexisting conditions. For example, the diagnostic of a psychologist that details the personality profile of a patient can't be protected by copyright.

Even an E.T. can create an OWA — with some help

A few years ago, a court was asked to decide whether a text that had been "authored" by celestial beings qualified as an original work of authorship — like asking whether Moses could have obtained a copyright on the Ten Commandments. In a thoughtful exercise of common sense sprinkled with a pinch of skepticism, the court declared that, so long as the text was transcribed, compiled, and collected by mortals, it was protected by copyright.

Substantive and nontrivial mental activity

To qualify as an OWA, the work must have significant complexity, scope, length, or duration. To test compliance with this requirement, you have to use different measuring sticks, according to the nature of the work.

Written, pictorial, and nonmusical works must have a certain degree of complexity or length.

✔ Titles, slogans, maxims, two-verse poems, and reproductions of common geometrical figures don't meet the test. On those grounds, the slogan, *"You got the right one, uh-huh,"* used to promote the Pepsi brand of soda, was denied copyright protection. That was also the fate of the folder icon by Apple Computer, Inc., that depicts a common cardboard folder together with the term *Waste Basket* to identify a discarded folder.

✔ A limerick barely passes the threshold of substantiality.

✔ A simple line drawing of a dove in the hand of Pablo Picasso, however, is certainly complex (and original) enough to get copyright protection.

Sounds are measured with a shorter yardstick than words are. In a musical composition, a single distinctive bar or even one original measure may be sufficient to deserve protection. The four opening notes of Beethoven's Fifth Symphony that are used as a hook throughout the symphony are a case in point. They would have enough substance to deserve copyright protection if they were composed today. Of a more recent vintage is the one measure "hook" of another commercial song used in connection with Pepsi products. Although it consists of only four repetitions of the phrase "Uh-oh" in rap music rhythm, that jingle was declared protected by copyright.

A nonfunctional creation

To qualify as an OWA, the work must not be primarily functional, such as a belt buckle or other useful article. However a degree of functionality in a work isn't necessarily fatal to its protection.

An architectural drawing has a function — to guide the construction of a building. But its functionality resides in the use of the drawing and isn't inherent in the drawing itself. The drawing embodies an imaginative rendition of a non-existing structure, including a representation of its shapes, proportions, arrangements of openings, and other characteristics that reflect the architect's talented vision, and so is copyrightable.

The rules of a board game are unprotected because they're purely functional steps. However, the decorative graphics on a game board, or the design of a chess piece that represents a whimsical character are non-utilitarian, protected creations. Indeed, the *ornamental design* of a useful article, as distinguished from the article itself, may be considered a visual OWA.

However, that rule applies only if the design can be identified separately from, and exist independently of, the article's function. For example, the shape of a belt buckle — no matter how creative — can't be separated from the buckle and isn't protected by copyright. But a medallion depicting a bucking bronco affixed to the face of a western-style buckle is protected because it isn't a primarily functional element.

An original work

The originality of an OWA doesn't imply that it's new, unusual, or innovative. The work is original if it isn't copied from a pre-existing source, but is independently created. It doesn't matter that the exact same work was created in another place or time by someone else, so long as the author wasn't exposed to or influenced by the earlier work.

If you create an OWA that's based on or incorporates one or more pre-existing works, the copyright attaches only to that part of the OWA that's exclusively yours. For instance, if you write a cookbook, you may select recipes from various sources, including previously published cookbooks. You then arrange those recipes in a sequence and format of your choice, describe them in your own words, and add comments and illustrations — all mental steps that together constitute an OWA protected by copyright. If you transcribe the recipes as you find them in a cookbook (with the authors' permission) you get no copyright in the copied text. The recipes themselves are mere functional processes that aren't protected by copyright.

Determining What Is Copyrighted and What Isn't

In order for a copyright to attach to your work, it must be an OWA meeting all the above-listed basic requirements and a few more spelled out in the Copyright Act. The concept of OWAs is very elastic and can occasionally be extended to cover newfangled things that the law hasn't anticipated. For example, video games, inconceivable a few decades ago, are now considered OWAs. But even if you're creating something in a genre that's been around for a while, it's good to know if it's protected by copyright.

Copyrighting categories

The law classifies OWAs into the following categories:

- **Literary works.** Any written or recorded sequence of words, numbers, or symbols, including the instructions that constitute a computer program.

- **Musical works.** All musical compositions and their accompanying lyrics, from commercial jingles to epic operas.

- **Dramatic works.** Any work that incorporates the spoken word, including accompanying music, to be performed by one or more characters.

- **Pantomimes and choreographic works.** Any non-vocal performance from classical ballet to "bump-and-grind" gyrations, from a trapeze act to a clown's silent routine.

- **Pictorial, graphic, and sculptural works.** Two- and three-dimensional works of fine, graphic, and applied art, including photographs, prints, art reproductions, maps, globes, charts, diagrams, models, technical drawings, and architectural plans.

- **Motion pictures and other audiovisual works.** Works that consist of a series of related images together with any accompanying sounds that are designed to be shown on a machine or device such as a projector, cassette or disc player, or other electronic contraption.

- **Sound recording works.** Works that result from the fixation of a series of musical, spoken, or other sounds on phonograph records, tapes, digital memory chips, or any other embodying device. This category doesn't include the sounds themselves, only the result of preparing, directing, recording, mixing, editing, and other steps in the recording process. (*Note:* This category excludes movies and other audiovisual works.)

- **Architectural works.** Building designs that are embodied in any tangible medium of expression, including buildings and architectural plans or drawings. Each architectural work includes the overall form, as well as the arrangement and composition of spaces and elements in the design. However, it excludes individual standard features such as doors, windows, and balconies.

These classifications were devised for practical administrative purposes and must be construed very loosely. A work may fit into several categories or incorporate several works falling in different categories. For example, a puppet show can be a dramatic work and a choreographic one. A motion picture is an audiovisual work that may include literary, musical, dramatic, choreographic, and pictorial works.

In addition, the Copyright Act also covers two types of hybrid works, although they don't meet all the required characteristics of an OWA:

✔ **Original mask works for semiconductor chip products.** Mask works look like photonegative films and are used to manufacture multilayered microchip circuits. They're used in photo-sensitive processes to form the intricate semiconductor layers and metallic connecting straps that constitute an integrated circuit.

✔ **Original designs of useful articles.** Protection applies to the original design of a useful article that makes the article attractive or distinctive in appearance to the public. So far, only ship hulls and their molds that have a utilitarian function (and not drawings, blueprints, or the mere portrayal of a hull) qualify as "useful articles" pertaining to ships.

Recently, Europe has greatly expanded and improved the protection of original designs of useful articles to all manufactured practical objects from safety pins to locomotives. The United States is expected to some-day follow suit and increase its coverage of the designs of useful articles under this section of the Copyright Act.

Works without copyright protection

Categories of works that don't benefit from copyright protection include:

✔ **Works generated by the U.S. Government.** Congressional records, census data, maps issued by the Department of the Interior, and so on.

✔ **Information in the public domain and containing no original presentation.** Calendars, scientific charts or displays, or statistical charts.

✔ **Clothing designs.** Fashion designers must resort to design patents to protect their creations.

✔ **Typeface designs.** However, computer programs used to generate unprotectable typeface designs can be protected by copyright. See the section on "Separating facts from expressions in computer programs" for more information.

✔ **Unsubstantial works.** Titles, names, short phrases, slogans, common symbols and designs, mere listings of ingredients or contents, bumper stickers, and traffic signs.

✔ **Transitory works.** Unrecorded improvised speeches, radio and television broadcasts, and dramatic or choreographic performances.

Whether a particular work falls into one of these exceptions isn't easily resolved because you can't apply any defined rule of thumb. Prior court decisions are narrowly drawn on the particularities of each case. Lawyers and judges must rely on common sense and a continuing familiarity with legal precedents when they give opinions or rulings on these issues.

The Scope of Copyright Protection

With this section, I get into one of the most subtle and critical aspects of copyright protection, which is the source of a great deal of misunderstanding and endless litigation. If you partied last night until early morning or are worried about the plastic toy your 3-year-old dumped into the toilet bowl, go take a nap or call the plumber and wait for a better time to read what follows.

The *golden rule* of copyright is simple to define, but it's not always easy to interpret. Copyright doesn't protect the *idea* behind an OWA. It only protects the *original expression* of the idea. There, I said it. Note that the idea may be a fact, and to further explain what is meant by idea, I quote subsection 102(b) of the Copyright Act:

> *In no case does copyright protection for an original work of authorship extend to any idea, procedure, process, system, method of operation, concept, principle or discovery, regardless of the form in which it is described, explained, illustrated, or embodied in such work.*

Distinguishing between the fact or idea embodied in a work and the manner in which the author expresses that fact or idea isn't always easy. I try to illustrate this kind of analysis in the following sections.

Just the facts, ma'am

Maggie, a reporter for the Daily Humdrum, witnesses a major traffic accident involving a famous rock singer. She writes her piece at the scene on her notebook computer and sends it to her editor, via unsecured e-mail. However, before Maggie's editor has a chance to read her message, KNAV, a local TV station, intercepts the message and broadcasts a special announcement relating the accident using only the facts in Maggie's pilfered message.

Does the Daily Humdrum have a cause of action for copyright infringement against KNAV? The answer, like the proper one to every legal question, is "It depends." It depends upon whether KNAV reported just the facts of the accident, which aren't protected by copyright, or copied Maggie's exact words and phrases — the manner in which she expressed those facts — in which case there may be infringement. However, if Maggie used a telegraphic style to draft her report, as in the next paragraph, the message doesn't have a substantial amount of original expression and no copyright protection can attach to it.

> Mond. - 4pm – Accident at 4th and Brdway – Rock WIGGLEBUTT's limo broadsides milk truck – Singer taken unconscious to SQUICKYGURNEY hosp. – suspected neck injury.

That was an easy one to resolve. Let me raise the ante in the next section.

Unlocking the flow of ideas

The purpose of the copyright golden rule is to permit the free flow of ideas, as the following example shows.

Sam writes a very successful novel about John Applebrown, a U.S. resident who traces his ancestry to a famous British lord and goes to England to look for remaining relatives. When he reaches England, he locates and eventually falls in love with a distant cousin who's heir to a great fortune.

Maxine, inspired by John Applebrown's story, decides to write the saga of Suho Chizu, a Japanese–American who discovers that her great grandfather was a powerful shogun. She travels to the Land of the Rising Sun and finds a cousin in a high government position who offers her marriage.

Do you think there's a copyright infringement here? Again, it depends. The concept of someone looking into his or her ancestry, discovering an illustrious foreign lineage, and then locating and eventually marrying a rich or powerful relative in his or her country of origin is what some judges would call a "scène à faire," which is Latvian for "wow, I'm smart; I can use foreign phrases." Just kidding. The phrase is French and loosely means "a story to be told," which is one of those basic ideas or concepts that are excluded from protection. However, if Maxine copied some of Sam's flowery sentences or used some of the same colorful characters that lend life and interest to Sam's book, Sam has a good cause of action against Maxine and her publisher.

As the details of a "scène à faire" are developed, protected expression begins to emerge. One can't copy a very complex plot with impunity, even if the imitator's writing style is quite different from the original author's. Determining when one crosses the line isn't always obvious. In a nutshell, basic plots such as "boy meets girl, boy loses girl, boy gets girl" are unprotected, unless the author adds distinctive twists to the basic scenario.

Separating facts from expressions in computer programs

In this section, I delve into the intricacies of copyrights and computer programs. If you haven't picked up this book with such issues in mind, feel free to skip to another section.

In what most people call a creative and welcome expansion of copyright protection, a few years ago the Copyright Act extended coverage to computer programs as literary works, in spite of the rumbling sounds detected over Emily Dickinson's and T. S. Eliot's graves.

Protected or not?

Some courts have returned to a concept called the abstraction-filtration-comparison test, which was first applied circa 1930 in a Universal Pictures Corp. case about the alleged copying of a play. According to this test, a work is dissected into a series of increasing generalities. At the bottom are detailed renditions of characters, situations, and activities, and at the top is the title of the work. The court then examines each level of abstraction, from the bottom up, in order to filter out those elements of the work that constitute unprotectable elements of ideas, processes, public domain information, merger material, and scènes à faire. Then, the protected elements are compared to those in the accused work. As soon as a match is found, that work is said to infringe on the rights of the copyright owner.

In one particular case, the test was applied to a set of 64-digit numerical command codes used by Mitel, Inc. to instruct a telephone call controller, a device that enhances the operation of a telephone system. Using the abstraction-filtration-comparison test, the court eliminated every element of the device, after determining that the selection of the codes was merely sequential or didn't evince any originality.

A contrary conclusion was reached in a case involving the copying of a font-shaping program by Adobe Systems, Inc. The program selects several curve reference points on a typeface and uses these points to alter its outline. The court found that the selection of the points was a matter of judgment, about which two programmers may disagree. Accordingly, the mere choice of reference point exhibited sufficient creativity to warrant copyright protection.

These two examples illustrate how closely the courts articulate their decisions and how complex their reasoning can be.

A *computer program* is a set of statements or instructions used to bring about a certain result, regardless of the form in which the program is embodied. Therefore, the program source code and the object code burned as ones and zeros into a read-only memory chip are protected by copyright. However, the process performed by the computer program isn't protected. Therefore, you can write a program to perform the same functions as someone else's, as long as you don't copy their code. For example, there are many accounting programs out there, and as long as each is written without copying the code from another program, all the programs are protected.

You can draw an analogy with the plot of a novel, like the one discussed earlier, to determine how much of the original program is protected. The process run by the computer corresponds to the "scène à faire" of the book. If the program is very simple and there's only one practical way to code the instructions, the expression of the process has no substance — it's merely an idea or concept — and therefore can't be protected. However, as the program becomes more elaborate, it acquires distinctive characteristics that reflect a unique way to code the program. Because this particular approach isn't the only way to "express" the program, the one selected by the original programmer is protected.

The issue of which components of a computer program are protected goes to the core of the idea/expression conundrum. This issue is extremely important because copyright has, by far, become the preferred method for protecting software. In a multitude of software infringement cases, the courts have refined the criteria used to separate protectable expression from unprotectable ideas and concepts. The last chapter on the subject probably hasn't been written yet, so if you're dealing with similar issues, check with a computer law specialist and peruse the "Protected or not?" sidebar in this chapter.

So What Does a Copyright Do for Me?

As the author of an OWA, you have some exclusive rights to control how your creation is used. For historical and practical reasons, these rights are collectively referred to as copyrights. However, they extend far beyond the right to prevent others from copying your work. Copyrights aren't absolute. Like patent rights, they're subject to a time limitation. Also, some exceptions allow others fair use of your work without your permission, in specific circumstances.

Reading your rights

The owner of an OWA holds a number of *exclusive rights* or powers that he or she alone can exercise. The following sections discuss the nature and scope of these exclusive rights as they apply to the various categories of works.

Thou shalt not copy

The primary and most important right held by the creator or owner of an OWA, regardless of its category, is to exclude others from duplicating the work. The mere copying is what's forbidden, even if the copy is never used:

- ✔ You can't make a copy of your own portrait bought from a photographer without infringing on the photographer's copyright. The fact that you paid good money for the original and some copies of the portrait doesn't automatically transfer the copyright to you.

- ✔ The minute you duplicate a pirated copy of a song or computer program onto your hard drive, you commit an act of copyright infringement.

- ✔ You can't download or install a legitimate copy of software without a license to do so.

- ✔ Using copyrighted popular music as background for your home video production is a clear violation of the composer or songwriter's rights.

Prohibiting preparation of derivative works

Based on one or more preexisting works, a *derivative work* can be a translation, musical arrangement, dramatization, fictionalization, motion picture, sound recording, art reproduction, abridgment, or other form in which a previous work is recast, transformed, or adapted. That last phrase covers many activities, such as making editorial revisions, annotations, elabora-tions, or any other modification that by itself is original and substantive enough to qualify as an OWA. Nobody has the right to make a derivative work of your OWA without your permission. Here are some examples of derivative works:

- ✔ A statue or puppet drawn from a cartoon character

- ✔ A TV sitcom based on a novel

- ✔ A photograph of a statue

- ✔ The modification of a computer program to make it compatible with a different hardware or software product

A young man wrote a script for a sequel to a popular motion picture. He sent it, unsolicited, to the movie's producer, asking for compensation if his script was used. When a film based on his script was released and the producer didn't respond to requests for payment, he sued claiming infringement of copyright. The producer counterclaimed for copyright infringement and won the case. The young fellow had no right to write a sequel to the original film without permission of the copyright owner, and consequently, acquired no right in his own creation. Worse, the script was an unauthorized derivative work that infringed on the copyright of the original film.

In order to spice up the sauce, let me mention a couple exceptions to the right that prevents making derivative works.

- ✔ The owner of the copyright of a sound recording can't legally prevent someone from making a recording that faithfully simulates the sounds of the original recording, so long as the new work records a different performance. However the owner of the copyright of the song or other recorded OWA can.

- ✔ A derivative work consisting of photographs or paintings of a building or other architectural work is permitted.

No handouts allowed

Distributing copies or adaptations of a work, whether by public sale, free distribution, rental, lease, or loan, is an infringement, even if you didn't actually make the copies. For example, copying a clipping from a newspaper or magazine about the impact of secondhand tobacco smoke and giving copies to all your chain-smoking relatives is a no-no. So is passing a copy of a spreadsheet program, licensed only to you, to one of your associates.

Barring public performances

You can prevent the public performance of a copyrighted work that falls under one of the following categories (see the "Copyrighting categories" section, earlier in this chapter): literary, musical, dramatic, pantomimes and choreographic, and motion picture and other audiovisual work.

If you own a copyright on a piece of popular music, you can prevent anyone else from playing a recording of it in public, such as background to an exercise class or a processional at a high school graduation pageant (see Chap-ter 19 about performing licenses).

A radio or TV station can't broadcast any copyrighted music or video program without a license from the copyright owner. In Chapter 19, I explain how public broadcasters obtain such licenses.

Proscribing public display

Not only the performance, but also the mere public display of a literary, musi-cal, dramatic, pantomime or choreographic work, pictorial, graphic, or sculp-tural work, or an individual image from a motion picture or other audiovisual work can be prohibited by its copyright owner. For example, an unauthorized display of a protected statue in an art gallery is a copyright infringement. In addition, public display of sheet music, textual documents, or photographs of a ballet performance are controlled by copyrights.

Quashing digital audio transmissions

The digital transmission of words or music from a copyrighted sound record-ing is forbidden without a license from the copyright owner. This restriction is key in the music industry's attempt to control the peer-to-peer music shar-ing practices that are so common between Internet users.

Protecting your artistic reputation

A *work of visual art* is defined as a painting, drawing, print, still photograph, or sculpture existing in a single copy or in a series of signed and consecutively numbered limited edition copies not exceeding 200. If you've created a work of visual art, during your lifetime, you have certain rights designed to give you credit for your work and protect your reputation even if you transfer your copyright in the work to someone else. You can

✔ Claim authorship of the work.

✔ Prevent your name from being used as the author of a work that you didn't create.

✔ Prevent any intentional distortion, mutilation, or modification of one of your works that is detrimental to your honor or reputation, as well as prevent your name from being used as the author of such a work.

✔ Prevent the intentional or grossly negligent destruction of any OWA of recognized stature, such as a piece of public art or the work of a renowned artist.

Knowing your limitations

So, did the last section make you a bit nervous about how many times you've infringed on a copyright? If all these copyright owners' rights were always enforced, we'd all be in jail. But those rights have numerous limitations, restrictions, exceptions, and exemptions.

Nothing lasts forever

In a major overhaul of the Copyright Act in 1978, the duration of copyright protection was considerably extended, but copyright renewal was abolished. (Before 1978, a copyright could be renewed for an additional 28-year term.) Because of numerous amendments to the Copyright Act since that date, the duration of any particular copyright depends on the date of creation and the nature of the authorship. Without getting into all the sordid details, here are some general guidelines to determine the duration of copyright protection:

✔ **Works created on or after January 1, 1978**

  • **By one or more identified authors:** Life of the last surviving author plus an additional 70 years.

  • **By one or more anonymous or pseudonymous authors:** 95 years from publication or 120 years from creation of work, whichever is shorter.

  • **In the employment of or under the control of another (also called *works made for hire*):** 95 years from publication or 120 years from creation of work, whichever is shorter. (See Chapter 12 for more on works for hire.)

✔ **Works created, but not published, by January 1, 1978:** Same duration as those created on or after January 1, 1978, but with no expiration before December 31, 2002.

✔ **Works published after December 31, 1977, but before January 1, 2003:** Same duration as those created on or after January 1, 1978, but with no expiration before December 31, 2047.

✔ **Works created and published with notice (see Chapter 13) or registered between January 1, 1964, and December 31, 1977:** 95 years from publication or registration, whichever came first.

✔ **Works created and published with notice or registered between January 1, 1950, and December 31, 1963:**

- **If renewed during their 28th year:** 95 years from publication or registration, whichever came first.

- **If not renewed:** 28 years from publication or registration, whichever came first.

A copyright always extends through December 31st of its year of expiration.

Losing control

Under the *first sale doctrine,* after you sell or otherwise transfer a copy or recording of your copyrighted work (see Chapter 12 for ownership-issues info), you can't prevent the resale or transfer of that copy and you can't continue to collect a fee or royalty every time the it changes hands either.

However, even the legitimate owner of a copy of a sound recording or computer program doesn't have the right to commercially exploit that copy by lease or rental, except to benefit a nonprofit library or educational institution. This prohibition doesn't apply to computer programs built into a machine or device, such as the program that controls the operation of a video game or your automobile ignition system. By the way, a computer program is never sold, but licensed to you exclusively as stated on the CD jacket or in the license you approve before downloading it: You can't sell it or give it away.

Playing fair

The concept of fair use allows others to use your copyrighted work (published or unpublished) without your permission. Of course, fairness is one of those subjective criteria about which you and the user of your work may disagree — so the law spells out what's fair use of copyrighted material:

✔ Reviews or criticism of the work

✔ News reporting

✔ Teaching (including making multiple copies for classroom use)

✔ Scholarship

✔ Research

Four factors determine whether the use of the original work is fair:

✔ The purpose and character of the use, including whether it is used for a commercial or a nonprofit educational purpose. A commercial, for profit activity is rarely characterized as fair use.

✔ The nature of the work. A work that represents a lot of talent or considerable labor is less subject to fair use than a cheap or trivial one. For instance, a dime novel carries less weight than a public monument or sculpture, and a homemade video production less than a sophisticated ballet performance.

✔ The amount and substantiality of the portion used in relation to the entire work. Lifting three or four pages from a three hundred page novel is more likely to be tolerated than reproducing an entire short poem.

✔ The effect upon the market or the value of the copyrighted work. A teacher can't routinely make and distribute copies of an entire textbook in order to save the students the cost of buying the textbook.

Licensing your work — Whether you like it or not

After you distribute a recording of a nondramatic musical work, such as a song, you're forced to grant a *compulsory license* (non-voluntary permission) to anyone else in the U.S. who wants to make and distribute new recordings of that work, either with physical copies or through digital transmission. The "gotcha" is that, each month, the person who takes advantage of the compulsory license has to pay you a royalty at a rate set by a permanent institution called the *royalty panel*, enthroned by the Copyright Office.

The person who takes advantage of the compulsory license can't just copy your recording, but must record his own. He may make a new arrangement of the music, so long as the new arrangement doesn't change the basic melody or the fundamental character of the work. The new recording isn't considered a derivative of your own work unless you consent to it. Keep in mind that you have a certain degree of control over a derivative work. In Chapter 19, I explain how the music industry deals with this provision of the law, and how you, as a songwriter, can benefit from it.

Also, in an effort to make radio and TV programs more accessible to people living beyond the broadcasting ranges of network stations, the law allows radio and TV stations to rebroadcast programs, under another kind of compulsory license and payment of a royalty, specified by the royalty panel, to the original broadcaster.

I could fill another book discussing the rules governing the compulsory licensing process, royalty rates, and arbitrating royalty-related disputes. I'll spare you for now — just know that these rules exist and usually require circumstantial interpretation by an IP lawyer.

Claiming exemptions and privileges

Some activities that would otherwise infringe on a copyright are allowed for specific nonprofit, charitable, or educational purposes.

✔ **Copies for the blind.** Non-dramatic literary works reproduced or distributed as copies or recordings in specialized formats exclusively for use by blind or other disabled persons are copyright exempt. Braille copies of a text are an obvious example of this type of exemption.

✔ **Libraries and archives.** Public librarians and archivists may reproduce and distribute one copy or phonorecord of a copyrighted work for a non-commercial purpose, providing that a notice of copyright appears on the reproduced copy or recording. They may also make up to three copies for preservation, security deposit, or research in another library or archive center.

✔ **Teachers.** Teachers can perform or display a copyrighted work for their students in a face-to-face teaching activity in the classroom of a nonprofit educational institution.

Don't confuse this with the fair use exception that allows teachers to make multiple copies of a reasonable portion of a protected work for distribution in the classroom, regardless of the status of the educational institution.

✔ **Nonprofit education.** Government agencies and nonprofit educational institutions may transmit, such as by broadcasting, by cable, and over the Internet or any other network, the performance of a nondramatic literary or musical work and the display of literary, pictorial, or any other type of work under these circumstances:

  • In a classroom or other teaching location.

  • To persons whose disabilities or other circumstances prevent their attendance in a classroom.

  • By officers and employees of a governmental body as part of their duties.

✔ **Religious activities.** In places of worship and religious assemblies, you can perform or display a nondramatic literary work, a musical work, or a dramatic-musical work of a religious character without consent of the copyright owner.

✔ **Charitable purposes.** With advance notice to the copyright owner, you can perform (although not transmit) a non-dramatic literary or musical work for nonprofit, educational, religious, or charitable purposes, unless the copyright owner objects at least seven days before the scheduled performance.

✔ **Private transmissions.** Retransmitting the performance or display of a work for public reception on a single receiving apparatus (such as a home theater) is exempt if the public is not charged and you don't retransmit it publicly. For example, if I appear on a TV show, I can receive the program on my regular TV set then rig a cable connection to communicate it to a large plasma screen on my patio for a viewing party.

✔ **Commercial establishments.** A small commercial establishment may retransmit a radio or television program free of charge to its customers. The law limits the number of speakers or TV sets you can use, depending upon the type and size of the business. This is the exemption that allows you to see 16 football games at one time at your local sports bar.

✔ **Agricultural fairs.** In the course of an annual agricultural or horticultural fair or exhibition, a government agency or a nonprofit agricultural or horticultural organization may perform a nondramatic musical work without license from the copyright owner.

✔ **Record shops.** Music and record shops can play or perform nondramatic musical works, including audiovisual works, for the benefit of their customers and to promote the sale of recordings of the works.

✔ **Transmissions to disabled persons.** You can transmit performances of literary works over ten years old to blind or other handicapped persons in nonprofit education or governmentally controlled circumstances. Don't confuse this right to transmit with the right to make copies mentioned at the head of this list.

✔ **Fraternal organization events.** Veterans' organizations and other nonprofit fraternal organizations can perform non-dramatic literary or musical works during a social function to which the general public is not invited. University fraternities and sororities can't benefit from this exemption unless the social function is held solely to raise funds for a specific charitable purpose.

✔ **In-house retransmissions.** Some secondary retransmissions of the performance or display of a work may be exempt under certain circumstances and settings, such as by a hotel or apartment house to individual rooms or flats and by cable companies (under a compulsory license as explained earlier under "Licensing your work — Whether you like it or not").

✔ **Ephemeral recordings.** Radio and television studios may make temporary recordings of their broadcast programs for internal use, under certain conditions.

✔ **Computer programs.** You may make one copy of a computer program as part of your use of the program or for your archives without permission from the copyright owner. You can also adapt that copy to your hardware. It isn't an infringement to let your computer generate an extra copy of a program to use for maintenance or repair. The archival copy may be transferred with the sale of the original program, but the repair copy must be destroyed when the maintenance or repair is done.

✔ **Personal use.** Finally, an exemption familiar to everybody. You may record a radio or television program while it's played on the air for later listening or viewing by you and the members of your household. You may not, without permission from the copyright owner, copy, sell, lend, or publicly play your recording.

Chapter 12

Untangling Ownership Issues

. . . .

In This Chapter

▶ Getting the copyright in a work made for hire

▶ Transferring your copyright

▶ Checking the copyright status of a work

. . . .

Copyright law casts a very broad net. It's hard to imagine a human endeavor that doesn't have a copyrightable component. Whether you write a book, peddle hotdogs from a street cart, coach aerobic exercises, teach a knitting course, sell real estate, or design a sophisticated, scientific instrument, copyright issues affect you.

This book is a literary original work of authorship (OWA) — it's copyrightable. Its illustrations — as well as the decoration on your hotdog wagon — are pictorial OWAs. While bouncing about your exercise studio, teaching your knitting class, or brokering house sales, you use recorded music, textbooks, audiovisual teaching aids, or multiple listing compilations, all works protected by copyrights. And the list of OWAs that you generate or use when developing, manufacturing, and marketing your scientific instrument — from advertising brochures and technical manuals to mask works and computer programs — is endless.

Each of these OWAs raises ownership and protection issues and conceals potential legal pitfalls for the unwary. And as you create your masterpiece or hire someone to do it for you, understanding who created an OWA, and consequently, who has the rights to it, is vitally important. An oversight or mistake in this area can have disastrous consequences.

In this chapter, I talk about how to decide whether you own a copyright (and if not, who does), how to give or sell your copyright to someone else, and how to track down copyright ownership. Often, it's fairly simple and you can figure it out yourself. But if it all seems incredibly confusing, your IP attorney can help you unravel the tangle of copyright ownership.

Staking a Claim: Making Sure That You Own the Copyright

Any original creation is a potentially valuable intellectual property. And when you start throwing the word *valuable* around, you know things won't remain simple for long. If you've been locked away in your home office writing the great American novel or developing the next world-famous pantomime routine, the question of who owns the original work of authorship (OWA) is probably simple — you do. However, if you developed a script while working for a movie production studio, or wrote the background music as a freelance composer, chances are that the studio owns the copyright in your creation. But, if you're reading this chapter, I'm guessing your situation is a bit more complex.

Many of the difficulties and costly litigations that you can have with copyrights involve questions of ownership. The usual participants in the great ownership debate are you and your associates, your employer or employees, collaborators, and contractors. Anyone who contributed to an OWA may have a full or partial interest in the work. You need to be aware of how the legalities of ownership affect your role in the creative process.

You and your associates

If you work (on your own and not as someone's employee) with a co-author, you two jointly own the copyright, unless you have an agreement to the contrary. Joint ownership of the copyright, just like a business partnership or a marriage, can be messy and quickly turn nasty when a disagreement surfaces. Contrary to patent law, which allows each co-inventor to exploit the invention independently without accounting to the other, joint owners of a copyright must account to each other for any benefit realized from the licensing or sale of the work or the copyright — and share the benefit. However, a joint owner can exploit the copyright or even transfer it to a third party without permission from the other owner — which can lead to very awkward situations.

If you can't avoid joint ownership of a copyright, you and the other joint owner should sign a written comprehensive agreement that spells out all critical and potentially contentious issues, such as:

> ✔ **Respective percentages of ownership.** The interest of co-owners of a copyright can be apportioned in any percentages the parties decide. If you can't agree, the law presumes that all parties have an equal, undivided interest in the copyright.

✔ **Joint or separate right to exploit the copyright.** Whether or not you and the other co-owner are equal owners, you can exploit the copyright jointly or allow each other to take advantage of any opportunity sepa-rately. You must also decide whether to pool your benefits or let each party keep his or her own receipts.

✔ **Right to prepare a derivative work.** A derivative work can become more lucrative than the original, even to a point where there's no more market for the original.

For example, John and Rob together devise an asset management com-puter program, tailored to Rob's tool-rental business. Both are co-authors of the program and co-owners of the copyright. Larry, Rob's friend who operates vending machines, hears about the program and asks Rob to help him write a similar program for his business.

Starting with the tool-rental management program, Rob and Larry develop a more sophisticated program to manage Larry's vending machine oper-ation. The new program adapts easily to other businesses. Rob and Larry, finding more and more applications for the program, embark on a very lucrative licensing venture.

Rob must account to John for all proceeds collected from the exploitation of the initial program. However, knowing that the new program is far more elaborate than the original program, Rob thinks that John only deserves a very small percentage of the proceeds from the second program (if any).

If John sues Rob and Larry for a reasonable share of those proceeds, a court would most likely award half of the proceeds to Larry (the half owner of the new program) and a quarter of the proceeds to each Rob and John, the owners of equal and undivided shares of the copyright in the original program, upon which the derivative work is based.

Here's why: Although John and Rob created the original program, when the second program was developed, Larry also became a part-owner. If John didn't want any more partners, he should've specified that each party has veto power over a joint authorship of a derivative work with a third party, in the original agreement.

✔ **Right to transfer one's interest to a third party.** If you aren't comfort-able with the idea of being in bed (joint ownership) with a stranger, you should arrange for each party to have first choice in buying the interest of the other.

✔ **Right of succession in case of death or disability of one party.** Success-ion laws vary from state to state. You can bypass those laws with a well-drafted agreement that guarantees an orderly transfer of the copyright to the surviving co-owner upon paying a stipulated sum to the deceased party's estate. You can fund and guarantee that payment by each taking an insurance policy on the life of the other.

All these considerations have important legal implications that deserve the attention of a competent lawyer. (Yes, trust me, there are incompetent ones.)

Work made for hire: When the creator isn't the author

A *work made for hire* (WMFH) is an OWA that's created by an employee within the scope of his employment, or one that is commissioned under a special agreement (see the following sections for details). In both cases the legal author of the work isn't its actual creator, but the employer, or the commissioning party, whether that's an individual or a corporation. The copyright in a WMFH never belongs to the actual creator of the work.

Employees' creations

Let me set the stage: An *employee* is someone regularly employed by another (the *employer* — groundbreaking stuff, huh?) and subject to payroll withdrawals. Freelance operators and independent contractors aren't considered employees in this context. (For more on those independents, see the next section.)

The law considers the employer to be the author of the work on the theory that an employee is just a robot that executes the task upon the direction of his boss: "Bob, fix me a cup of coffee. And while you're at it, write me a computer program." It's all in a day's work. *Just a note:* This aspect of copyright law is totally inconsistent with patent law, which requires that only the genuine inventor, not the boss, be listed on a patent application (see Chapter 10). Logical? No. But there's little logic in the madness of the law. So, what's new?

Works commissioned from non-employees

A creation by a non-employee is classified as a WMFH if it falls within one of the nine qualifying works categories in the following list and the work is specifically commissioned under a written contract signed by both parties.

✔ **Contribution to a collective work:** A *collective work,* such as a periodical, anthology, or encyclopedia, contains a number of separate and independent contributions assembled into a collective whole. Any contribution to such a work is classified as a WMFH.

When two non-employee authors jointly contribute to the text of a book, and both perform tasks such as writing and editing, and in the final work their contributions are merged into inseparable or interdependent parts, they create a joint work — not a collective one (see the "You and your associates" section, earlier in this chapter). A joint work by non-employees can never qualify as a WMFH under contract or by law. But when two or more non-employees contribute separate portions of a single work under a requisite agreement, the employer legally becomes the sole author and is presumed to have authored all its employees' contributions.

✔ **Part of a motion picture or other audiovisual work:** Composing background music or designing graphic stage sets for a film, writing a script for a teaching video cassette, or laying out a dancing act for a movie ballroom scene are examples of qualifying works.

✔ **A translation:** Translation of written or aural text from one language to another.

✔ **A supplementary work:** A work prepared for publication that is adjunct to a work by another author, such as an introduction, preface, foreword, epilogue, afterword, conclusion, illustration, explanation, revision, update, commentary, map, diagram, chart, table, editorial notes, musical arrangement, answer sheet, bibliography, appendix, glossary, index, or anything that may assist in the use of the principal work.

✔ **A compilation:** A work formed by collecting and assembling preexisting materials or data. The way that this material is selected and arranged creates a work that, as a whole, constitutes an OWA. A collective work is also a compilation, but a compilation can be authored by a single person. Reference works such as dictionaries and lexicons, directories, cookbooks, and anthologies qualify as compilations.

✔ **An instructional text:** Any work intended for use in a systematic teaching activity, ranging from scholarly treatises to simple ABC books used by kindergarteners.

✔ **A test:** Such as the S.A.T., or any literary or graphical work that solicits a subject's written, oral, or physical answers or reactions.

✔ **Answers for a test.**

✔ **An atlas:** Any collection of territorial maps and related textual material.

The requisite contract to create a WMFH out of a non-employee's contribution must be signed by all parties and must include a clause substantially equivalent to the following:

> *Any original work of authorship created by XXX (the "Creator") under this agreement shall be a work-made-for-hire pursuant to 17 U.S.C. 101 and the copyright in said work shall vest in YYY (the "Commissioning party"). The Creator shall assign to the Commissioning party any work that doesn't qualify as a work-made-for-hire. Both parties have signified their consent to this agreement by their respective signatures below.*

When you have a choice

If you're the boss, you must either let the actual creator of the work acquire the copyright, which he then *assigns* (legally transfers) to you after the work is completed (see "Knowing when to assign," later in this chapter), or have him work under a WMFH agreement. In the latter situation, you get the copyright, but for a different duration than a standard non-WMFH (see Chapter 11). The best alternative depends upon the age of the creator, and other factors discussed in the next paragraph. If the creator is relatively young, the copyright life will be longer if it's kept in his or her name. If the creator is of advanced age, a WMFH may yield a longer copyright duration.

The commissioning party retains complete control over the copyright in a WMFH, even more than in a case of assignment (see the next paragraph about cancellation upon the contributor's demise). On the other end, if you're not in the driver's seat, but are hired to perform a task that's subject to WMFH status, you should carefully consider all the ramifications of working under a WMFH agreement instead of your simple promise to assign. You should pay particular consideration to the following right-to-cancel provision.

Besides the difference in copyright duration in a standard work versus a WMFH, the assignment of a standard work to a commissioning party can be cancelled by the assignor or by their heirs, in whole or in part, under certain circumstances such as the author's death. If you're concerned about these matters, you probably need to consult an IP attorney.

In certain states, notably California, the law classifies a person working under a WMFH agreement as a full-fledged employee, subject to all the benefits and payroll withdrawals of a regular employee. If you're in one of these jurisdictions (check your state labor and insurance codes, or ask your attorney), only use WMFH agreements when commissioning corporate entities, and not with individuals. If you don't withhold taxes and other deductions from their paychecks, you'll be breaking state and federal laws.

Handling non-qualifying WMFH agreements

Because of the advantages WMFH agreements often provide to the commissioning party, companies routinely use them to hire outside contributors. But many of these agreements are inappropriate because they are for nonqualified types of works. For example, a publisher may commission an author to write a book under a WMFH agreement, even though the work doesn't fit into any of the nine categories listed in the previous section. What happens to the copyright under these circumstances? Does the contract confer any right to the commissioning party?

As always, the answers to these questions depend on the particular circumstances of the case in question. The courts tend to treat these improper agree-ments as nonexclusive copyright licenses granted by the creator to the commissioning party to use the contemplated work while reserving to the creator the right to do whatever he wants with the work and copyright.

In other words, he can authorize someone else to use and exploit the work and also do that himself in competition with the commissioning party.

Changing Owners: Transferring Interest in a Copyright

The copyright to an OWA can be sliced like salami into separate ownership portions (legally called interests) that you can then assign (transfer) to different people. You can also assign to different parties all the various exclusive rights of a copyright owner that I painstakingly list in Chapter 11. For example, a motion picture studio can get the right to make a TV sitcom from your story, while a magazine can serialize it over a number of weeks.

Knowing when to assign

The law is very clear that an OWA isn't created until it is *fixed* (in a tangible or reproducible state, described in Chapter 11). Furthermore, when a work is prepared over a period of time, the portion of it that is fixed at any particular point in time constitutes the work as of that time.

You can only transfer copyright ownership on what is fixed at the time of the transfer. The transfer doesn't automatically cover any part of the work that will be created and fixed in the future. Accordingly, if you ask a contractor to assign (transfer) a copyright on his contribution to a project before the work is started or fixed, the assignment document will have no legal effect.

I'm sure you're wondering how you can ensure, at the outset, that the copyright on a future work will be transferred to you. In your hiring agreement, have the contractor or prospective author sign an agreement to assign the copyrights of every OWA created within the scope of the job to you. Then, have a formal assignment document ready for signature as soon as a work is fixed.

Drafting a binding assignment agreement

The basic rule of transferring an entire copyright interest is to get it in writing. Any transfer, other than by court order, inheritance, or other automatic manner specified by law, is invalid unless it's in a written conveyance (the transfer of an interest from one person to another) signed by the owner.

Note that the conveyance of a partial interest, such as a non-exclusive license (see Chapter 19) need not be in writing to be legally effective. But who would be foolish enough to enter into a license agreement by oral agreement?

A written conveyance assignment effectively transfers copyright ownership. But you need to go one step further. You must have the conveyance notarized (or sworn before an authorized person) to use it in court as *prima facie evidence* (evidence admissible without any further proof) of the transfer.

If you assign the copyright abroad, have it witnessed by a U.S. diplomatic or consular officer or by a foreign official authorized to administer oaths (much as a notary would be here). Make sure that the official certifies his or her authority, for example with a seal or stamp.

For a simple example of a copyright assignment, see Figure 12-1.

---

*For good and sufficient consideration, I, _____ ,
the undersigned hereby assign and transfer to: _____
all my right, title and interest in the entire copyright in the United States of America and
anywhere in the world for the original work entitled: _____
_____ , authored by
_____ a copy/photograph of which
is attached hereto, and to the Copyright Registration No.: _____ .*

_____ *Assignor*

*STATE OF_____)
) ss.
COUNTY OF_____)
On _____ before me, the undersigned, Notary Public and for said
State, personally appeared_____ , known to me or proved to
me to be the person whose name is subscribed to the above instrument.
WITNESS my hand and official seal.*

_____ *NOTARY PUBLIC*

Figure 12-1:
Copyright
assignment.

If the work for which you want to own the copyright hasn't been created yet, the hiring agreement with your contractor should include the following promise to assign clause:

Contractor agrees to assign to Developer [that's you] any original work or authorship created by Contractor within the scope of this agreement and will diligently execute, at the request of Developer, any assignment or other document reasonably necessary to transfer the copyright in said work to Developer. The phrase "original work of authorship" shall comprise any such work authored by any person under the control or direction of Contractor, including employees and subcontractors. Contractor shall make any contractual arrangement necessary, with such persons, to allow Contractor compliance with this agreement.

This is the type of hiring agreement clause that can be used when a WMFH agreement isn't applicable or advisable as explained under "When you have a choice," earlier in this chapter.

After the work is completed, you ask the creator to sign an assignment in the form shown in Figure 12-1.

Investigating the Status of a Copyright

Imagine yourself in one of these situations:

- You're writing a coffee-table book about Renaissance gardens. You found an encyclopedia containing beautiful engravings of wild roses, and you'd like to use them to illustrate your own work. You need to find the owner of the copyright covering these engravings and get permission to copy them.

- You're writing a short skit for a high school performance and want to use the music of a popular song with your own lyrics. You need permission to create your derivative work from the song's copyright owner.

- You own a small bronze statue of a Tom Sawyer character that you'd like to reproduce as part of a painting or photographic print. You can't do it without permission from the copyright owner.

- You want to incorporate a number of preexisting OWAs in your own creation, but don't have the time or resources to obtain necessary licenses or permissions from copyright owners. These preexisting works are in the *public domain,* which means they were never or are no longer copyrighted.

Your course of action in any of these four situations isn't easy. In addition, the older the work, the harder identifying the current copyright owner becomes. If you're lucky enough to identify and find the copyright owner, getting a license or permission can be like pulling teeth, unless you're ready to plunk down a good amount of cash.

Before you spend time and money searching for a copyright owner, keep in mind that finding the owner is no guarantee that you'll readily get the license or permission you need. The copyright owner may be unwilling to grant you one or may be under a legal obligation to prohibit anyone from using the work. The price you can pay for the permission or license isn't worth what the copyright owner's attorney might charge to prepare the necessary paperwork.

If you can't secure the permission, don't even think of using the copyrighted material without it. As I show you in Chapter 20, a copyright owner can get a relatively large damage award for a single infringement act — without having to prove any loss resulting from the infringement. Not good news for you.

Here are some general guidelines for your quest to find a copyright owner and secure permission — good luck.

✔ If you're certain that a work has been on the market or that the copyright has been registered for more than 95 years, you can safely assume the work is in the public domain. However, make sure you're not copying a more recent edition that may still have a copyright.

✔ For a book, first contact the publisher. You may get lucky and talk with a very understanding attorney or licensing agent who can answer all your questions and give you the license or permission you're after. Based on my own experience, even if you find him, he's unlikely to be that cooperative. Unless you get a final refusal by the copyright owner, you need to keep digging. To find the copyright owner, first check the copyright notice on the work.

✔ If you're interested in a musical work, start with the record company. If you have no luck there, try to contact a mechanical licensing agency — a clearing house that a song writer or a music publishing company uses to license record companies. The most famous is The Harry Fox Agency, Inc., 711 Third Avenue, New York, NY 10017. A smaller agency is The American Mechanical Right Agency (AMRA), 333 S. Tamiami Tr., Venice, FL 34285.

✔ When dealing with a statue or other sculptural work, consult an art dealer if you can't decipher a recognizable name on the work. She may be able to identify the author and the approximate date of distribution.

✔ Search the records of the U.S. Copyright Office. Online, you can access works registered and documents, such as assignments, recorded since 1978. Older papers must be searched manually. You can do it yourself or ask the good people in the Copyright Office to do it for you for a fee of $75 per hour (last time I checked). I recommend that you download or request *Circular 22, How to Investigate the Copyright Status of a Work.*

✔ As a last resort, consult a copyright attorney.

Chapter 13

Giving Your Copyright Fangs

In This Chapter

▶ Registering your copyright

▶ Depositing copies of your work in the Library of Congress

▶ Putting the correct copyright notice on copies of your work

▶ Drawing on government resources

As I explain in Chapter 11, you don't have to do anything to get a copyright, except to create and own an original work of authorship (OWA). However, if you're a U.S. resident, before you can go to court and stop a copycat, you must first register your copyright with the Copyright Office (a part of the Library of Congress). Luckily for you, in most cases, the registration is a relatively simple and inexpensive process that you should be able to handle by yourself after you read this chapter.

If you have an unusual case and you face a complex situation that raises a legal issue (I flag them along the way throughout this chapter), consult a copyright attorney. But there's more to the copyright story. Congress wants its library to accumulate a collection of every substantial OWA that's published in this country without paying for it, so you're obligated by law to deposit copies of the best edition of your work in the Copyright Office.

In this chapter, I tell you how to comply with both registration and deposit requirements in the most practical and economical way. Then, I explain the purpose, advantages, and proper manner of applying a copyright notice on copies of your creation. I also explain how to take advantage of government resources and take care of some administrative and housekeeping matters.

Making It Official: Registration

Registering a copyright consists essentially of filling out an official application form provided by the Copyright Office, filing it along with a nominal fee ($30 at the time of this writing), and submitting some material that identifies your creation. When the good people in the Copyright Office get to your application in three to six months, they'll either stamp it and return it to you as a proof of registration, send you a request for more info, or heaven forbid, flatly reject it because you didn't follow my directions.

Seems pretty straightforward, doesn't it? Hold your horses. As with all legal formalities, a few tricky twists and turns await you along the way that require careful consideration: when to apply for registration; which form you should use; how to answer some of the cryptic questions on the form; and what kind of identifying material to send. Don't worry. I go over all that, but as an incentive to register your copyright, I start by telling you all the good things the registration will accomplish for you.

Courting the benefits of registration

Registration, contrary to deposit, isn't mandatory. If no one ever tries to copy or unlawfully use your work, registration doesn't really matter. But because discretion is the better part of valor (or of a savvy business mind), and the bad guys really are out there, registering is well worth the effort.

Getting to court

The main reason for registering your copyright is to give you the right to file an action for infringement in a U.S. district court. Basically, *infringement* is the unauthorized use of a copyrighted work (see Chapter 11 for an explanation of copyright infringement and Chapter 20 for ways to stop infringers in their tracks). Unless you're a foreign resident, you can't file a complaint against a copycat if you didn't register your copyright.

Foreigners don't have to register their copyright before going to court, because on March 1, 1989, the U.S. joined an international treaty called the Berne Convention that says: *"The enjoyment and the exercise of copyright shall not be subject to any formalities"*. However, this prohibition applies only to *"countries other than the country of origin"*. This means that the U.S. can't impose any formalities upon foreign copyright claimants, but can subject you and me to any red tape Congress may devise.

The Copyright Office may take months to process your application and confirm the registration, but don't fret — it's supposed to be effective on the day it reaches the Office. You can send your application today, and file an infringement complaint tomorrow. If the judge finds your application in good order and upholds your complaint, she may direct the U.S. marshal to seize infringing goods and issue a restraining order to suspend all infringing activities. If the validity or your application is iffy, she may wait to see what the Copyright Office does with it before issuing her orders (see the "Getting help from Uncle Sam" section, later in this chapter, to expedite the review).

A registration made within five years of the publication of your work becomes *prima facie* (legally sufficient) proof that your copyright is valid. After you introduce the registration in evidence, the burden of proof shifts to the infringing defendant, who must then establish the invalidity of your copyright or use another persuasive defense like "The devil made me do it."

Registration puts potential infringers on notice that your work is copy-righted, preventing copycats from pleading ignorance. Imagine that some deceitful character named Zook convinces The Bamboozle Company that he's the author of your work or the owner of the copyright. For a fee, Zook feloniously grants Bamboozle a license to perform your work. In an action brought against Zook and Bamboozle, the latter can't plead ignorance and innocent infringement. The law presumes that the company checked the ownership of the copyright in the records of the Copyright Office.

Making the most of your day in court

I hope you never have to bring a legal action to stop an infringement of your copyright, but if you do, it's good to go into court as soon as you can, armed with all the evidence you need to win your case.

- ✔ **Collecting more at court:** If you registered before the infringement, you can ask for statutory rather than actual damages. *Statutory damages,* contrary to actual damages, don't require proof and accounting of your losses. Instead, the judge looks at the conduct of the defendant to deter-mine how much to give you, much like with punitive damages in a per-sonal injury action. If you haven't yet exploited your work, you may be unable to show actual loss that you can attribute to the defendant's conduct. That's when statutory damages are a better deal. Even better, the law specifies minimum statutory damage amounts — which may top the amount of losses you could document and prove in court.

  Having your registration on file before your copyright is infringed also allows you to receive an award of the attorney's fees when you win the infringement action. Considering what lawyers charge these days, that award may far exceed any actual or statutory damages.

- ✔ **Getting a second chance:** Your registration may be refused for a number of reasons, such as lack of substantiality, lack of original creativity, or mere functionality of the work (see Chapter 11). Of course, the refusal is the opinion of an application examiner and is never final. Talk to your copyright attorney. If, in her opinion, your application for registration has some merit, she'll suggest an appeal to a federal district court. An appeal takes time. (That's why it's always advisable to file your applica-tion for registration as early as possible and get the matter settled before you need to sue someone.)

  If you don't have time to pursue an appeal and want to go after an infringer right away, file a lawsuit despite the refused application, and name the Register of Copyright as additional defendant. The judge will first decide whether the denial of your registration was justified. If you win this first round, you're back in the game. If you lose it, you can either appeal to a federal circuit court of appeals or give up.

Other benefits

Although getting to sue infringers is a primary benefit to registering your copyright, there are others:

- ✔ **Cash in on your copyright:** Your registration is a public notice of your copyright claim. People interested in licensing your work or creating a derivative version can check the records of the Copyright Office, find your address, and offer you the deal of your life.

- ✔ **Stop imported knockoffs:** If you file your certificate of registration with the U.S. Customs Service, its agents can stop the importation of counterfeit works without you having to go to court or know the identity of the infringer. The suspected goods will be impounded and destroyed after a period of time, unless their owners challenge the seizure in court within a specified period. I get into this in more detail in Chapter 20.

Timing is everything: When to register

To get the maximum protection, you should register your copyright within three months from first sale, distribution, or other disposition of your work. Any of these acts constitutes a *publication* of your work. That way you're covered for any infringement that took place right after the publication and before registration. But you don't have to wait that long. You may gain the following advantages by doing a pre-publication registration:

- ✔ Your pre-publication application allows you to confront and resolve any eventual registration problems very early in the game.

- ✔ The pre-publication registration acts as an early notice of your claim. It allows you to ask for statutory damages and attorney's fees from an early copycat or other infringer.

- ✔ The requirements for a pre-publication registration are less stringent than for a post-publication registration — you need to submit only one informal copy of your work, such as a manuscript.

- ✔ You don't have to file a post-publication registration unless you have added copyrightable material to your work.

- ✔ In a pre-publication application, you may group a number of related works, such as a series of posters or postcards in a single application. After publication, you can only bundle works that were published together, forcing you to file multiple applications.

- ✔ If you are creating a computer program or database that will be sold on CD-ROM, you can delete or block out trade secrets and other sensitive information from the copy of the program you submit with your pre-publication application. However, if you don't register until after publication, you can't omit anything from the required CD-ROM deposit copy. (See the sidebar "Preserving trade secrets in computer programs.")

Finding and Filling Out Forms

You must apply for registration using one or more of the forms supplied by the Copyright Office, whether you're applying for a pre-publication or post-publication registration. The choice of forms is dictated by the nature of the work in accordance with the categories listed in Chapter 11 or some special circumstances as I explain below. On these forms the applicant is referred to as the *copyright claimant* rather than the copyright owner, because until your application is approved, you can't be certain that you own a valid copyright.

- ✔ **Form TX:** Non-dramatic literary works and computer programs.
- ✔ **Form VA:** Pictorial, graphic, sculptural, and architectural works, and any other unlisted visual art you may have created.
- ✔ **Form PA:** Musical, dramatic, pantomimes, and choreographic works. Motion pictures and other audiovisual works.
- ✔ **Form SR:** Sound recording works.
- ✔ **Form SE:** Serial works published in successive, numbered, and dated issues such as newspapers, magazines, newsletters, and other periodicals.
- ✔ **Form G/DN:** Complete month's issue of a newspaper.
- ✔ **Form GR/CP:** Group of individual contributions to a periodical, used always in addition to an application on form TX, VA, or PA.
- ✔ **Form RE:** Renewing a pre-1978 copyright registration.
- ✔ **Form CA:** Correcting or amplifying a prior registration, but not for changes in the content of a work (that requires a brand new application). Also for correcting errors in the copyright notice (see "Marking Your Copyrighted Work," later in this chapter) appearing on the deposited copies or to reflect changes in ownership that occurred on or after the registration date.

You can use short versions of Forms TX, VA, and PA if you and your work satisfy these four requirements:

- ✔ You're the sole author and owner of the copyright (see Chapter 12 for info on ownership issues), and you're still alive (check your pulse).
- ✔ The work doesn't incorporate any preexisting material (see Chapter 11).
- ✔ The work isn't a work made for hire (WMFH; see Chapter 12).

Get application forms by writing to the U.S. Copyright Office at 101 Independence Ave. S.E., Washington, DC 20559-6000 or by calling 202-707-9100. You can also access forms online at www.copyright.gov/forms.

Handling multi-category works

Your work may include materials that fall into different categories. For instance, a book about impressionist paintings probably contains a literary work and a number of pictorial works. A video production may include pictorial, dramatic, and choreographic works. You don't have to file a separate form for each work — just use the form for the work that's most prevalent in your creation. One registration will cover multiple copyrights in a single work, as long as you list all the categories on the application.

As with other legal matters, there are exceptions. Courts have been inconsistent when deciding whether a registration for a computer program on Form TX also covers the graphics generated by the program and displayed on a computer screen. Most judges have ruled in the affirmative, but it's a good idea to also file Form VA to cover the screen displays.

Avoiding common mistakes

Although copyright registration forms come with guidelines on how to fill them out, many applications are rejected or delayed because of errors. Most errors are because the applicants (and even their attorneys) misunderstand the terminology used on the forms or the basic concepts behind copyright law.

The U.S. Copyright Office will ask for a correction if your application is defective, but if the examiner can't detect errors because facts are missing from your application, you may end up with a defective or completely invalid registration. Unfortunately, you could be in the middle of an infringement action before you discover a mistake that's fatal to your case.

In the following sections, I address the most common mistakes people make when filling out these forms and give you some additional guidelines — sometimes those on the forms aren't perfectly clear.

Lack of a title

Just like every file in your computer needs a name, the Copyright Office needs a handle to process your application. So make sure you enter a title, any title, for the work in Section 1 of the application form. "My Creation: Volume 1" will do if you can't think of something more specific (but being a creative person, I'm sure you'll do better than that). The same title must also appear on the first page of the copy of your work you submit with the application.

Classification errors

Verify the category (or categories) to which your work belongs by reviewing the definitions in Chapter 11. Then pick the appropriate form from the list earlier in this section. "That's so simple," Simple Simon says. Yet misclassifying your work is one of the most common mistakes found in copyright registration applications. The consequences can be costly.

Ruth wrote a catchy tune entitled "Pop Went the Zit" and licensed it to Hype, Inc., an advertising agency that used it in a TV commercial. Her attorney, Ira C. Blunder, Esq., filed a copyright registration using a videocassette of a performance of the song as a deposit copy. Ira used Form PA, identifying the work as an audiovisual production rather than a musical work. A short time later Ruth filed a copyright infringement against Hype, Inc., for using her song beyond the term of the license. Here comes the judge and dismisses the case because Ruth didn't have a copyright registration for her song.

Her registration was invalid because it claimed an audiovisual work created by Hype, Inc., and not by Ruth. Her legal eagle then compounded his mistake by filing a correction of the registration using Form CA. Ruth gingerly runs back to court, sure that she now has a valid registration for her song. The judge quickly rules that she still can't register her song because you can't use Form CA to correct the nature of a work.

The moral of this story: Do your homework. Read the instructions on the forms, brush up your expertise by rereading this chapter, and carefully review all the forms before you send in your registration application.

Authorship errors

Many registration applications are rejected or found defective or invalid because the authors and the nature of their creations are improperly stated on the application form.

In a non-WMFH situation (see Chapter 12), each author's complete name and the nature of her contribution must be carefully entered in Section 2 of the application form, as shown in Figure 13-1. The nature of the contribution relates to the author's action — editing text or directing an audiovisual work.

You may list an author by either his or her full real name, with a pseudonym, or skip it altogether and check the Anonymous box. But watch for the effect of your selection on the duration of the copyright as explained in Chapter 11. You can skip the birth date. But the date of death of an author is mandatory.

When registering a work or a portion of one created as a WMFH, you need list only the name of the employer or commissioning party, as Section 2c in Figure 13-1 illustrates. In this case, the editorial revisions were made by employees of Rising Tide Studios, Inc.

So many people are confused about the WMFH issue that the application examiner sometimes asks whether you really intended to designate a contribution as a WMFH. By the time you respond, the registration certificate is delayed by another month. So I suggest that you attach an explanatory note like the one in Figure 13-2 to your application and then mark the appropriate box. Doing so tells the examiner that you understand the nature of a WMFH and speeds up your application.

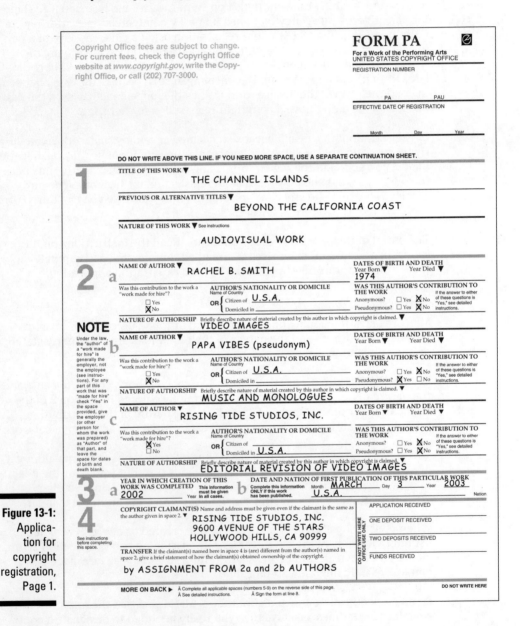

Figure 13-1:
Application for copyright registration, Page 1.

Figure 13-2:
Explanation
of a
contribution
as a WMFH.

The contribution of author _____ *is a work made for hire because it was created:*

☐ by an employee of author.

☐ under a work made for hire contract.

False dates

You must give the completion date of the entire work in Section 3a of the application form. That's easy enough. If the work was published, indicate the date and country of first publication in Section 3b. Giving a false date, especially one that's later than the actual date, can invalidate your registration. If you don't remember the exact day or month, enter the earliest date you earnestly believe your work may have been published.

Publication occurs when you dispose of *copies* of your work, which means that you temporarily or permanently give up possession and control of at least one copy of the work by sale, rental, lease, or free distribution. For example, temporarily lending your novel to a publisher for consideration isn't publication. But, passing around copies of your manuscript to your friends is.

Publication concerns physical copies that can be passed around. Disposing of the original isn't a publication. Neither is performing or displaying it publicly or transmitting it over the airwaves.

Incorrect ownership

Enter the name and address of the current copyright owner as the claimant in Section 4 of the form. A copyright owner isn't necessarily the person in possession of the original work, but the entity holding the copyright. If the owner is different from the author named in Section 2, you must indicate how the copyright passed to the claimant — by contract, assignment, will, or other form of conveyance (see Chapter 12).

An assignment or transfer of exclusive rights must be in writing and signed by the transferor. A handshake agreement won't do.

Improper or missing source designation

Failing to correctly identify preexisting material incorporated in the work can be fatal to your registration because, you're claiming authorship of something you didn't create. Preexisting material can be anything you borrowed or copied from a previous work. I show you how to avoid misstating the source of the work on your application for copyright registration (see Figure 13-3).

Section 5 of the form is self-explanatory and doesn't present any serious challenge, so long as you understand the differences between published and unpublished works, and between author and copyright claimant.

Be sure to use the latest application form. A few years ago, the Copyright Office published some forms stating in the second line of Section 5 that if your answer is "no" to the preceding question, you may go to Section 7. That was wrong. You must fill out Section 6 whenever the work incorporates any preexisting material, whether or not there was a previous registration.

EXAMINED BY	FORM PA
CHECKED BY	
☐ CORRESPONDENCE Yes	FOR COPYRIGHT OFFICE USE ONLY

DO NOT WRITE ABOVE THIS LINE. IF YOU NEED MORE SPACE, USE A SEPARATE CONTINUATION SHEET.

PREVIOUS REGISTRATION Has registration for this work, or for an earlier version of this work, already been made in the Copyright Office?

☒ Yes ☐ No If your answer is "Yes," why is another registration being sought? (Check appropriate box.) ▼ If your answer is No, do **not** check box A, B, or C.

a. ☐ This is the first published edition of a work previously registered in unpublished form.

b. ☐ This is the first application submitted by this author as copyright claimant.

c. ☒ This is a changed version of the work, as shown by space 6 on this application.

If your answer is "Yes," give: **Previous Registration Number** ▼ PA XXXX   **Year of Registration** ▼ 2002

5

DERIVATIVE WORK OR COMPILATION Complete both space 6a and 6b for a derivative work; complete only 6b for a compilation.

Preexisting Material Identify any preexisting work or works that this work is based on or incorporates. ▼

ENTIRE WORK EXCEPT UNDERWATER SCENES

a

6

See instructions before completing this space.

Material Added to This Work Give a brief, general statement of the material that has been added to this work and in which copyright is claimed. ▼

UNDERWATER SCENES INCLUDING
MUSIC, MONOLOGUES AND EDITING

b

DEPOSIT ACCOUNT If the registration fee is to be charged to a Deposit Account established in the Copyright Office, give name and number of Account.

Name ▼   **Account Number** ▼

a

7

CORRESPONDENCE Give name and address to which correspondence about this application should be sent. Name/Address/Apt/City/State/ZIP ▼

JON J. JONES
  RISING TIDE STUDIOS, INC.
    P.O. BOX 9999
  HOLLYWOOD HILLS, CA 90998

Area code and daytime telephone number (800) 000-1111   Fax number (999) 000-1112

Email J.J.@RTS.com

b

CERTIFICATION* I, the undersigned, hereby certify that I am the

Check only one ▶
☐ author
☐ other copyright claimant
☐ owner of exclusive right(s)
☒ authorized agent of RISING TIDE STUDIOS, INC.
    Name of author or other copyright claimant, or owner of exclusive right(s) ▲

of the work identified in this application and that the statements made by me in this application are correct to the best of my knowledge.

8

Typed or printed name and date ▼ If this application gives a date of publication in space 3, do not sign and submit it before that date.

JON J. JONES   Date APRIL 1, 2003

Handwritten signature (X) ▼

☞ x _Jones_

Certificate will be mailed in window envelope to this address:

Name ▼	RISING TIDE STUDIOS, INC.
Number/Street/Apt ▼	P.O. BOX 9999
City/State/ZIP ▼	HOLLYWOOD HILLS, CA 90998

YOU MUST:
• Complete all necessary spaces
• Sign your application in space 8

SEND ALL 3 ELEMENTS IN THE SAME PACKAGE:
1. Application form
2. Nonrefundable filing fee in check or money order payable to Register of Copyrights
3. Deposit material

MAIL TO:
Library of Congress
Copyright Office
101 Independence Avenue, S.E.
Washington, D.C. 20559-6000

Fees are subject to change. For current fees, check the Copyright Office website at www.copyright.gov, write the Copyright Office, or call (202) 707-3000.

9

*17 U.S.C. § 506(e): Any person who knowingly makes a false representation of a material fact in the application for copyright registration provided for by section 409, or in any written statement filed in connection with the application, shall be fined not more than $2,500.

Figure 13-3: Application for copyright registration, Page 2.

In Section 6a, briefly identify the preexisting material. If the preexisting material is the bulk of the work, you can just write "The entire work except . . ." and identify the new material as shown in Figure 13-3.

If your work is a compilation, such as a cookbook that incorporates a number of previously published or uncopyrightable recipes, you must list in section 6b your own contributions, such as collecting, selecting, and arranging the recipes and any illustrations, ratings, or commentaries.

Administrative matters

Section 7a is for attorneys and firms that have frequent dealings with the Copyright Office and have a deposit account from which fees can be paid.

Before you mail in the form, be sure to sign the application and enclose your check for the filing fee. I cover required identifying material for deposit in the "Depositing Copies of the Work" section, later in the chapter.

Depositing Copies of the Work

In a separate section of the Copyright Act, and in addition to registration, the law requires that you deposit in the Copyright Office two copies of the best edition of your creation for use by the Library of Congress. The rule applies to any substantial OWA. The word *substantial* is key — the Library of Congress isn't interested in miscellany, such as commercial labels, postcards, and Aunt Helen's speech to the Garden Club annual banquet.

However, as with every legal matter, there are exceptions, exemptions, and loopholes. In this section, I explain how to take advantage of them, and in particular, how to kill two birds with one stone (Sorry P.E.T.A. persons) by sending material with your application for registration that in most cases will dispense you from the deposit requirement.

The deposit rules are lengthy, complex, and often changed. As much as I try to streamline them and translate the legalese, you may get lost. When in doubt, don't hesitate to run for help to a copyright attorney.

Meeting the deposit requirement with your application for registration

With your application for registration, you must submit one copy of the work if it is unpublished, has only been published abroad, or consists of a contribution to a collective work. For a work published in the United States, you must submit two copies of the best edition of the work within three months of the publication date. (If the work is a sound recording, you must also provide the printed material that normally accompanies the recording, such as a jacket or insert.)

Selecting the copies

Send in the most recent version of your work. So long as the same author created any previous, unregistered version, the registration will cover both versions. For example, the application for registration illustrated in Figures 13-1 and 13-3 would cover the original work. *Note:* In the sample, there was a previous registration mentioned in Section 5 of the form.

If you're not sure which version to send, choose the one that will be exposed to the public and is most likely to be copied.

Marcel sketched a line drawing, obtained a pre-publication registration for it, and applied a version of his design on T-shirts, which became hot sellers. Soon Keith, Marcel's competitor, copied the design, so Marcel sued Keith for infringement of the copyright in his T-shirt — that's for the entire design on his T-shirt including an adaptation of his drawing.

"Marcel and his T-shirt are all wet," Keith tells the judge. "They're not covered by a registration." "You're so right," answers the magistrate, "I can see straight through it." He throws the case out of court. The drawing and the T-shirt are two distinct and different OWAs. Marcel should've sued for infringement of his drawing, or he should've filed an application for registration of his T-shirt design before going after Keith.

Sending photographs of three-dimensional works

Three-dimensional objects and flat objects exceeding 96 inches in any dimension should be deposited as photographs, photoprints, or some other two-dimensional representation, except in the following situations where you must provide the real McCoy:

- Post-publication registration of a globe, relief model, or relief map.

- Post-publication registration of a game consisting of multiple parts that are packaged in a container with flat sides and dimensions no greater than 12-x-24-x-6 inches, such as a Monopoly brand of board game.

- Works reproduced on three-dimensional containers that can be readily opened out, slit at the corners, or otherwise made flat for storage and don't exceed 96 inches in any dimension, such as a cardboard model of a building.

- Jewelry made of base metal (not gold, silver, or platinum) not exceeding 4 inches in any dimension.

- Works or articles that are part of the registration of a published educational kit where the kit also includes a literary or audiovisual work.

The photographs or photoprints must disclose the entire work shown from every side. If the work is already published, the copyright notice must appear in one of the photographs. You may add a close-up of the notice if it's not clearly visible on one of photographs. Mark all photographs or photoprints with the title of the work.

You must provide at least one dimension of the work by placing a ruler next to it when taking a picture or marking its dimensions on the back of a photograph or photoprint.

Exceptions: Submitting a single copy of a published work

In some cases, you only need to send one copy or set of identifying materials with a post-publication registration:

- ✔ Three-dimensional cartographic representations, such as globes and relief models.

- ✔ Diagrams that illustrate scientific or technical information in linear or other two-dimensional form, such as architectural or engineering blueprints or mechanical drawings.

- ✔ Greeting cards, picture postcards, and stationery.

- ✔ Lectures, sermons, speeches (including Aunt Helen's), and addresses that are published individually and not as a collection of works.

- ✔ Musical compositions published in printed copies only, or both printed copies and electronic sound recordings, if the only publication took place by rental, lease, or lending.

- ✔ Published multimedia kits or any part thereof.

- ✔ Literary, dramatic, and musical works embodied in sound recordings. This exemption doesn't apply to the registration of a sound recording itself (see Chapter 11 for a definition of a sound recording).

- ✔ Choreographic works, pantomimes, and literary, dramatic, and musical works published only as part of motion pictures.

  Two-dimensional games, decals, fabric patches or emblems, calendars, instructions for needlework, and craft kits.

- ✔ Works appearing on three-dimensional containers such as boxes, cases, and cartons.

- ✔ Motion pictures. However, see the section on special deposit requirements later in this chapter.

- ✔ Computer programs with deleted portions as explained in the "Preserving trade secrets in computer programs" sidebar.

Preserving trade secrets in computer programs

Computer programs often include proprietary processes you don't want to disclose to your competitors. Although material deposited in the Copyright Office for the Library of Congress may be accessible to the public, you can prevent unscrupulous copying by taking the following steps.

CD-ROMs are subject to more stringent post-publication requirements than other forms of recordings. If you plan to distribute your computer program on CD-ROM, make sure you file your application for registration before publication. If your computer program will be embodied in another type of machine-readable medium such as magnetic tapes or disks, punch tapes or cards, or firmware, you may wait until after the distribution of copies to file your registration.

However, you don't have to submit entire copies of your source code, but only *identifying material* (material that's sufficient to recognize your computer program without revealing the whole contents), consisting of partial source and object code, in one of these five formats:

✔ The first and last 25 pages of the source code, including the page bearing the copyright notice in the case of a post-publication deposit. You can block out pages containing sensitive information, if the blocked-out portion is smaller than the remaining portion.

✔ The first and last 10 pages of the source code listing with no blocked-out portion.

✔ The first and last 25 pages of the object code, together with 10 or more consecutive pages of the source code with no blocked-out portion.

✔ For computer programs consisting of 50 pages or less, the entire source code listing with up to 49 percent blocked out.

✔ If you're claiming the copyright in a revised portion of the program not contained in the first and last 25 pages, you must add 20 pages of source code representative of the revised material with no blocked-out portion. Alternately, provide any 50 pages of the source code representative of the revised material, with up to 49 percent of these 50 pages blocked out.

Watching for special deposit requirements

The copyright registration of some types of works requires the submission of additional material:

✔ **Motion pictures:** The published or unpublished copy must be accompanied by a separate description of its contents, such as a synopsis or press book. (This goes for the video of your toddler's first steps, too.)

✔ **Works published on CD-ROM (including computer programs and databases):** The submission must consist of the entire CD-ROM package, including the instruction manual, and a printed version of the work embodied in the CD-ROM. In the case of a computer program, you must also submit a printout of the first and last 25 pages of the source code.

✔ **Holograms:** The submitted copy must include precise instructions for displaying the holographic images and photographs or other identifying material that clearly shows the displayed images.

✔ **Works published in both machine-readable and visually-perceptible material:** The submission must consist of both types of materials. If the machine-readable material is on CD-ROM, however, you only need to include the identifying portion of the CD-ROM material: the title of the work, the copyright notice, and a portion of the work representative of the copyrightable contents.

Asking for special relief

If the required material would cause you hardship, you may ask the Register of Copyrights for special relief, such as an alternate form of submission or the return of a valuable deposit copy. For example, supplying a copy of an expensive limited edition of a print may be prohibitive, or supplying an entire copy would be easier than providing any required identifying material.

Formal deposit of the best edition

If you followed my instructions about the submission of material with your application for registration, you've probably fulfilled the requirement to deposit copies of the best edition of your work. However, if you only filed for a pre-publication registration, the Copyright Office may decide that the material you submitted isn't fit for conservation in the Library of Congress and request two published copies. If you don't comply, you face more than $2,500 in fines plus an invoice to cover the cost of purchasing the two copies on the open market.

If you didn't register your copyright (you'd be foolish not to), you must deposit two copies within three months of publication.

Marking Your Copyrighted Work

Placing a copyright notice on every published copy of your work, in one of the forms outlined below, fulfills some important functions:

✔ Warns people that the work is covered by copyright and deters infringement.

✔ Prevents a person charged with infringement from claiming innocence.

✔ Increases damage awards for willful infringement.

- ✔ Improves your chance of foiling infringers with procedures such as restraining orders, preliminary injunctions, and seizure of counterfeit goods. A restraining order or a preliminary injunction stops the infringer until a trial on the issue or an amicable settlement of the case.

- ✔ Identifies the copyright owner.

- ✔ Informs the public of the date of publication.

Formatting the copyright notice

A copyright notice consists of three elements:

- ✔ The word *Copyright,* the abbreviation *Copr,* or the symbol ©. Use the *circled P* in the case of a sound recording.

- ✔ The year the work was first published (distributed).

- ✔ The identification of the copyright owner (name, abbreviation, or symbol by which the name can be recognized).

Always use the © symbol. It's the only one recognized by certain countries under the Universal Copyright Convention.

If your creation incorporates material generated by the government, such as statistical tables, maps, or census data, exclude that material in your notice:

©2003 Jane Deer excluding census data tables.

©2003 Jane Deer text excluding tables and maps.

Placing the notice

Depending on the nature of the work, you need to place the notice in a conspicuous place:

- ✔ **Book:** On the first page, the title page, or the back of the title page.

- ✔ **Magazine or other periodical:** Same as for a book or near the title, volume number, and date. One notice covers all articles in the periodical, except for advertising by someone other than the magazine owner.

- ✔ **Collective work:** On each separate contribution under or near the title or at the end of the contribution.

- ✔ **Work on machine-readable media:** Disks, tapes, or CD-ROMs must display the notice at sign-on, near the title, at the end of the screen-displayed image, on printouts, or on the medium or its container.

✔ **Movie or other audiovisual work:** Embodied into the work's medium, so that the notice appears near the title, at the beginning or end of the work, or with the cast of characters or credits. If the work lasts 60 seconds or less, the notice can be on the film or tape leader. The notice must also appear on the permanent housing (cassette body) or container (cardboard pocket).

✔ **Pictorial, graphic, or sculptural work:** On any visible part of the work. If the work is too small or doesn't have a front or back surface that can bear the notice, use a label or tag attached to the work.

✔ **Phonorecord:** On the label or any visible portion of the phonorecord.

You don't have to place a copyright notice on the original work, only on copies. If the work is not yet published, you don't need to have a notice, but displaying it on copies anyway is a good idea — just in case they fall into some unscrupulous person's hands. Just write it as ©*2003 Jane Deer (unpublished)*.

Getting Help from Uncle Sam

During the last few years, the Copyright Office has greatly expanded the assistance services it provides to the public. Take advantage of the following resources (hey, they're free):

✔ A well-designed Web site at www.copyright.gov.

✔ An instant information service, available by calling 202-707-3000. The TTY line is 202-707-6737.

✔ User-friendly forms and very informative brochures that you can download from the Web site or order by phone at the previous numbers. Call 202-707-2600 to have explanatory circulars on most copyright topics (but not forms) faxed to you.

Use the 24-hour Publication Hotline (202-707-9100) if you know which circular or form you need.

Direct mail enquiries to Library of Congress, Copyright Office, 101 Independence Avenue, S.E., Washington, DC 20559-6000.

Under these very limited, extenuating circumstances, you may request to have your application expedited (which means your certificate of registration will be sent to you within two or three weeks instead of in months):

✔ Copyright litigation.

✔ Import of counterfeit copies into the United States. File your registration with U.S. Customs so that its agents can seize the infringing goods.

✔ Contract or publishing deadline that depends your copyright registration.

You must request special handling in a letter accompanying your application for registration, explaining how you meet one or more of these special circumstances. You must pay an additional fee of about $600, along with the regular registration fee. Send your request and application to the Special Handling Department of the Copyright Office. For the P.O. Box number and specific fee amount, check Circular 10 on the Copyright Office Web site, `www.copyright.gov`, or call 202-707-3000.

Recording Copyright Documents

Documents such as copyright assignments, license agreements, court orders, and other legal papers affecting the rights of a copyright owner may be recorded in the Copyright Office where they're accessible to the general public and act as *constructive notice* to anyone. For example, you may want to record an assignment to you of Bill's copyright in his song, in order to warn people that they should deal with you and not Bill if they want a license to use the song.

You can send a copy in place of an original document providing it's accompanied by a sworn or official certification that it's a true copy of the original. Consult an attorney about what may constitute a valid certification. It varies depending upon the type of document and its source.

You should include a document cover sheet, available from the Copyright Office, and your check for the applicable recording fee.

Part IV
Making Your Mark: Protecting Your Commercial Identity

The 5th Wave   By Rich Tennant

Disney Corp. vs. Diznee's Magic Kingpin Bowling Alleys

Okay, we'll change the name of the bowling alleys, but about our bowling ball caps, do these really look like mouse ears, your honor? I mean really now...

In this part . . .

Sure, you're probably familiar with that little ™ trademark symbol. But did you know that several other
types of commercial identifiers, including trade names and
service marks, are just sitting there waiting for you to put
them into the game as well? All these commercial identifiers have a common purpose — to put an exclusive (and
hopefully favorable) brand on your goods and services,
giving you an edge over your competition. I devote this
part to breaking down the Xs and Os so that you can use
the right commercial identifier for the job at hand.

I also demonstrate (with plenty of examples) what makes
an effective mark and what types of identifiers you should
avoid. And after you decide to draft one or more of these
players, you still need to make sure that they're the best
pick. I lay out a game plan that walks you through the
search for look-alikes (and sound-alikes) and outline how
to register and use your trademark or service mark.

Chapter 14

Solving Your Identity Crisis

. . . .

In This Chapter

▶ Understanding the roles and functions of commercial identifiers

▶ Making the most of your trade name or trademark

▶ Appraising the weight of a commercial identifier

▶ Striving for exclusive rights by using a distinctive moniker

. . . .

A *commercial identifier,* such as your company name, the brand on your product, or the street name of your service facilities, is a goodwill ambassador, a herald, a promise — it's the first thing a customer sees or hears about your firm or your product. This first contact often determines the customer's attitude toward the business or product that the name identifies. Your commercial identifiers are your prime marketing tools. They also help the customer choose among a range of similar products or services.

When you start a new business or introduce a new product or service, you get a chance to create value out of nothing. By selecting strong, protectable, and effective commercial identifiers, you get inexpensive protection for your enterprise and the chance to catapult your products or services into a dominant market position. Yet the majority of business people don't give this process much thought.

In this chapter, I define some terms and lead you through the maze of business names, trademarks, servicemarks, and other commercial handles and signposts. I also lay out how these commercial identifiers play a key role in any business, and perhaps most importantly, give you some ideas on what constitutes a distinctive and legally protectable trade name or trademark.

Hitting the Right Mark: A Commercial Identifier Inventory

I confess that I misused the term *trademark* in the title of this book. A trademark is actually just one type of commercial mark — the one that you apply to a product rather than a service establishment — even though it's commonly used to generically designate all kinds of commercial identifiers. But commercial identifiers are actually divided into three groups:

- **Product identifiers:** Commonly known as brands and formally called trademarks.

- **Service identifiers:** Include servicemarks, certification marks, and membership marks (or association marks).

- **Company identifiers:** Also called *trade names* — typically these are business names and logos.

In the sections that follow, I look at each of these identifiers in depth.

Marking a product

The product identifiers most folks are familiar with are trademarks. A *trademark* is any name, word, phrase, slogan, symbol, design, shape, or characteristic that, when associated with a product, distinguishes it from other similar products. For example, the word KODAK is a trademark.

But any non-functional characteristic of a product or package can act as a product identifier. Without reading the words on the package, you know that a yellow package identifies Kodak film, while a green box identifies Fuji Film.

Distinctive shapes, colors, and ornamentations of products, packaging, or places of business can act as product identifiers and are referred to as either *trade dress, configuration marks,* or *design marks.*

Here are some well-known examples of product identifiers:

- DR PEPPER, a mark identifying a soft drink

- WHEN IT RAINS IT POURS, found on salt containers

- The STAR symbol on the hood of a German car

- The log cabin shape of a maple syrup container

- The pink color of an insulating glass-wool material

- The characteristic exhaust sound of an American-made motorcycle

The list is endless. Anything that customers can associate with a product that influences buying decisions qualifies as a product identifier (see Figure 14-1).

Figure 14-1:
Configura-
tion mark or
trade dress.

Identifying a service

A *service identifier* is any name, word, phrase, slogan, symbol, tune, design, or characteristic that distinguishes a service from similar services offered by others. These include servicemarks, certification marks, and membership marks. For example, the mission church facade and tiled roof of a food service establishment identifies TACO BELL fast-food services. A squat building with a red-lined, square-topped roof designates a PIZZA HUT restaurant. Here are some other well-known servicemarks:

- MR. GOODWRENCH for an automotive repair service
- PRUDENTIAL for financial services
- A RED CROSS for the services of an international charitable organization
- The grey color of an airplane that tells you it's part of United Airlines services
- The clownish character of the JACK-IN-THE-BOX chain of fast food restaurants (see Figure 14-2)

As with product identifiers, there's no limit to what you may use to singularize your business and catch the attention of the customer.

A *certification mark,* as shown in Figure 14-3, is a service identifier used to approve or certify the quality, accuracy, safety, performance, or authenticity of another's product or service. Some well known certification marks are

> ✔ The GOOD HOUSEKEEPING seal
>
> ✔ The UNDERWRITERS LABORATORY seal

A certification mark differs from any other type of mark because its owner can't use it to qualify its own goods or services, but only the products or services of others.

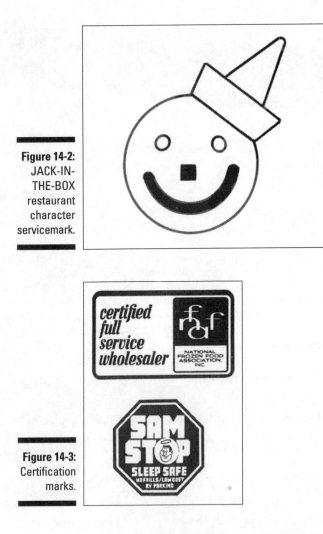

Figure 14-2: JACK-IN-THE-BOX restaurant character servicemark.

Figure 14-3: Certification marks.

A *membership* or *association mark* is another category of service identifier that indicates affiliation with an association. Membership marks are placed on badges, cloth patches, membership cards, pennants, and letterheads. They include political parties' emblems and distinctive religious symbols. See Figure 14-4 for an example. Some well-known membership marks are

  ✔ The TOASTMASTERS INTERNATIONAL logo
  ✔ The GIRL SCOUTS OF AMERICA trefoil design

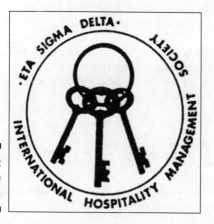

Figure 14-4:
Membership
mark.

In general, servicemarks fall under the same laws and regulations as trademarks. Certification marks and membership marks, however, are subject to special formalities and requirements that I address in Chapter 17.

Naming a company

A company identifier, or *trade name,* identifies a firm and takes a few different forms:

  ✔ **Legal name:** This identifier appears on tax returns, judicial and administrative documents, and other official papers. Two well-known trade names are GENERAL MOTORS CORPORATION and ALLSTATE PROPERTY AND CASUALTY COMPANY.

  ✔ **Shortened version of an official name:** Examples include GENERAL MOTORS, GMC, or ALLSTATE. This abbreviation is sometimes called a *d.b.a.* (doing business as).

  ✔ **Adorned names:** These identifiers are also called *logotypes,* such as the word ALLSTATE under the drawing of two superimposed open hands.

Occupying multiple domains

A word or phrase can be used as a trade name, trademark, or servicemark. For instance, the letters GMC on a building could act as a trade name indicating administrative offices of the General Motors Corporation, a servicemark advertising automotive services, or a trademark promoting automotive vehicles or parts. Does it really matter? Yes, because the law treats each type of commercial identifier differently, giving more legal clout and protection to a trademark than to a trade name, as I explain in Chapter 17.

Domain names, which identify Web sites on the Internet, also fulfill both roles. A domain name is primarily a trade name when it resides on the World Wide Web. But it can also act as a trademark or servicemark when it's part of an advertisement, such as DITECH.COM on TV.

Putting Commercial Identifiers to Work

An effective commercial identifier, be it your trade name, trademark, or servicemark, plays three roles in your business scheme:

✔ Promotes your products or services.

✔ Protects you against copycat imitations and other unfair appropriation of your reputation and goodwill.

✔ Generates profit when you exploit or trade it.

If a name is distinctive and appealing, it advantageously positions your products or services on the market, giving you a greater degree of promotion, protection, and profit. Customers easily remember and recognize the name and, therefore, are motivated to patronize your store or buy your product.

The distinctiveness of the identifier translates into legal clout, which in turn helps to protect your market position. (See the "Testing the Legal Strength of Commercial Identifiers" section, later in this chapter.) As the identifier gathers strength and reputation, it becomes a valuable commodity that you can lucratively exploit.

Promoting your product or service

A good commercial identifier motivates the person who sees or hears it to buy the product or service it identifies, or it steers the potential customer toward the company that uses it as a trade name. Here are a couple examples:

✔ The trademark MOUNTAIN DEW, with its refreshing imagery of Alpine meadows under glittering dewdrops, suggests refreshment to the thirsty individual and motivates him to buy the soft drink it represents.

✔ A traveling businesswoman arrives in town after a long overnight flight. She has an important interview and needs to have her hair professionally done. In the phone book, she spots listings for ROMANCE STYLISTS and ERNIE'S SALON. The lady has no idea about the reputation of these two establishments. But, chances are, she'll select the classy, glamorous-sounding listing and give poor Ernie the cold shoulder. The owner of the ROMANCE STYLISTS shop has gained another customer, thanks to her motivating servicemark.

After a customer experiences and appreciates the quality of a product sold under a particular mark, he'll naturally return to it whenever he's faced with a choice between the known brand and several similar products. He'll also tend to recommend the product to a friend, who identifies it by its label.

Products that are identified with an inspiring and motivating trademark may promote themselves with little or no publicity. But if your identifier isn't very stimulating, your products must rely on their own merits or on a well-orchestrated and costly advertising campaign.

When you launch a new product under a unique and inspiring handle, the product acquires an advantageous market position that may be impregnable if subsequent competitors can't use that identifier or a similar one. For example, there's no patent or other legal impediment keeping you from manufacturing and marketing hook-and-loop fabric fastener strips. But how can you make any inroad into the market without using or referring to the VELCRO mark, which confers a dominant market position to the preexisting product, and contributes to the product's promotion and protection.

On the other hand, a mark like TREADMILL on a line of treadmill exercisers is too generic to give you much marketing clout. Because you're not the only one making treadmills, your mark would also benefit your competition. And, if you later manufacture other exercise equipment, that mark won't fit.

Protecting your product or service

When one talks about protecting a product, the first thing that comes to mind is a patent. However, the percentage of products on the market that are protected by patents is relatively low compared to products that derive their exclusive or advantageous market position from a strong identifier.

Choosing marks over patents

Entrepreneurs and companies attempting to introduce a new product on the market shouldn't underestimate the broad and easily enforceable protection they can get by using a strong commercial identifier either in place of or in addition to the more costly patent protection. The legal community hasn't fully appreciated the protective role of distinctive trade names. It's no wonder that business and marketing people are, in general, unaware of the extent of protection that they can get from an effective moniker or a distinctive product configuration.

A fledgling company on a tight budget and needing effective protection for its new product should seriously consider adopting a good identifier. An identifier may be more appropriate and,

in the long run, more effective at competitively positioning the product than a patent, which takes several years and large expenditures before it is granted and is difficult and expensive to enforce. A patent involves a public disclosure of the product's composition or manufacturing process and has a limited life. By contrast, a commercial identifier can be readily created, is valid as long as it is used, and can be expeditiously enforced as I show you in Chapter 20.

Depending on your product, a commercial identifier is no substitute for a strong patent, but a good one may offer just the right degree of protection necessary to propel a product or service to a secure market position.

Brand loyalty

An effective identifier favorably positions a product on the market against the competition. And anybody who introduces a new product or service can give it a protected name or mark that nobody else can use or even come close to. If the mark is fitting and memorable, the public will forever associate the mark with that product.

I'll bet my favorite pet Doxie that you can't name a competing brand to VELCRO. What name comes to mind when you're in dreaming of feminine lingerie? Probably VICTORIA'S SECRET. These exemplary identifiers say nothing about the products, yet how effective they are!

After a customer is used to referring to a particular product or service by an effective *proprietary name* (legal jargon for a name that can only be used by its owner), that customer tends to ignore similar products or services offered by other companies with less familiar or less inspiring designations.

The long arm of the law

After a product or service is favorably positioned on the market, a strong identifier protects it against unfair competition. The misappropriation of a trade name, trademark, or servicemark, or using a confusingly similar one, is prohibited by law. Such acts can be stopped by judicial orders, which are sometimes accompanied by seizure and destruction of the counterfeit goods or the closure of the offending establishment. See the "Testing the Legal Strength of Commercial Identifiers" section, later in this chapter, for all the ins, outs, and upside-downs on commercial identifiers and the law.

Creating a new source of income

In ancient Egypt, names were believed to have an existence of their own, separate from the persons or things they designated. Commercial identifiers have turned this belief into a reality. Not only do commercial identifiers have an existence of their own, but they're also assets worth a lot of money. When you sell the business, that value can be converted into cold, hard cash. However, you can even "sell" the name and still own it, if you exploit the identifier in one of these ways:

- ✔ **Licensing:** This arrangement allows someone else to manufacture your product under your mark. For example, a shirt sold under the HANG TEN trademark may have been manufactured by a licensee of Hang Ten International.

- ✔ **Merchandising:** Under this method, you lease the use of your mark to others on a multitude of unrelated goods. Have you ever played with STAR WARS toys? If so, you can see how the force is with LucasFilms.

- ✔ **Franchising:** A *franchise* is a contractual arrangement authorizing another firm to render services under your commercial identifier, such as MCDONALD'S or BEST WESTERN. Franchising often includes some transfer of know-how and technical assistance by the franchisor to insure the success, quality and reputation of the products or services.

In a licensing, merchandising, and franchising venture, the company that owns the underlying commercial identifier is responsible for the wholesomeness and safety of the products or services. That company must, by law, exercise effective quality control over the products or services. I discuss all these options in greater detail in Chapter 19.

Although commercial identifiers aren't expressly bought and sold, they're indirectly the most traded commodity. Let me count the ways:

- ✔ When you buy a burger and fries from McDonald's, you're paying a few cents for the use of the famous name by the restaurant's owner, along with the dollars you're handing over for the meat and potatoes.

- ✔ If you're selling a business, you're not only selling your inventory and equipment, but also your *goodwill,* the company's reputation and recognition in the marketplace, that's represented by the company's trade name and trademarks.

> ✔ When stocks are bought and sold, investors are influenced by the value and performance of the company, represented by its trade name or trademark. For example, CONSOLIDATED FOODS changed its name to SARA LEE in order to increase the value of that company's stock. The strategy worked and was the prime factor in doubling the value of the company's shares within the following 12 months.

Testing the Legal Strength of Commercial Identifiers

Every IP right is based on a number of subtle legal concepts, and commercial identifiers are no different. Your right to the *exclusive* use of a commercial identifier and your ability to prevent imitations depend on two factors — its *distinctiveness* and the *unlikelihood of confusion* with other preexisting identifiers. The more unique the trade name or trademark and the more dissimilar it is from commercial identifiers already in use, the easier it is to get court orders against a competitor trying to confuse the public with names that look, sound, or even feel like yours.

Working towards distinctiveness

In "Putting Commercial Identifiers to Work," earlier in this chapter, I detail how distinct identifiers can help you promote products and services and turn a profit. But in this section, I concentrate on how distinctiveness affects your ability to legally protect your name or mark in the courts.

Trade names and trademarks have different degrees of distinctiveness. You can't protect a name or mark that exhibits no distinctiveness at all — and who would want to? If the mark isn't distinctive, it's completely useless and can even jeopardize your legal rights, as described in Chapter 17.

But as the level of distinctiveness increases, so does the legal strength of the moniker. By the term *legal strength,* I mean its clout — the ability to prevent others from using the same (or a confusingly similar) trade name or trademark. Position your company or product on an impregnable pinnacle by selecting very distinctive identifiers. The distinctiveness of a commercial identifier (or lack of it) can be laid out on a four-part legal strength scale:

> ✔ Generic
> ✔ Descriptive

✔ Suggestive

✔ Arbitrary

Only suggestive and arbitrary identifiers are inherently distinctive. Descriptive names or marks can sometimes become distinctive over time. A generic term is a dud incapable of identifying or protecting anything.

In case you're tempted, the law doesn't extend much protection to family names, and their registration as trademarks or servicemarks is subject to severe restriction. Check out Chapters 15 and 17 for information on the pitfalls of using your name.

Starting with the generic

Generic trade names and trademarks (also *commonly descriptive* ones) have no legal strength at all because they're mere dictionary definitions that apply to all products or services of a kind no matter their sources, and the courts allow no one to monopolize the common language.

How about a simple example? Previously, I pointed out that using the trademark TREADMILL for treadmill exercisers isn't very creative or effective from a marketing standpoint. It also brings other baggage:

✔ Somebody else probably is already using the same word as part of a trade name or trademark for a similar product, which is likely to drag you into damaging conflicts, consumer confusion, and costly litigation.

✔ Legally, it would be impossible to register, and therefore difficult to enforce, such a generic label against future imitations.

Selecting that mark would be a pretty dumb move. Yet hundreds of entrepreneurs make this mistake every day when they name their companies or products.

One such company is a bedroom- and bathroom-product retailer who chooses BED & BATH as a servicemark. They then get upset when a competitor comes up with BED BATH & BEYOND, because the newcomer is likely to steal much of the goodwill already accumulated under the mark BED & BATH. However, the original retailer couldn't do anything about it because the only two terms appearing in both servicemarks are common English words that name the type of products sold by these businesses.

Similar reasoning shows you that a muffler shop that operates under DISCOUNT MUFFLERS can't prevent another muffler shop from placing a "Discount Mufflers" sign over its door. Likewise, IMPORTED AUTO PARTS, DISCOUNT TOWING, and AUTO REPAIR SPECIALISTS are also ineffective marks.

Don't succumb to the temptation of picking a generic term for your company or product because it confers no distinctiveness to your trade name or trademark. If you go generic, you're buying a heap of trouble.

Moving on to descriptive

One notch above a generic term is a descriptive trade name or trademark. It's not quite the dictionary definition of your product or service, as a generic name often is, but a *descriptive* trade name or trademark still only describes a common characteristic or function of the product or service without distinguishing it from similar names.

VISION CENTER is a descriptive trade name for optometric services. It's not a common definition, but it tells you a lot about the services provided.

Although a descriptive name is a vast improvement over a generic one, it's not the best choice unless you can put up with a degree of risk.

The law recognizes that a descriptive trade name or trademark may eventually acquire some legal strength, and be considered distinctive, through continuous and exclusive use, extensive advertising, and the development of a reputation. Eventually, the name takes on a *secondary meaning* that identifies a specific company, product, or service.

After five years of steady and exclusive use, you can file an application for registration to legally protect your name or mark as I explain in Chapter 17, but you still have to tolerate close imitations by competitors.

The following names have acquired secondary meanings:

- The mark MARINELAND for a theme park featuring live sea animals is highly descriptive of any attraction featuring marine life. However, after many years of use, it's now associated with a chain of marine parks in Florida and California.

- About 100 years ago, FORD was just a family name. Now, it has become a very distinctive brand (trademark) of automotive products.

Reaching distinctiveness

A distinctive name is so unique that it may have no relation to the product that it identifies, or it may merely hint at some characteristics of the product. A distinctive name gives you the biggest marketing advantage and the greatest degree of legal protection. Distinctive commercial identifiers fall into two categories:

✔ **Suggestive:** A suggestive identifier implies, rather than describes, a characteristic of the designated product or service:

- REJUVIA for skin care products doesn't describe anything specific, but does suggest rejuvenation, a fountain of youth.

- OLD HEARTH for bakery goods immediately reminds you of old-style bread making in wood-fired ovens.

- VISA for credit card services tells you that, armed with that company's card, you can go anywhere to buy anything.

✔ **Arbitrary:** An arbitrary or fanciful identifier is either a known word or phrase that has been given a new meaning or one that's totally made up. Both types are unique, original, and unlikely to be accidentally used by another business:

- JELLIBEANS for a skating rink

- OPUS ONE for wines

- EXXON for automotive fuels

- LEGO for sets of building blocks

Arbitrary identifiers have the most legal strength. They're protected against imitation from the outset. They can muster a very broad scope of protection that goes beyond strongly similar terms, and extends over identifiers that merely suggest a relationship with existing designations as shown in the following section.

Courting success (and failure): Distinctiveness on trial

The protection and legal clout a trade name or mark provides is proportional to its distinctiveness, as demonstrated by the following court decisions. Although the strength or weakness of the identifiers wasn't the only factor weighed by the courts, the verdicts pretty much followed the rule that a good, distinctive identifier deserves a wide scope of protection, but a weak, descriptive one must endure close competition.

✔ The owner of the distinctive LEGO trademark stopped a competitor from using the mark MEGO.

✔ The operator of a skating rink under the very original JELLIBEANS servicemark obtained an injunction to prevent a competing rink from using the servicemark LOLLIPOPS.

✔ Stouffer Corporation, owner of the descriptive LEAN CUISINE mark couldn't prevent a competitor from using the mark MICHELINA'S LEAN 'N TASTY.

> ✔ FIRST NATIONAL BANK OF SIOUX FALLS, with a foolishly common and weak trade name, couldn't prevent another bank from using the equally insipid name FIRST NATIONAL BANK OF SOUTH DAKOTA.

Look at the wide difference between JELLIBEANS and LOLLIPOPS. Yet the court thought that the latter servicemark infringed on the former. By contrast, although FIRST NATIONAL BANK OF SOUTH DAKOTA closely resembles FIRST NATIONAL BANK OF SIOUX FALLS, the court didn't find any confusion problem. The proof is in the originality (distinctiveness) of the name.

Avoiding the likelihood of confusion

The second factor that affects the protection afforded to any commercial identifier is the unlikelihood of confusing it with preexisting identifiers. State and federal laws forbid the commercial use of any trade name or trademark that is *"likely to cause confusion, or to cause mistake, or to deceive."*

When you buy a yellow package of film, you expect to find a high-quality product manufactured by the Eastman Kodak Company without reading the name on the package. You rely on the yellow color. You'd be very upset, with good reason, if you later discover that the product was made by some fly-by-night outfit.

Fortunately for you — and Kodak — that can't happen in the United States because the law gives the Eastman Kodak Company several very powerful means to weed out unscrupulous entrepreneurs who try to ride on a well-known mark's trade dress (the yellow color of the package) to deceive and bamboozle unsuspecting consumers.

How far can a company go to prevent competitors from using monikers or configuration marks that are copies or imitations of its own trade names and trademarks? Or, looking at it from the opposite perspective, how close can you get to an existing commercial identifier when you select a name or trade dress (without getting your hand slapped)?

The short answer is very simple: It depends. The full answer is more complex. You need to consider several critical factors to assess the likelihood of confusion between commercial identifiers. The most important is the distinctiveness of the preexisting trade name or trademark. Other factors to consider are the similarity of the names or marks, the similarity of the goods or services, the respective channels of commerce through which the goods are marketed, the costs of the goods, and the sophistication of the typical buyer. I address this issue of likelihood of confusion in more depth in Chapter 16.

For now, just remember that the *likelihood of confusion* test in combination with the concept of *distinctiveness* determines how much protection your commercial identifier will enjoy.

Chapter 15

Creating the Next Household Name

*U*nfortunately, good commercial identifiers almost never come to mind in a flash of inspiration, and they're rarely found by accident. They can't be collected from the public through naming contests. Instead, they must be built painstakingly from the ground up, piece by piece, keeping the legal and marketing ramifications in mind. You can't use arbitrary or subjective, and consequently unreliable, approaches to find an effective name — you need to apply a structured methodology.

I'm not here to magically turn you into a professional name-smith. But I do spell out the basic steps of this methodology so that you can recognize a good commercial identifier when you see one — and come up with your own. Even more importantly, I give you the savvy to avoid the worst naming mistakes.

Laying out all the name-coining rules would take a dozen or so chapters. So I simply give you the basic principles behind coining effective names the same way lawyers learn the law — by studying a few prior cases.

After defining the basics, I analyze a number of commercial identifiers, some more desirable than others, before suggesting some practical naming techniques.

Marketing Muscle: The Components of Good Commercial Identifiers

Commercial identifiers should be evaluated under two distinct criteria: marketing power and legal clout. *Marketing power* is the ability to attract customers and favorably position the business, product, or service against the competition. *Legal clout* is the capability to prevent competitors' use of the same, similar, or even vaguely related identifiers.

In Chapter 14, I touch upon the legal aspect of identifiers. Legally speaking, a good commercial identifier must be:

- Distinctive
- Unlikely to be confused with another identifier

Good news! An identifier that meets these two legal factors also provides marketing power. This situation is one of those rare cosmic events where the law is pretty much in synch with the real world. And the reverse is also true: An identifier that packs a good marketing punch is also granted broad protection by the law.

Commercial identifiers aren't limited to names. The category also includes graphics, logos, and three-dimensional configuration marks. The same rules apply for all types of identifiers. If you use a drawing of a bicycle to identify your bicycle shop, you're using a generic designation that anybody is free to copy — and customers are free to ignore. Instead, call your bike shop TOUR DE FRANCE and use the EIFFEL TOWER as an icon to make your shop memorable and distinctive.

You must be wondering, "How can I give marketing power to my business name or other commercial identifier?" In this section, I start you down the Marketing Superhighway by outlining the three tasks a successful identifier must accomplish and by providing some case studies. Later, in the "Trying the Tricks of the Trade" section, I'll clue you in on tools you can use to build a savvy commercial identifier.

If you can foot the bill, I recommend working with a specialized marketing firm or a naming consultant to develop your commercial identifier. With the info in this chapter, you can be an informed client, take an active role in the process, and ensure that the identifier reflects your vision. If consulting an expert is just too costly, don't fear. This chapter shows you what to look for in a name, and provides hands-on methods you can employ to create a great identifier on your own.

The A-B-Cs of building a commercial identifier

Commercial identifiers are your goodwill ambassadors and your best advertisements. Think about a radio or TV commercial. Its purpose is to turn the customer on to a company, service, or product. A good and effective commercial identifier does the same thing by:

A. Attracting the attention of the targeted customer.

B. Establishing a bond, relationship, or common interest with the potential customer.

C. Offering a concrete or abstract benefit to the customer.

In a TV commercial, these three tasks are often done in 30 seconds of words and images. Your challenge in creating a commercial identifier is to perform all these tasks with a single word, a short phrase, a graphic image, or a unique package.

Dissecting success stories

The following examples show you how a number of successful commercial identifiers have mastered their ABCs.

HANG TEN: A trademark for beachwear.

A. This mark gets attention with its hard-hitting sound and its intriguing word association for those who aren't familiar with its meaning.

B. The phrase is borrowed from southern Californian and Hawaiian surfer jargon and means keeping your ten toes on the surfboard. That meaning is reinforced by the accompanying logo of two footprints, shown in Figure 15-1. Because the mark speaks their language, surfers, surfer wannabes, and other "beach bums" immediately recognize it and develop a feeling of kinship toward the product it identifies.

C. The mark screams: "Buy and wear my clothes, and you'll become one of those legendary curl-riders — or at least look like one."

Figure 15-1:
Hang Ten
trademark
name and
logo
combination.

APPLE COMPUTER: The trade name of a computer manufacturer (in case you didn't know) whose logotype is show in Figure 15-2.

A. Two wizards from Silicon Valley broke through the clutter of minicomputer manufacturer names like CONTROL DATA, DIGITAL EQUIPMENT, and other quasi-generic, nerdy, techno-geek monikers by selecting a fresh, somewhat incongruous, and pleasantly evocative name that immediately caught the attention of the newbies and spurred a cult-like loyalty among many of them.

B. The company initially targeted the educational market, of which the company still keeps a considerable share. What more endearing (and enduring) symbol of education than the legendary apple Johnny takes to his teacher?

C. That bonding symbol is reinforced by a sharp logo of an apple with a bite taken out of it. This is a powerful invitation to take a bite of the good life the company's products will bring to you.

Figure 15-2:
Apple
Computer
trade name
and logo
combination.

AMAZON.COM: The domain name of a bookseller on the Internet.

A. The name is arbitrary and consequently very distinctive. It's at the beginning of the alphabet, quickly noticed, and very easy to remember.

B. Amazon is a very simple, easily spelled word that triggers three friendly and fascinating impressions among potential customers. First, the reference to the Amazon River conjures adventure. Second, it subliminally suggests amazement. Third, the image of Amazon warriors suggests strength. The term is fluid, yet strong, and reinforces the imagery of strength and adventurous discoveries. It is the epitome of a customer-friendly name.

C. The imagery of the longest river on earth with all its tributaries spread over an immense basin symbolizes the many and vast resources of the company. It tells you that you can find anything you want on its site.

You can really see the strength and marketing power of AMAZON.COM when you note that the company very handily survived while other dot-coms were dropping like dot-flies. Compare this success to the early collapse of companies with generic or highly descriptive domain names, such as PETS.COM, GARDEN.COM, FURNITURE.COM, and all the rest.

NYQUIL: A trademark for cough medicine.

A. Here's a distinct coined name with a fanciful sound that's concise, yet stretched out by its fluttering ending. Pure poetry, I'd say.

B. To the person afflicted with an annoying cough, the term is soothing and endearing.

C. The name is composed of two word fragments reminding us of "night" and "quietness" or "tranquility," and so promises a peaceful night.

Trying the Tricks of the Trade

Name-smiths have a broad palette of elements and concepts they can draw on to paint powerful commercial identifiers. In this section, I briefly go over some of the basic and most effective technical and artistic name-coining approaches.

One of the biggest mistakes you can make is to focus too much on your company, product, or service and forget your target audience. Take some time to analyze your potential customers, and you have a better chance of choosing a name that packs a powerful punch. You can look at a number of factors to define the audience:

✔ **Geography:** New England and the Southwest are very different parts of the country. The servicemark DEL TACO may not ring a bell for many New Englanders. By the same token, many Southwest residents may have no idea what SCARBOROUGH FAIR "should" conjure up in their minds.

✔ **Age group:** Know who you want to attract. The mark TWINKIES is perfect for children; HEALTHY CHOICE probably couldn't help you there, but it does speak to an adult population concerned with their health.

✔ **Educational level:** You don't have to be a rocket scientist to understand and respond to marks such as MR CLEAN, COVER GIRL, and RAINBIRD. By contrast, ARPEGGIO and REJUVIA are addressed to a more sophisticated audience. MICROKERATOME (for an eye surgery tool) speaks only to the highly educated specialist.

You can play with other factors such as income level, ethnicity, and even political leanings to further focus your identifier toward a specific group of customers.

Defining the message

You have to decide what message you want your commercial identifier to convey to your targeted audience. Here again, think market rather than product or service. Don't tell the homemaker that your vacuum cleaner has a high-tech motor-and-blower assembly with sound baffles. Tell her that it's quiet enough to use next to her sleeping infant. Forget features. Think results. In the NYQUIL name, the message isn't about the therapeutic ingredients of the cough medicine — it's the promise of a good night's sleep.

Using your imagination

I'm always amazed at how clever and entertaining entrepreneurs are when naming their dogs or pleasure boats, but how trite and dull they can be when selecting their commercial identifiers. They're too close to their creations and can't take their noses off the grindstone long enough to look at the market. DIGITAL EQUIPMENT and CONTROL DATA are trade names developed by blind techies; APPLE COMPUTER is a name devised by people with vision.

Devising a commercial

Because your commercial identifier operates as an advertisement, why not begin the naming process by writing a script for the best commercial you can dream up for your company, product, or service?

Be serious about it. Carefully analyze whether your commercial conveys a basic concept or term around which you can coin a new name. This is exactly what professional name-smiths do. Have your associates or marketing gurus do the same. The process helps you get a consensus about what you can offer to the customer. After you agree on the message that the identifier must convey, it's all downhill to the selection of that perfect name.

Playing the scale of name-coining options

Your commercial identifier can't simply define your company, product, or service, or the name won't have any legal clout or protection (see Chapter 14). Don't make it too descriptive either. The more descriptive a commercial identifier, the less protection it carries. But, what you can't say explicitly can be implied or suggested by a mere word or phrase.

Coining a new term

Instead of using words from the English language or another language, coin a brand-new word:

- ✔ **Join two or more words:** KITCHENAID on kitchen appliances or SUNKIST on citrus fruit

- ✔ **Fuse two words by sharing some letters:** TRAVELODGE (travel and lodge) for roadside inns and WESTAFF (west and staff) for employment services

- ✔ **Tack a prefix or suffix onto a word:** MICROSOFT for computer software and WOOLITE on a fabric detergent

- ✔ **Clip the beginning or end of a word:** FANTA (from fantastic) on soda

- ✔ **Abbreviate and then merge words:** JAZZERCISE (from jazz and exercise) for aerobic studios

- ✔ **Imitate a common word:** NUMBERJACK (which imitates lumberjacks) for accounting services

Making allusions

What you can't say directly, you can convey in a roundabout way:

- ✔ **Use a symbol:** GREYHOUND suggests the speed of a bus service and COUGAR reflects the strength and agility of a muscle car.

- ✔ **Evoke an image or sensation with a reference:** MOUNTAIN DEW on a soda, or SEVEN SEAS LODGE for a coastal resort.

- ✔ **Turn a common, descriptive term into an attention-catching phrase:** TWO BIT TOW is equivalent to DISCOUNT TOWING, but a lot more elegant and distinctive.

- ✔ **Provide a role model:** CRAFTSMAN on tools and COVER GIRL on cosmetics.

Personalizing your mark

Using a fanciful character as a mark, like the JOLLY GREEN GIANT on canned vegetables, MR CLEAN on cleaning preparations, or DUTCH BOY on cans of paint, offers a good opportunity to devise very clever commercials because people tend to bond with a friendly cartoon character. The character mark turns into an effective and inexpensive advertising agent.

Jazzing up the name

The aesthetic qualities of a commercial identifier have a great deal of impact on its powers of attraction and retention. *Aural impact,* the harshness or softness of a term, can help convey the right image. NYQUIL has a soothing sound. Jazz up a name with an *onomatopoeia* (a word whose sound imitates nature), such as jingle, splat, peck, and pop. For example, COUGAR expresses the roar of a wild cat, and CASCADE imitates the sound of falling water.

Joking around (tastefully, of course)

Humor is a great attention getter. Don't overdo it, but the right amount can impress your commercial identifier indelibly into the psyche of your potential customer. BANANA REPUBLIC as a servicemark for active-wear stores and SOCIAL SECURITY on a cologne have just that right touch of witticism that I like in a name. JOGSTRAP on clutches used to hold weights while running and NO DEER NOT TONIGHT on a wildlife repellant spray are pushing the boundaries of good taste, but they're certainly unforgettable.

COCA COLA — The real story

COCA COLA is probably the best-known mark in the entire world. For good or bad, this product is an icon of American culture, and COCA COLA is often cited as a model mark. Well, not so fast.

In 1886, the drink was originally touted as a medicinal elixir by its inventor, Dr. John Styth Pemberton, for it contained a narcotic extract from coca leaves and a caffeine-loaded extract derived from kola nuts. Back then, people believed that those two extracts had therapeutic qualities (and they didn't need to take drug tests). With the product rather than the public in mind, the drink was named COCA COLA. If you've read this chapter this far, you know that the mark merely described the ingredients of the drink and therefore was initially unprotectable.

After the use of the coca leaves extract was banned, the first half of the mark was no longer descriptive and became merely suggestive. In the meantime, COLA, had become a generic

name for a type of soda. Those guys at Coca Cola Co. ended up with a mixed bag, but through extensive advertising, they boosted that mark to the pinnacle where it stands today.

However, the mark has its problems: Every time COCA COLA is advertised, other brands such as PEPSI COLA and RC COLA derive at least half the promotion benefits. When Coca Cola Co. opens a new market in an underdeveloped country, the other cola manufacturers take a free ride on its coattails because the Coca Cola Co. has already familiarized the new consumers with the term COLA. That wouldn't happen if the mark didn't contain a generic term.

I'm the last one to denigrate the many aesthetic qualities of that mark. It's well-balanced, sonorous, and rhythmic because of its double alliteration and syncopated syllables. However, I personally prefer another type of bubbly — DOM PERIGNON, after the monk who put the fizz into champagne.

Heeding the muse

Don't be afraid to take a bit of poetic license and give your commercial identifier flamboyance, but not pretension. JELLIBEANS and NYQUIL are both smooth, melodious words. FRUIT OF THE LOOM is another pleasant moniker. Try the following literary techniques:

- ✔ **Use alliteration:** The repetition of sounds in syllables, as in CASCADE and TWO BIT TOW.

- ✔ **Think rhythm:** Put some rhythm in your name, as in COCA COLA or DOM PERIGNON.

- ✔ **Match sight and sound:** Use the coincidence of sound and image to emphasize your message. A great example is the mark COUGAR, where the harshness of the word combines with the image of the ferocious wildcat to convey the power and machismo of the sports car.

Avoiding the Seven Deadly Identifier Sins

Knowing how to avoid commercial identifiers that could to lead you into a marketing fiasco, or an embarrassing situation, is essential. The cardinal sins of commercial identifier development are platitudes, pride, puffery, and plagiarism. Also, make sure that no scarecrow, skeleton, or scatology lurks behind the name you create . . . Let me explain.

Platitudes

Using *platitudes* (trite, commonplace words and phrases) to identify your business, product, or service is a no-no. A generic phrase like THE BUILDER'S MART for a construction-material outlet, DISCOUNT MUFFLER for a muffler shop, or LITE (or LIGHT) on a low-calorie brew identifies nothing because the phrase can't distinguish you from anyone else. Miller Brewing Company made the mistake of introducing the first low-calorie beer in the industry under the commonly descriptive (no better than generic) mark LITE and spent a lot of dough promoting it. Within a few months, several of its competitors were marketing their own light beers.

A platitude is born from the strong temptation to use a commercial identifier that tells people about your business or product. If you insist on doing so, do it with style and imagination by using some of the tricks I suggest earlier. THE

ROSE COLORED GLASSES for optometric services is merely suggestive and therefore quite distinctive. You may also add a generic term to a distinctive and fanciful one, as in APPLE COMPUTER.

If you need to be more specific, add an explanatory term or phrase to your distinctive identifier (see Figure 15-3).

Figure 15-3:
Distinctive
servicemark
with
explanatory
phrase.

Many companies are burdened with the surnames of long departed founders or a descriptive technical name that no longer fits its product line. In these situations, the management may resort to crunching the cumbersome corporate identifier down to an acronym or a few initials. For example, NATIONAL CASH REGISTER turned into NCR, and MINNESOTA MINING AND MANUFAC-TURING morphed into the 3M Company. However, because you have only 26 letters to play with, there's a high probability of conflicts with similar names. Furthermore, initials carry no message and therefore are not distinctive, motivating, or memorable.

Pride

To be effective in the marketplace, a name should be distinctive and, if possible, unique. In most cases, there's nothing distinctive in a surname. The Yellow Pages directories are replete with SMITH BROTHERS, INC., SMITH COMMUNI-CATION, SMITH & SONS, and so on. But these are very common names, say you? Trust me on this one: Just about any surname you think isn't common probably is, and others have used it repeatedly.

Except in those instances where a personal name has already acquired notoriety, like GEORGE FOREMAN or YVES SAINT LAURENT, identifying a company product or service with a personal name is never advisable.

Using a name that describes an outstanding characteristic of your product is also a pit of personal pride. The developer of the CHEMDRY mark for carpet cleaning services may be very proud of the process she developed, but the homeowner doesn't give a hoot how the carpet is cleaned, as long as it's cleaned. The term CHEMDRY is pretty descriptive and uninspiring. A competitor could closely imitate the name with impunity.

Puffery

Highly laudatory phrases, such as THE BEST BEER IN AMERICA, are considered merely descriptive and are neither registrable nor protectable.

Plagiarism

You may be tempted to copy or imitate a successful commercial identifier in order to take a little ride on your competitor's coattails. After the impressive commercial success of a chain of toy stores operating under the servicemark TOYS "Я' US, a plethora of "Something 'Я' US" names appeared on the market. These copycat businesses soon had to change their names, at a great loss in goodwill and reputation — and in damages and attorney's fees. In Chapter 20, I show you how easy it is to shoot down the imitator of a distinctive name. So don't fall into temptation and let the evil of plagiarism spoil your business venture.

The three main reasons for staying clear of names similar or too close to an existing name are

✔ To protect yourself against accusations of infringement.

✔ To avoid restraining orders, injunctions, or seizure of your goods.

✔ To avoid being forced to change your commercial name after developing some goodwill and reputation under the infringing name.

Scarecrows, skeletons, and scatology

When selecting a commercial identifier, stay away from words that may have negative connotations. Terms that suggest death, suffering, and other painful implications may sometimes creep into a commercial identifier. For example, the word "pane" may be misunderstood as "pain."

Also, make sure that the name you choose doesn't have another meaning or connotation in a different language. If your product is destined for foreign distribution or a predominantly Hispanic or Asian market in this country, verify that your identifier doesn't evoke something morbid, ridiculous, or obscene in the foreign idiom:

✔ In Japanese, the word *shi,* which means four, has the same sound as the word for death. The Korean word *sa* has a similar problem. Avoid both sounds when branding a product to be exported to Asia.

✔ The mark NOVA on a car, with a shift of emphasis to the last syllable, means "It won't go" in Spanish.

✔ In Germany, the term *mist,* as in the curling iron mark MIST STICK, stands for *manure.*

✔ The French word *camelote* means shoddy merchandize.

✔ The PSCHITT brand of Perrier soda means *fizz* in French. I don't have to tell you how that term is perceived in an English-speaking market.

✔ When the slogan used to promote PARKER pens, "It won't leak in your pocket and embarrass you," was translated into Spanish, it read, "It won't leak into your pocket and make you pregnant."

In view of the ever-increasing importance of global trade and the vital necessity for American manufacturers to export their products, make sure that all new commercial identifiers are compatible in any market where they may be introduced.

Chapter 16

Conducting an Availability Search

*Y*ou're very excited — you've just come up with the perfect name for your new business. But is that name up for grabs? Probably not. Finding an available trade name or trademark on your first try is a bit like winning the lottery! Count on researching at least three options before you stumble upon an available moniker.

In this chapter, I fill you in on what an availability search is (and what it isn't) and the purpose of a search. I then describe what an appropriate availability search involves, outline a search strategy that you can use, and explain how to analyze your findings.

I restrict my comments to word identifiers. There's no practical way to research prior use of graphic and configuration marks except by thumbing through thousands of pages of trademark registers and electronically searching for keywords in the description of these marks that can be found in some of these registers.

Practicing Prudence

An *availability search* is a careful look at a whole range of commercial identifiers that can be found on the World Wide Web and various business and legal databases (including state and federal trademark registers) to find out, as a first step, whether anyone else is already using your choice of trade name or trademark.

After you uncover one or more prior uses, two questions must be answered:

✔ Can you use your choice of moniker without infringing the rights of the prior users?

✔ Can you obtain the benefits of a federal registration (which I outline in Chapter 17)?

An availability search is essentially a legal process. Deciding what and where to search and analyzing the results of the search requires a good understanding of the legal-strength and likelihood-of-confusion concepts I explain in Chapter 14. Although you may be able to do some of the basic legwork, you may have to consult your IP professional to decide whether your trade name or trademark is available and registrable. (See the "Analyzing the Results" section, later in this chapter.)

What an availability search is not

I can't overemphasize the need to conduct an appropriate availability search before you place a commercial identifier in business. (See Chapter 14 to review the types of commercial identifiers.)

Many people (business attorneys included) believe that the secretary of state's office, whose role is to regulate corporations and limited liability companies, "clears" a name before accepting it as a company identifier. Working under this assumption, these folks don't bother searching any farther than the secretary of state's office.

But the secretary of state only checks the name for direct conflict with other names on the state corporate register — he or she couldn't care less if other laws prevent you from using that name. Reserving a business name in your secretary of state's office or having it accepted as a corporate identity doesn't mean that you can use the name commercially whether locally or nationwide.

A renowned osteopathic hospital asked its corporate attorney to "clear" the phrase HEALTH CARE CHOICE to identify its health care insurance program. The attorney checked with the secretary of state and confirmed that the identifier was available. But this confirmation offered no defense to the frustrated directors of the hospital when a major health insurance provider sued them for infringement of its mark CHOICE.

If you're operating in one of the more enlightened venues, such as California, you're particularly at risk because the courts there give precedence to the first user anywhere in the United States. Some other states allow you to use a mark that's used in another state as long as you're the first local user.

Reasons for conducting an availability search

Just in case you're not quite convinced of the necessity of conducting an availability search, here are a few legal and financial difficulties a search can help you avoid:

- ✔ **You can get sued:** Adopting a commercial identifier that copies or imitates one that's already used may be an actionable act of infringement.

- ✔ **Judges get angry:** If you're convicted of infringing on the rights of a prior user and you carelessly neglected to conduct a search before using the identifier, the court won't treat that as a show of bad faith, but could penalize you for your negligence by increasing the damages awarded to the plaintiff. However, if evidence exists that you had a prior warning or strong suspicion that the mark was already taken, the judge may consider your failure to do a thorough search as willful and intentional infringement, and order you to pay the offended party's attorney and other court costs.

- ✔ **Your application for registration can be denied:** The disappointment and financial losses associated with the United States Patent and Trademark Office (USPTO) denying your application for federal registration because your mark conflicts with an existing one are substantial. (I discuss federal registration in Chapter 17.)

- ✔ **You may face a costly change of identifier:** If you launch your company or product under an infringing name, you'll soon have to change it. Think about the loss of goodwill that you'll incur and the cost of promoting a new name.

- ✔ **You may find yourself in bad company:** I'm assuming you're a straight shooter — you took the time to buy and read this book — so you probably want to do an availability search because you believe in your company, service, or product and you want it to stand on its own in the market. You don't need to piggyback on the goodwill developed by a similar trade name or trademark, and you don't want the public to confuse your commercial identity with some organization with a bad reputation.

Defining the Scope of Your Search

The extent of your search depends on the identifier that you want to register. So before you get ready to search, make sure that you understand your own identifier. You can then set search boundaries.

Practicing self-analysis: Assessing your choice of identifier

The scope of your search and the interpretation of your search results (see "Analyzing the Results," later in this chapter) depend upon two factors:

- ✔ The legal strength of the identifier
- ✔ The intended field and territory of use

The *legal strength* of a commercial identifier is its ability to prevent other businesses from using the same or confusingly similar identifiers. So your first order of business in the great name search is to assess where your prospective commercial identifier falls on the *legal strength scale* — generic, descriptive, suggestive, or arbitrary — which I outline in Chapter 14.

After you've taken your legal-strength reading, you need to delineate the anticipated *field and territory of use.* In other words, you need to define the nature and utilization, collectively referred to as the *definition,* of your goods or services and the geographical areas where they'll be marketed. Doing so is a three-step process:

1. **Write a concise definition of the nature, role, or function of the business, product, or service for which you want to use the prospective identifier.**

   Here are some examples:

   - A business manufacturing automotive engine parts

   - An engineering inspection and certification service for dwellings

   - A single retail shop for high-end female fashion apparel

   - A series of medical tomography scanners

   - A nationwide fast-food restaurant chain

   - An adult table game

2. **Compare your product or service definition with those found in the** *International Classification of Goods and Services* **in order to determine which** *international class* (IC) **you should search.**

   The International Classification is a multinational system of grouping goods and services into different categories. You can read the definition of each IC in Chapter 1400 of the *Trademark Manual of Examining Procedure* (TMEP), accessible on the USPTO Web site (www.uspto.gov).

3. **Translate the territory of use into governmental entities.** This refers to one or more counties, a state, or a number of states.

The identifier of any commercial activity that affects foreign or interstate commerce is considered as used in the entire country. This includes businesses serving tourists and travelers, such as hotels and restaurants.

Setting boundaries

Good news! Unlike the patent search that forces you to consider everything published anywhere in the world (see Chapter 6), U.S. commercial-identifier-protection laws, although subject to a few limited situations that I explain in Chapter 18, make you search for trade names and marks only used within the United States and, in some cases, only in their actual territory of use.

So, you've narrowed your search down to the good ol' USA and to one or more ICs. But that's still a pretty big sea to swim in — you need to narrow it even further. Enter your old friend — the legal-strength scale:

✔ **Distinctive:** If your commercial identifier is distinctive because it's either suggestive or arbitrary, you must extend your search to practically all areas of commercial activities. The trademark KODAK, for example, could refer to anything, so you'd need to look wider than the photographic industry and into every IC.

Folks who've come before you already have a ton of legal protection for their distinctive marks. But the upshot is, after you clear your distinctive mark, you're afforded the same protection.

✔ **Descriptive:** If your commercial identifier is merely descriptive, you can limit your search to fields related to your own industry. If you're searching for the trade name BOSTON BREWERS, you can limit it to the wine, beer, and liquor classes. The downside is that even if you find no one else using your mark, a descriptive mark offers very little protection against infringers.

✔ **Generic:** If your commercial identifier is generic, don't bother searching because anyone is free to use it.

Check out Table 16-1 for an idea on where to draw your search boundaries.

Table 16-1	Search Parameters for Sample One-Establishment Beauty Parlor Names	
Position on Legal Strength Scale	*Mark*	*Search Boundaries*
Generic	HAIR & NAILS	No search necessary

(continued)

Table 16-1 *(continued)*

Position on Legal Strength Scale	Mark	Search Boundaries
Descriptive	PERMANENT WAVES CALIFORNIA CARE	County cosmetic-products and personal-care businesses found on the Web and state and county commercial registers
Suggestive	A CUT ABOVE SHEAR DELIGHT BEAUTY AND THE BEST	State cosmetics-and-toiletries-goods and personal-care businesses found on the Web and state and county commercial registers
Arbitrary (existing word unrelated to goods or services)	PASSION FLOWER ARABIAN NIGHT DOMANI	U.S. cosmetic-and-toiletries-goods and personal-care businesses found on the Web and state and federal trade-mark registers
Totally arbitrary (newly coined word)	XOKKOX CAPIX JUVERA	All categories of goods and services nationwide found on the Web and all state and federal trademark registers

Commercial identifiers: The world tour

Currently, the laws regulating the protection of commercial identifiers stop at our national borders. This is incompatible with the globalization of trade, especially because the names of foreign establishments, products, or services are now familiar to many Americans.

Even when foreign companies or products have no commercial presence in the United States, their names are easily recognized. Most people know that LA SCALA identifies an opera house in Milan, and that LE LOUVRE is the name of a museum in Paris. An American customer seeing an art print bearing the name LE LOUVRE would probably think that the production and distribution of that print are sponsored by the French museum. In France, the term CHAMPAGNE doesn't designate just any old bubbly, but the highly praised product of a small territory east of Paris. In fact, the generic use of the mark CHAMPAGNE in the United States is causing a lot of friction between our commercial representatives and their indignant French counterparts who like to wash down their frog legs and escargots with le vrai CHAMPAGNE, sacré bleu!

Slowly, legislation is catching up with the new global economy. Most industrial countries are moving toward standardization of their trademark laws, and the United States is joining more international treaties and conventions. Soon, we can expect to have a worldwide system regulating the use of trade names and marks.

Carrying Out Your Search

Unlike many countries, the United States has no authoritative, centralized national register that you can check to make sure no one has already acquired your prospective identifier.

In the United States, your exclusive right to use a commercial identifier is based on you using it first — and continuously — in commerce (or filing an *Intent to Use* application for registration on the Federal Register, as I explain in Chapter 17).

The states and the Fed maintain non-mandatory registers of product and service identifiers commonly called *trademark registers.* As to company identifiers, various registration systems exist at the state level, but not at the federal level. Most county administrations maintain registers of fictitious commercial identifiers, including sole proprietorships and partnerships operating under an assumed name as part and parcel of their administrative and regulatory activities. For the same reason, state governments keep records of corporations, limited liability companies, and partnerships.

Millions of commercial identifiers are used in this country, but only about one-fourth of them are registered in the United States Patent and Trademark Office. But even the hundreds of thousands of commercial identifiers that aren't recorded in any readily searchable register are protected against unintentional imitation. Therefore, an availability search can never provide you with 100 percent assurance that your prospective identifier isn't already taken — just your luck, right? — but it can improve your odds, so here you go.

In order of importance, there are four excellent places to search. If you find the name you had in mind already taken on your first go around, at least you've saved some time that you can devote to coming up with another name.

Internet

The Internet, this cornucopia of information, is a bonanza for name searches. You need only type in a word and the search engine fetches hundreds — sometimes thousands — of references. Sometimes, the volume of information you retrieve is so overwhelming that you need to narrow it down by adding words to the search criteria. If that happens, you can request an advanced search, where you can search on a number of keywords or an exact combination of words. For example, if I search for *tornado* as a mark for a drain cleaner, I get over three million references with one search engine. But if I enter the combination *tornado* and *drain,* I get only around 27,000 results. At least it's a start, right?

If you don't find your moniker on the Internet, you have a pretty good chance that nobody is already using it. But unless you have coined a very unique term like KODAK or XAKKOX, you're more likely to hit so many references that you have to sift through and then interpret them, as I explain in the section "USPTO database," below.

Some marks that haven't been used in commerce may have been reserved by *Intent to Use* applications for registration with the USPTO. Because they aren't being used yet, the marks may not appear on the Internet. So don't think you're safe using your chosen identifier just because you didn't spot it on the Internet. You must go to the next step and search the USPTO database.

USPTO database

The USPTO maintains a comprehensive database of all marks that have been applied for, including those that were refused. The database also contains a record of all marks with current or expired registrations. You can access this database through the *Trademark Electronic Search System* (TESS) on the USPTO Web site at www.uspto.gov.

Federal registration is open only to marks used in interstate or foreign commerce. Therefore, only those marks are included in the USPTO database.

Choose the **Search** option under **Trademarks** to get started. First, click the **New User Form Search (Basic),** where you can enter a single word, a combination of words, or an exact phrase. Note that you can also search by serial number or owner.

If you get too many hits, go back to the Search Form page and click the **Structured Form Search (Boolean).** This search lets you specify different criteria on which to search, such as the actual mark; the classification; the publication, filing, or registration date; or the description. For example, if you're searching ALIBI for a bar, enter **ALIBI** as a search term and select "Non-Punctuated Word Mark" from the corresponding drop-down field list. Then, enter **43** (lodging, food, and drink establishments) as the second search term, and select "International Class" from the second drop-down box. For a washcloth, search for RUBADUBDUB as a "Non-Punctuated Word Mark" with 24 (textile goods) as the "International Class."

You can also focus your search by specifying the exact product or service, such as *ALIBI and bar* or *RUBADUBDUB and washcloth,* using the Goods & Services category from the drop-down field box. Make sure you try different definitions of your goods or services. For example, after you enter *bar,* try some synonyms, such as *tavern, barroom, saloon,* or *lounge.* After plugging in *washcloth,* see whether terms like *towel, sponge, bathrobe, bathtub,* or *washbasin* return any results.

State trademark registers

Many states and counties have their public records on the Internet so you can easily check the records of corporate and other limited liability company identifiers and fictitious business names and marks that have been registered in the states that are part of the territory of use. Some private databases also provide access to state registers, as well as some business name records. To determine which state registers you need to search, see the "Setting boundaries" section, earlier in the chapter.

State registers only record marks used within that state.

Private database services

A few private companies provide trademark search services or direct access to some name databases. The best-known are Dialog and LexisNexis. You can conduct an in-depth search for a mark, including USPTO records and state trademark registers, on dialog.com. If you want someone to do the search for you, dialog.com can refer you to a professional researcher in your field by clicking on **Search Services** on their site. Lexisnexis.com gives you access to a huge warehouse of information, but it isn't organized for a practical and thorough commercial identifier search. You can search it to find some names and information about their use.

Access to these databases is restricted to paid subscribers; however, most private database services allow you to pay as you go by credit card.

Foreign searches

If you're planning to export your products or services overseas, you may want to verify that your mark doesn't conflict with any mark used in those countries.

Most foreign trademark registers aren't accessible online. Use a native trademark agent to conduct this type of search. Most intellectual property (IP) attorneys have correspondents in major industrial countries whom they call upon for international inquiries.

The World Industrial Property Organization (WIPO) in Geneva, Switzerland, maintains databases of European trademark applications. For trademark info, look on the organization's site, www.wipo.org, and work your way from the intellectual property section to the trademarks area. The organization's

Madrid Express Database (`http://ipdl.wipo.int`) provides anyone with a listing of trademark applications. However, data about registered marks is available only to subscribers.

The laws pertaining to commercial identifiers vary from country to country. In most parts of the world, you can only acquire exclusive rights by registration. I recommend that you consult an IP attorney before you spend time and resources checking foreign trade names and marks.

Analyzing the Results

Remember, finding no reference to your prospective name in all the available sources of commercial identifiers is no guarantee that it's available. Because so many commercial monikers are unregistered and unsearchable, the possibility of inadvertently infringing on some obscure yet protected trade name or trademark is always there. On the other hand, finding out that your baby is already in use doesn't necessarily prevent you from using it as well.

If you do find that your commercial identifier (or something resembling it) is already in use, you have to consider the legal issue of whether using this identifier is likely to cause confusion in the marketplace.

Only an IP specialist can give you a fairly reliable answer on this complex question, but even that would only be a guesstimate. Because the standards for determining likelihood of confusion are so imprecise and dependent upon the circumstances of the case, many attorneys and law firms plainly refuse to issue a definitive opinion on the subject. Foolish would be the attorney who cleared a name of all risks of infringement.

Yet you have to make that judgment, unless you decide to drop any candidate name that is identical or vaguely similar to one already in use. Because of the sheer number of names and marks already used in commerce, you may have to change your selected name dozens of times before you stumble on that unblemished pearl nobody has seen before. The best I can do for you is to lay out the most common criteria that the courts use to decide the issue of infringement of commercial identifiers and give you a few examples.

Determining likelihood of confusion

Common sense is your best guide in analyzing likelihood of confusion between your commercial identifier and those you uncover during your search.

Likelihood of confusion, like pornography, is hard to define. As a famous judge once quipped on the subject of pornography, "I can't tell you what it is, but I can recognize it when I see it." Courts are still trying, without great success or consistency, to quantify likelihood of confusion. It really boils down to a logical, honest, fair evaluation of all the circumstances.

First, ask yourself earnestly, "Am I trying to launch my product or business on the coattails of a well-known one?" I've noticed that many people do just that without admitting it to themselves. I mention elsewhere that the service-mark TOYS "Я" US triggered a flurry of imitations. Then there was the DEPOT craze: HOME DEPOT, OFFICE DEPOT, AUTO DEPOT, and so on; and the CLUB vogue: SAM'S CLUB, PRICE CLUB, and a few others. Avoid this type of piggy-backing if you want to steer clear of legal problems.

Although the various courts use slightly different standards to determine the likelihood of confusion between two commercial identifiers, I describe the most used factors in the following sections.

Legal strength or weakness of the preexisting identifier

The protection afforded to a commercial identifier is proportional to its distinctiveness (see Chapter 14 for more on this). You can't apply an arbitrary term to any kind of product or service, no matter how your predecessor used it. The Eastman Kodak Company was able to prevent the use of its unique mark on watches and other products totally unrelated to photographic goods.

If the name you want is suggestive of your product or service, you may be able to use it — even if it's already used for a different type of product or service — because a suggestive term doesn't immediately make the customer think of a specific product or service. For instance, in order to make the connection between the servicemark TOUR DE FRANCE and a bike shop, you have to know what the famous competition is about, then speculate that bicycles or bicycle-related goods or services may be involved. Finding that the mark has already been used in connection with casual wear wouldn't, under normal circumstances, prevent you from using it for your bike shop.

If you settle for a descriptive term like THE HAIR PALACE for your beauty shop, salons in other states or counties with the exact same name are no problem. The controlling issue here is the likelihood that some customer may frequent both establishments.

Quality of the prior goods

A mark used on high-quality goods is entitled to more protection than one used on average or low-quality merchandise. For example, if you plan to sell expensive, high-fashion dresses for "full figured" ladies under the mark STRONG &

STRIKING, you might not be in conflict with the owner of the same mark who sells run-of-the-mill women's wear because there's little chance that your customer would patronize the other manufacturer.

Similarity of the two identifiers

The similarity in appearance, sound, and meaning of the two identifiers is taken into account. Obviously, the more your commercial identifier resembles the preexisting one, the more likely the confusion among the customers.

The courts tend to give more importance to the sound of a mark than to its look, so you can't get away with misspelling an already established name. For example, CAUDDAC won't differentiate your goods from KODAK, and PLEIDOW won't distinguish your product from PLAYDOH. That said, adding a distinctive logo may be enough to negate any likelihood of confusion, especially when the marks are descriptive.

Similarity of the goods or services

You need to give considerable weight to the similarity of your goods or services to those of your predecessor. Again, a small difference between the marks or the goods may get you off the hook if you're dealing with a descriptive or generally weak mark, but you won't get away with imitating a suggestive or famous mark even if your goods or services aren't similar. For example, a toiletry manufacturer was allowed to use the mark SPORT STICK in connection with its deodorants, despite the fact that another party was already using the mark SPORT-STICK on a lip balm. The slightly descriptive or highly suggestive mark SURE on an underarm antiperspirant didn't prevent another company from using SURE & NATURAL on feminine protection shields. However, you can't sell or do anything under the mark PLAYBOY because it's such a famous, and, therefore, strong name.

Likelihood of bridging the gap

You must also anticipate that the person already using your selected identifier for different goods or services may one day bridge the gap by offering the same goods or services as yours. What's the likelihood that CURRICULUM.COM may offer a college transcript processing service in the future? If that's a possibility, you may be opening yourself up to infringement problems. Use your best judgment. Don't guess. If in doubt, err on the side of caution.

Marketing channels

Are your goods likely to appear next to those with the similar mark? Could your loan brokerage services and other services with the same mark be offered by the same bank or financial establishment? If so, that would cause customer confusion, so you must abandon the name. If the identifier is descriptive, a slight difference in marketing channels may be sufficient to preclude likelihood of confusion.

Sophistication of the buyer

The likelihood of confusion is increased when goods sold under similar marks are relatively inexpensive and subject to impulse buying. Candies and popular magazines fall into this category. More expensive and complex products, such as computers, are less subject to name confusion because they require more customer consideration of their functions and capabilities. Very expensive or customized equipment for discriminating buyers is almost immune to the likelihood of confusion.

Putting it all together

In the end, the only way to analyze the results of your search (especially if you found an identical or similar identifier) is to look at *all* the criteria I list to determine whether your prospective mark is a good choice.

Imagine you're about to market a new type of CAT scan machine to be sold for at least a quarter million dollars to medical groups, hospitals, and health research centers. Your marketing group has coined the mark NOVARAD, but an availability search uncovers NOVARAY, which is used for X-ray equipment and is also marketed to the healthcare and medical research fields. Take a look at each of the factors for determining likelihood of confusion that I outline in the previous sections and see where you come out:

- NOVARAY is suggestive and deserves a broad scope of protection.

- The NOVARAY X-ray equipment has been sold for many years and maintains a good reputation in the field.

- RAY and RAD (short for radiation) are quasi-synonymous words, making the marks NOVARAY and NOVARAD very similar.

- The two brands of equipment are used in the same field, by the same people, for the purpose of looking into someone's anatomy.

- The manufacturer of the NOVARAY device may someday expand its product line to CAT scan equipment, as has already been done by companies like GENERAL ELECTRIC and SIEMENS.

- The two machines are sold through the same channels of distribution.

Here you've already gone through six of the seven criteria mentioned above, and you've come up with six good reasons to send your marketing team back to the drawing board to coin another moniker. However, the "sophistication of the buyers" test will save the day and trump all the other factors. Is there any chance that the MDs and PhDs who purchase your equipment will be confused about the source and purpose of such an expensive piece of equipment? No way. Therefore, the first six negatives present no obstacle to using the NOVARAD mark.

By now, you've probably realized that there's no foolproof way to analyze the likelihood of confusion between two commercial identifiers. Although some factors, such as the strong legal clout of the senior mark, carry more weight than others, a certain factor may override all the other factors, as in the NOVARAD example. Common sense, my friends, must be your guide. If you follow that advice, you'll go a long way toward ensuring a good choice and an excellent chance of avoiding any legal difficulties.

Chapter 17

Establishing and Registering Your Commercial Identifier

*I*n the United States, you acquire your exclusive rights to a distinctive commercial identifier by simply making commercial use of it. However, you enhance your ability to prevent others from copying your identifier when you register it as a mark on state or federal trademark registers.

In this chapter I cover the ins and outs of how to gain rights to your commercial identifier and how to register it. I focus on federal registration of marks because state registration is relatively simple and varies from state to state. After I take you through the application for registration process, I provide some info on the follow-up work you need to do after obtaining registration.

In these few pages I can't cover all the complex aspects of applying to register a mark. Filling out, filing, and processing your application for registration in the U.S. Patent and Trademark Office (USPTO) usually raises intricate legal issues and requires some tough choices on your part. Moreover, your application will be handled by a USPTO trademark attorney, so unless you're using the services of a competent lawyer, you'll be at a great disadvantage. Even though the standard application forms are adequate in most cases, any unusual circumstance requires some legal massaging beyond what these forms allow. The bottom line? Don't dispense with the advice and services of a good intellectual property (IP) professional if you want to avoid the many potholes on the road to a successful registration.

Gaining Exclusive Rights to a Commercial Identifier

In order to secure exclusive rights to a commercial identifier you must do two things. First, you have to select a distinctive identifier (described in Chapter 14). Second, you have to use that identifier in connection with commercial activities. In the following list, I describe activities that qualify as commercial use for each type of identifier:

- ✔ **Trade name, corporate identity, and fictitious business name:** Entered on state or county records; applied to a sign, advertisement, or distributed promotional material; or used on business cards, letterhead, checks, offers, estimates, shipping papers, invoices, or other documents

- ✔ **Trademark:** Put on labels, tags, containers, point-of-sale displays, documents accompanying the product, or on the product itself

- ✔ **Servicemark:** Used on signs, business cards, letterhead, clothing patches, promotional materials, offers, job estimates, or other documents

- ✔ **Membership mark:** Used in the same manner as a trademark or servicemark or on cards, emblems, or other items carried or used by members

- ✔ **Certification mark:** Used on a document or article to show compliance with certain certification requirements

Registering Your Commercial Identifier

The most effective way to shore up the exclusive rights you have acquired through use of a commercial identifier is to register it as a mark with the USPTO — and in some cases, on one or more state trademark registers.

Registration isn't readily available for company identifiers, but only for product and service identifiers — in other words, for marks. But you can often dress up a company identifier as a mark that you can then register. Here are a few examples:

- ✔ You've named your manufacturing company "Ionic Scientific Manufacturing Company, Inc." Strip that name down to IONIC SCIENTIFIC and establish that moniker as a trademark by applying it to your products. Then register the mark to protect and bolster both your mark and company identifier.

> ✔ You've named your business "Bean Brain Accounting Services Associates." Highlight BEAN BRAIN on your business cards and put "Accounting Services" under it as an explanatory legend. Then register BEAN BRAIN as a servicemark.

In this chapter, I deal mainly with registering a mark with the USPTO — a rather complex and lengthy process. Registration of a mark on a state trademark register varies from state to state but is relatively uncomplicated.

State registration may give you certain state legal remedies that attach only to locally registered marks. State registration may be your only resort if you can't qualify for federal registration. Let your IP professional decide whether state registration is a good idea for you.

The USPTO registers your mark on the Federal Principal Register (or the Supplemental Register, which I discuss in the "Going to jail: Switching to the Supplemental Register" section, later in this chapter) and grants a registration certificate if your application survives a USPTO trademark attorney's thorough examination and any eventual opposition by some other dude displeased by your mark (which I cover in the "Getting published and dealing with opposition" section, later in the chapter). The process is similar to that for a patent application (see Chapter 9).

In general, registering your mark doesn't give you any ownership rights that you didn't already have, but it does give you a procedural advantage to stop an infringer. More specifically, your registration does the following:

✔ **It arms your attorney:** It's a really big stick to beat away someone trying to copy or imitate your mark.

✔ **It acts like the deed to your house:** It tells the world that the USPTO has investigated your mark, confirmed your ownership, verified its commercial use, and concluded that the mark is valid and enforceable.

✔ **Anyone doing an availability search will find your registration:** Anyone as smart and honest as you will keep clear of your mark.

✔ **The burden of proof shifts to the infringing defendant:** In a legal action, introducing your registration certificate shifts the burden of proof away from you. Without a registration, you'd have to prove that you own the mark by introducing evidence that you used the mark first.

✔ **You can get temporary restrictions placed on the infringer:** Registration makes it easier to get a restraining order, preliminary injunction, or seizure of counterfeit goods while awaiting trial. These temporary, but very effective and often decisive, remedies stop an infringer dead in his tracks.

✔ **You get federal protection:** When you register your mark, you're protected by federal laws. Federal courts have broader jurisdiction and powers than state courts. And without a federal registration, you can't go before a federal judge without proving that the accused infringer is headquartered in a different state.

✔ **You can stop the entry of infringing foreign goods:** U.S. Customs can seize imported goods bearing your marks and eventually destroy them if the importer doesn't challenge the seizure.

✔ **You can obtain cancellation of domain names that conflict with your mark:** See Chapter 20.

✔ **International registration is easier:** Federal registration makes it easier to register your mark abroad under many international treaties and conventions (in some foreign jurisdictions, it's a requirement).

✔ **The registration certificate looks great on your living room wall:** That fancy gold seal and red ribbon are mighty impressive.

Establishing eligibility

To qualify your mark for federal registration, you must use it *in commerce*. For the purposes of registration, "use in commerce" means that you've used your mark in connection with goods or services in interstate commerce, in foreign trade, or in any other activity regulated by Congress.

Lodging and food service establishments, shops, and other commercial enterprises catering to tourists and travelers are considered to be in interstate commerce.

About those symbols

Allow me to clear up some common misconceptions about the TM, SM, and ® characters you see next to some commercial identifiers. TM (for *trademark*) and SM (for *servicemark*) have absolutely no legal significance. They simply indicate that someone is claiming the identifier as a mark. If the mark is distinctive and properly used, as I explain at the end of this chapter, the status of the identifier should be obvious without the symbol. If the mark is descriptive and weak, using such a symbol doesn't do much to improve its status.

The ® symbol is another matter. It's an international symbol indicating that the mark is registered at the national level (in the U.S., that's on a federal register). Using the ® symbol before registration is a misrepresentation that can torpedo your application. Failure to use it after registration precludes you from collecting monetary damages from a convicted infringer.

Any mark that meets these criteria, including configuration marks (see Chapter 14), can be registered, except for a mark that:

- Contains immoral, deceptive, or scandalous material

- Incorporates the flag, coat of arms, or other insignia of either the United States or any individual state, municipality, or foreign nation

- Is a geographical indication of the origin of a wine or spirit

- Disparages or falsely suggests a connection with any person, institution, belief, or national symbol

- Uses a name, portrait, or signature that identifies a living individual without his or her written permission

- Includes the name, signature, or portrait of a deceased U.S. president during the life of his widow, without her written permission

- Is generic, commonly descriptive, functional, or misleading

- Is likely to cause confusion with a commercial identifier still in use by another

- Is primarily a surname

Restrictions are subject to interpretations developed by court precedents. For example, the two first prohibitions didn't prevent the registration of a representation of a condom decorated with stars and stripes, suggesting the American flag. My explanation highly steeped in legalese: Go figure!

As I'm sure you know, laws are often complicated and confusing — why should trademark laws be any different? But although the U.S. trademark laws have so many exceptions that even lawyers can get tangled in the web, keep in mind that you can register an ineligible mark after it acquires a secondary meaning (see Chapter 14). This exception covers marks that comprise a surname or one that's merely descriptive or functional. You can go ahead and enter your ineligible mark on the Federal Supplemental Register, however, until it acquires a secondary meaning (see the "Going to jail: Switching to the Supplemental Register" section, later in this chapter).

Timing is key: Putting your intentions to good use

You can have the world's most original, distinctive, marketable, ironclad mark or name, but unless you legitimately use it in commerce, you don't have a leg to stand on when you submit a regular application to register it with the USPTO. However, in the interim, you can get some protection by stating your intentions (but no false pretenses, please). You have two filing options:

✔ **In-Use application:** You can wait to file your application for registration until the mark is used in commerce as what I'll call an *in-use* application.

✔ **Intent-to-Use (ITU) application:** This application reserves your right against any other subsequent applicant to obtain a registration for a great mark you've created but haven't yet used in commerce. However, you can't get a certificate of registration based on an ITU unless you use it in commerce and file a regular application within one year. Accordingly, there's no good reason to delay filing an application for registration after you settle on a distinctive mark.

A trademark or servicemark must be genuinely used in the general course of business and not as a token mark for the purpose of registration only. Unless you're already in business and able to sell your goods or provide the services, don't even try to file an in-use application because a false application may result in an invalid registration. Instead, file an ITU application.

You're not a bird, and you don't want a worm, but in the world of ITU applications, being early gets you the following advantages:

✔ The filing date of your ITU application retroactively becomes the date you acquire your mark after the registration is granted. This is how the ITU protects your mark — after you file, you can even stop someone who uses the mark in commerce before you, but after your application.

✔ Your ITU application is posted on the USPTO and other databases where it can be discovered during an availability search.

✔ A USPTO trademark attorney examining another application for the same or a similar mark can cite your ITU application to provisionally refuse registration to that applicant.

✔ Your ITU application allows you to file an application in another country. If you file the foreign application within six months of your ITU application, the U.S. filing date is recognized as the priority date abroad.

Preparing Your In-Use or ITU Application

The process of registering your mark begins with preparing and filing your application. (I detail the rest of the process in the "Pushing Your Application Through the USPTO" section, later in this chapter.) You can file either by mail or via the Internet. To get the application forms you need, log onto the USPTO site. Go to the trademark filing area where you can choose to file electronically or print the application in order to file by mail.

Whichever option you select, click on the link to apply for a new mark and then on **Trademark/Servicemark Application, Principal Register**. You can also get special application forms for registering collective membership marks, collective trademarks/servicemarks, and certification marks. (A *collective trademark/servicemark,* such as SAM STOP for RV parks, is a mark adopted by an association for use only by its members in connection with their goods or services to distinguish them from those of nonmembers. By contrast, a *collective membership mark,* such as HELLS ANGELS, simply indicates membership in an organization, but is not used in connection with any goods or services.)

Filing an online application is advantageous for several reasons:

- ✔ Electronic applications get to the USPTO instantly and are given priority over mailed-in applications.
- ✔ The USPTO will soon require an extra filing fee for mailed-in applications.
- ✔ As soon as you file your application with the USPTO, you can trace it, amend it, and generally keep better control of it via the Internet.

If you want hard-copy forms, you can get them from the USPTO by fax or mail. However, your lawyer may have her own forms that accommodate exceptions or special circumstances.

You're now ready to fill out your application. In the next few sections, I guide you through the form, pointing out the critical legal issues and how to handle them along the way.

Warming up with the wizard

If you access the application online, the USPTO provides you with a set of preliminary questions — a wizard — to tailor the application to your needs.

If you don't want to use the wizard, you can request the Standard Form, but this will just complicate matters — following the wizard ensures that you don't forget anything.

- **Filing basis:** See the "Timing is key: Putting your intentions to good use" section, earlier in this chapter, for info on the Intent to Use/Use in Commerce designations. If you've applied to register the same mark for the same goods or services in a foreign country during the last six months, check Yes under Right of Priority based on Foreign Application (Section 44(d)). If you already hold a registration in a foreign country, check Yes under Foreign Registration (Section 44(e)).

Order a certified copy of your foreign application or registration now. You have to submit it to the USPTO within six months of your current application date.

✔ **Goods and/or services in multiple classes:** See the "Classifying and defining your goods or services" section, later in the chapter, for determining the number of classes to register your mark in.

✔ **Joint applicants and signers:** For tips in this regard, see the "Providing applicant info: Defining the owner" section, later in this chapter.

✔ **Is an attorney filing this application?** If you've listened to my advice, your hotshot attorney will answer *Yes.*

✔ **Do you wish to appoint a domestic representative?** If you live outside of the United States, you must appoint a U.S. resident or company to receive and accept papers on your behalf.

✔ **Do you wish to enter an additional statement?** For Pete's sake, just say no. Don't go blabbing about how you branded your lamps with the trademark LUCERNA because that's what they're called in Italian. You'd reveal that LUCERNA is an unprotectable and unregistrable generic word (even though it's not in English). In other words, the less said the better. But your lawyer may use this space for entering an appropriate legal statement about the history or composition of the mark that'll enhance the application and expedite its examination.

✔ **Signing options:** I suggest you select the first option, and sign electronically as I explain later.

The section numbers after each option refer to the Lanham Act, also known as Title 17 of the U.S. code.

After you answer the eight basic questions, select Continue to see the official application form. See the sections that follow for information on how to fill out all those little boxes.

Providing applicant info: Defining the owner

You may file the application on behalf of:

✔ Yourself, as an individual

✔ A corporation

✔ A general partnership

✔ Another type of business entity, such as two or more individuals jointly, a marital community, a trust, a limited partnership, or other limited liability company

This isn't a matter of choice but a question of fact. The mark and its registration must be owned by whomever stands behind the product or service because the mark carries an implication of warranty of quality and commercial fitness of the goods or services it identifies. If the product fails or is adulterated, the owner of the mark can be sued for any resulting losses or injury to the customer.

The owner must sign the declaration at the end of the form either when the application is filed or later as requested by the examiner. Here's the skinny on who must sign a non-individual application:

✔ In a joint application, all applicants must sign the papers. To avoid this inconvenience, you can call the joint venture a general partnership.

✔ For a partnership, at least one general partner must sign the application.

✔ An officer, such as the president, CEO, COO, or CFO (and *not* a director or manager), handles the honors for a corporation.

✔ For a limited liability company, the manager signs on the dotted line.

✔ The trustee of a trust puts pen to paper.

Defining the mark

Marks that incorporate graphics, shapes, colors, or other non-verbal characteristics require special attention. In the sections that follow, I provide some insight into graphic marks and trade dress, and then I provide form-specific instructions.

Your mark may consist solely of one or more colors applied to a particular object, such as a product, a packaging, a store sign, or a building. A color mark, just like a product shape, isn't considered inherently distinctive until it has acquired secondary meaning. Therefore you can't register it on the Principle Register until that time. (For information on the Supplementary Register, see the "Going to jail: Switching to the Supplemental Register" section, later in this chapter.)

Graphic mark

If your mark comprises verbal and design elements (including fanciful lettering), such as the one illustrated in Figure 17-1, you can file for:

✔ **The literal part (made of one or more typed standard characters):** The character, word, or phrase only

✔ **The design part:** The graphics only, if they can stand alone and aren't part of the lettering

✔ **The whole enchilada:** Both the characters and graphics

Note: A mark that consists only of standard characters is commonly called a *word mark,* even if it consists of a single punctuation character.

Figure 17-1:
Combined
word and
design
mark.

To obtain the maximum coverage, register only the part that exhibits the greatest legal strength.

✔ If you have a strong word mark, you can get broad coverage by filing for the literal part only. A person needs only to copy or imitate that part to create a likelihood of confusion among the public.

✔ If you have a non-descriptive and motivating design, you may want to obtain registration for that design only.

The odds that someone would copy both parts of the mark are relatively low. You can catch more flies with a limited form of the mark.

If you have a weak word mark, combining it with a graphic, even a fanciful one, won't save the mark from rejection.

Configuration mark

Distinctive shapes, colors, and ornamentations of products, packaging, or places of business can act as marks and are referred to as *trade dress* or *configuration marks* (see Chapter 14).

You can only register the trade dress or packaging of a product or the style of a business establishment if that unique approach isn't practical or functional. When defining such a mark, describe only its non-functional aspects.

For instance, if the product is a screwdriver with a series of diamond-shaped engravings on the center of the handle, the mark should only define a series of diamond-shaped engravings around the mid-section of a screwdriver handle, not the screwdriver or the screwdriver handle. The drawing must depict the engraving in full line and the rest of the screwdriver in dotted lines. See the section "Entering the mark and preparing the drawing," later in this chapter.

The shape of a product normally isn't considered to be inherently distinctive until it has acquired a secondary meaning, but a package design can be. Don't bother filing for registration of a mark that's not inherently distinctive before it's been in commerce for a few years and you can submit some evidence of secondary meaning in the form of testimonials or a public survey. Until then, you can file for registration on the Supplemental Register (see "Going to jail: Switching to the Supplemental Register," later in this chapter).

Entering the mark and preparing the drawing

If your mark consists of a word or phrase with nothing other than standard English punctuation or sanctioned typographical elements, check Typed Format on the application and enter the mark in the box in all uppercase. For a design or configuration mark, check "Stylized or Design Format" and submit an image file drawing as instructed. The drawing must be in black and white lines only, including shading. The lines must be sharp, solid, and uncrowded. Gray tones or tints aren't permitted.

If you're applying for a mark consisting of mixed upper- and lowercase letters or with foreign punctuation, such as WeedWrestor or PROVENÇAL PROMENADE, check the "Stylized or Design Format" box, but simply submit a sheet with the word mark simply typed in the middle of it.

A graphic mark should be easily reproducible in any media. Tell your designer to avoid complex graphics, halftones, and blending colors. Ideally, your mark should be suitable for rendition on a rubber stamp. Such a mark greatly simplifies the preparation of your application.

Classifying and defining your goods or services

How you classify and define your goods or services not only influences the protection your mark will get, but also determines the types of prior marks that can be cited against your application.

If you haven't already done so, define the areas of commerce where your mark is used and then compare that definition to the International Classification listings, detailed in Chapter 16. (You can find the International Classification listings in Chapter 1400 of the *Trademark Manual of Examining Procedure* (TMEP) on the USPTO Web site.)

You can use the same mark on goods or services that fall into several classes. For example, if you're manufacturing leather articles, you may have to select all the following classes:

- Class 18 (Leather goods) for handbags, briefcases, luggage, wallets, purses, and belts

- Class 14 (Jewelry) for watch straps

- Class 16 (Paper goods) for desk pads and checkbook holders

- Class 20 (Furniture) for jewelry cases

- Class 25 (Clothing) for jackets, pants, shoes, and boots

- Class 26 (Fancy goods) for leather belt buckles

- Class 34 (Smokers' articles) for cigar and cigarette holders

In the box labeled Listing of Goods and/or Services on the form, enter a definition for each type of good or service associated with your mark. Don't use a code, but find a description that's as close as possible to one found in the International Classification.

Filing for in-use versus intent-to-use classes

The type of application you're filing affects the classes that you list:

- **In-use:** On a regular application, list only goods and services already offered in commerce.

- **Intent-to-use:** No limit on the types of goods or services you can list in each class. You can always drop items later when you need to prove you've used the mark in commerce (see the "Providing evidence of commercial use" section, later in this chapter).

If you have a combination of goods and services already in commerce and not yet in commerce, you may file a cost-saving single application. Simply check Yes on both Intent to Use and Use in Commerce on the wizard page and fill out both Basis for Filing sections on the form. However, you should watch for the pitfall discussed below under "Completing the ITU process."

If you're trying to keep costs down, keep in mind that your filing fee is based on the number of classes you specify in your application. At the time of this writing, the filing fee is $335 per class. Therefore, the filing fee for the leather products example earlier in this chapter would be $2,345. Ouch!

Specifying the dates of first use

If you're filing a regular application, you must enter two dates for each class or goods or services:

- First use of the mark anywhere, including limited use within a single state

- First use of the mark in commerce, as defined earlier in this chapter

The two dates are the same if the goods or services were placed in commerce at the outset.

Providing evidence of commercial use

In a regular application, you must submit one specimen of use for each class of goods or services. You may use an image file showing the trademark on a label, tag, container, or the product itself. You can also show a servicemark on a sign, advertisement, business card, letterhead, brochure, proposal, invoice, or other document that describes the goods or services.

Signing and filing the application

To electronically sign the declaration at the end of the application, you may use any name, word, letters, codes, or symbols you choose between slashes, such as */jd signature/*. Then, file the application by clicking on **Validate,** and following the fee payment instructions. Alternately, you may print and mail it. Your electronic or mailed application will be accepted without a signature (not recommended), but you'll be asked to mail a signed declaration later.

Pushing Your Application Through the USPTO

After you hit the "Validate" button or place your application in the mail, you may think you're home free. Think again. The journey of an application through the USPTO may be longer than Dorothy's journey down the yellow brick road.

About six months from your filing date, your application lands on the desk of a trademark attorney. That's when the fun begins. An in-use application that's not challenged takes about 18 months to mature into a registration. Each interim action by the examiner adds another six months — and an opposition (see "Getting published and dealing with opposition," later in the chapter) adds 16 to 24 months. For an ITU, you must add about six months to these figures, plus whatever time (up to 36 months) you take to place your goods or services in commerce after you receive a *notice of allowance* (see "Completing the ITU process," later in the chapter.)

Contrary to a patent application that can be expedited for a number of reasons (see Chapter 8), the Commissioner of Trademarks very rarely gives any application priority.

The examination of an application for registration of a mark parallels the examination of a patent application (see Chapter 9). One difference, though, between the two processes is that your mark application isn't confidential. The bad news? Anyone can see what you're up to. The good news? You can check the current status of any pending application or registration — including your own — online at www.uspto.gov.

The rules outlined in the *Trademark Manual of Examining Procedure* (TMEP) guide the examination process. The TMEP is periodically updated and available by subscription from the Superintendent of Documents (see Chapter 24) or you can download it free from www.uspto.gov/go/tmep.

In the sections that follow, I tell you how your application for registration is processed. This information applies to in-use and ITU applications, but the ITU process has a few additional steps, which I outline in the "Completing the ITU process" section, later in the chapter. And, alas, not everything in life is easy, so check out the next section for information on when bad things happen to good applications.

Passing (or failing) the examination

When your application hits the USPTO, an examining trademark attorney is assigned to your case. Your first contact with the examining trademark attorney may be a request for corrections to some technical defects in your application, such as insufficient fees or missing information. Then, after the examiner completes a thorough availability search on your mark, you receive a first report on the status of your application, between six and ten months from your filing date.

The examiner's report may include a combination of objections and refusals to register. The report always specifies the time (in most cases six months) you have to answer. Objections and refusals are never welcome, but they don't necessarily put an end to your pursuit.

The report is in formal language, by and for an attorney, and cites controlling authorities, such as sections of statutes, regulations, and court decisions. I echo my former words — don't go it alone; consult your IP attorney.

You have to answer the report by filing an amendment with supporting arguments. An *amendment* is a legal document that answers every objection or ground for refusal and either accepts or contests each of the examiner's findings and decisions. The name comes from the fact that it often includes a modification of the application. There's no fee required unless you have to split the goods or services into one or more additional classes, in which case you must pay the standard filing fee for each added class.

Finding the right lawyer

Any attorney who practices in one of the 50 states or the District of Columbia may represent you before the USPTO during the examination and prosecution of your application. He or she doesn't need any special certification or examination, unlike patent attorneys.

Although many lawyers who aren't IP specialists will take a mark-registration case, you can't

expect these occasional trademark practitioners to give you the same quality of service as an IP professional who keeps up with the frequent changes in the laws pertaining to commercial identifiers. Carefully investigate the qualifications of any professional before you hire him or her to advise and represent you.

After a couple of exchanges with the examining attorney, you'll either get a preliminary approval or face a final refusal to register the mark. After the preliminary approval comes the publication step, which I explain below. A final refusal leaves you with two options — appeal the decision or let the application lapse and pick another mark.

Promptly answer any communication from the examining trademark attorney. Failing to do so may cause your application be declared abandoned.

If your application has been declared abandoned because you failed to timely answer the examining attorney, or pay a fee, you can apply to revive it. File a petition to the Commissioner of Trademarks within two months of the notification of abandonment, alleging that the abandonment was unintentional.

Dealing with examiner objections

The most common objections are improper listings (examiners prefer to use the word *recitations*) of goods or services or a wrong classification. In most cases, the examining attorney suggests a new recitation of goods or services and their appropriate classifications.

Don't blindly accept suggestions from the examiner without considering their impact on the scope of your mark and the cost of the registration. You know your product or service better than the examining attorney. Her suggestion may miss the mark (Ha! Ha!) and not give you the coverage you need. Also, each added classification raises the filing fee and other subsequent fees.

The examining attorney may also ask you to disclaim a descriptive part of your mark and even suggest a wording for the disclaimer. In other words, you're asked to agree that you don't have any exclusive right to that portion of your mark. If you don't agree that that portion is merely descriptive, present a convincing argument against the need for a disclaimer.

Facing rejection

If the examiner's report contains a refusal to register, all is not lost. You can also contest that decision. The following list outlines the most common grounds for refusals and the ways that you can rebut them. You must answer a refusal to register the mark with an amendment. There's no fee involved in answering a rejection:

- ✔ **Likelihood of confusion with a registered mark or company identifier:** If the refusal is based on likelihood of confusion, you must try to distinguish your mark from the trade names or marks cited by the examining attorney by applying the tests outlined in Chapter 16. To be more effective, your argument should rely on pertinent court decisions and other authorities that can overcome those cited by the examining attorney.

- ✔ **The mark isn't distinctive, but merely descriptive or primarily a surname:** If registration is refused on the ground that the mark isn't distinctive, you can show evidence of the contrary in the form of intensive advertising campaigns, commentaries culled from newspapers and other publications, or written testimonials by competent individuals.

  If you've used the mark in commerce for at least five years, you may establish secondary meaning by filing a statement, terminating with a declaration (similar to the one at the end of the application filing form, preferably with the same type of supporting evidence) asserting that the mark has been in substantial, exclusive, and continuous use for five years and has become distinctive.

- ✔ **The mark is disqualified under the eligibility requirement:** If your mark is declared ineligible for registration, there's a good chance you made a fatal mistake in your selection. However, a good attorney can sometimes get you past the most formidable obstacle. With laws, nothing is set in concrete. It's mostly a question of time and money. (See the "Establishing eligibility" section, earlier in this chapter.)

Going to jail: Switching to the Supplemental Register

If your mark was rejected on the grounds that it isn't distinctive, the examining attorney will routinely suggest that you switch your application to the Supplemental Register until you can show that it has acquired secondary meaning. One big advantage is that after your mark is on the Supplemental Register, examining attorneys can cite your mark against other applications for an identical or similar mark.

You can apply for registration on the Supplemental Register at the outset if your mark isn't inherently distinctive, such as a new color mark. However, think twice before doing this because registering on the Supplemental Register amounts to putting your mark in jail for those few years. You're publicly admitting that it's merely descriptive and very difficult to enforce against an imitator.

Moreover, such a registration does not carry all the advantages attached to a Principal Register entry, even though it allows you to file an infringement action in a federal district court.

Choosing the Supplemental Register depends upon your situation. If you've already used the mark for a few years, and there's little chance you'll have to sue someone in the near future, a Supplemental Registration could work for you. However, if you just started and have five years ahead of you to establish secondary meaning, and if you may have to go to court before then, you're better off without the stigma of a descriptive mark imposed upon you by a registration on the Supplemental Register.

Getting published and dealing with opposition

Upon preliminary approval, the examining attorney sends you a *notice of publication.* This notice gives you the date upon which your mark will be published in the *Trademark Gazette* for oppositions. This weekly publication of the USPTO contains, among other items, a list of applications that have recently been granted preliminary approval for registration. (You can access the *Trademark Gazette* on the USPTO Web site at ww.uspto.gov.)

Anyone who objects to your registration can file an *Opposition* with the USPTO within 30 days of the publication date. People with objections can also file requests for an extension of that 30-day period. You receive copies of these requests. If someone files an opposition, your application is sent for a spin before the Trademark Trial and Appeal Board (TTAB).

The TTAB conducts a trial to determine whether your mark and that of the opposing party are in conflict and if so, who has priority of use. Needless to say, this is a complex and costly battle that must be fought between lawyers.

Opposition is usually based on a perceived conflict between a mark to be registered and a commercial identifier used by the opposition. But opposition can come from other quarters as well. Anyone who can demonstrate that he could be adversely affected by your registration can file and fight an opposition. If I think your mark disparages my person or ethnic group, or even offends my moral or religious beliefs, I have a basis for opposition.

Your worries aren't over yet. Before your mark becomes incontestable, as I explain below, a person who misses the deadline for opposition gets a second chance to attack and cancel your registration on the same grounds. A *cancellation* is conducted before the TTAB according to the same rules and procedures as an opposition.

Receiving the USPTO's seal of approval

If you encounter no opposition or the opposition is settled in your favor, the next step depends upon the type of application. If you filed a regular application, your registration will be issued without further ado, about three months from the end of the opposition period (or any extensions).

After you receive your certificate of registration, you must place a notice of registered status next to the mark. The notice can consist of the legend *Registered in the United States Patent and Trademark Office,* the abbreviation *Reg. U.S. Pat. & Tm. Off.,* or the international symbol ® placed next to the upper-right corner of the mark when possible. Failure to use the notice may prevent you from collecting damages and legal expenses from an infringer, although you may still stop the copycat.

Completing the ITU process

If you filed an ITU application, your travails are far from over. About three months after the expiration of the opposition period (or your successful fight against objections), the examining attorney sends you a *Notice of Allowance.* That means your mark is registrable pending use in commerce.

You now have six months from the date of the Notice of Allowance to use your marks and submit a *Statement of Use* with the required fee ($100 per class at the time of this writing). A registration is usually issued about three months after the filing of the Statement of Use.

You can't get a registration until you use the mark in commerce.

You can file your Statement of Use electronically by logging on to the USPTO Web site. Simply visit the trademarks area and select the option for responding to a Notice of Allowance.

You can extend the period before you have to file your Statement of Use in six-month increments, up to six times, for a total of 36 months from the date of the Notice of Allowance by filing a Request for Extension of Time for Filing a Statement of Use. Each time, you have to pay the required extension fee, which is currently $150 per class. Your first request is automatically granted, but with each subsequent request, you must provide some credible reason why you haven't yet used the mark in commerce.

If you miss a deadline, the entire application is declared abandoned.

A few circumstances call for special procedures. Here are the most common:

✔ **Amendment to Allege Use:** If you've used the mark in commerce between the date of your ITU application and before the approval for publication, you may file an *Amendment to Allege Use* during that interim period. When the USPTO receives the amendment, your ITU application turns into an in-use application. Simply use the same form (and the same fee) as for a Statement of Use.

✔ **Splitting the application:** If you've only used the mark in commerce on some of the goods or services listed in your application, you can revise your application after receiving the Notice of Allowance in either one of two ways:

- Delete the unused goods or services and file a Statement of Use covering the goods or services already in commerce.

- Divide your application into two — one for goods or services already in commerce, the other for the ones that aren't. Each application may cover a different category of goods or services. You may have to pay an additional filing fee to cover a divided class.

You can only split the application in an amendment to your original application, because there's no form available for this type of filing.

If you filed an application combining in-use and ITU goods or services, when the entire application is approved, you'll get a Notice of Allowance for the in-use part. However, no registration will be issued for either ITU or in-use goods or services until you file a Statement of Use on the ITU items.

If you miss a deadline, the entire application will be declared abandoned. This is one reason that filing a combined application is not recommended.

Appealing an adverse decision

You can appeal — all the way to the U.S. Supreme Court, if you want to — an adverse decision by the examining attorney. Figure 17-2 illustrates the appeal routes. Basically, you can appeal an adverse decision by the examining attorney on a purely regulatory matter, such as a final request to submit a drawing or amend a recitation of goods or services, by petition to the Commissioner of Trademarks. However, you must appeal an adverse decision on a substantive matter, such as a refusal to register the mark, to the TTAB.

If the Commissioner of Trademarks or the TTAB goes against you, you can appeal either to the Court of Appeals for the Federal Circuit (CAFC) or to a federal district court. If you appeal in the federal district court, you can introduce new evidence because a new trial or examination of the facts will be conducted in that forum.

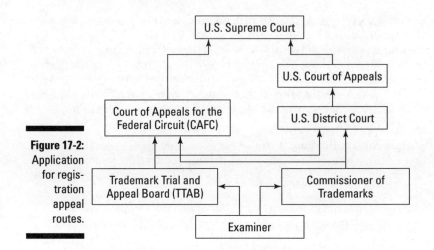

Figure 17-2:
Application
for regis-
tration
appeal
routes.

Any adverse decision by the federal district court can be appealed to a U.S. Court of Appeals. A decision by either the CAFC or the U.S. Court of Appeals can be appealed to the U.S. Supreme Court. And if the U.S. Supreme Court says no, you're out of luck. I don't think God has a trademark office.

If the mark you want to register is already used, but not in your market area, you may apply for a *concurrent use proceeding* to obtain exclusive rights to use the mark in the territory not occupied by the senior user. You may apply by amendment after the examiner cites likelihood of confusion as grounds for refusing you registration. The matter goes to trial before the TTAB, where you become the plaintiff and the senior user is the defendant. The procedure is akin to an opposition.

Keeping Your Registration Up to Snuff

You don't have to pay maintenance fees after your mark is registered, but you do need to take some steps to prevent automatic cancellation.

Preventing cancellation

At its sixth anniversary, your registration is automatically canceled unless, during the preceding year, you file a Section 8 Affidavit stating that your mark is still used in commerce. Along with the affidavit, you have to provide evidence of its commercial use by submitting a specimen of the type required with the original application.

Making your mark and registration incontestable

If, after five years, no court has decided against your ownership of the mark, and no one is currently challenging it, you can sew up your registration for good by filing a Section 15 Affidavit before the mark's sixth anniversary. The affidavit must state that the mark has been in continuous use for the last five years, is still used in commerce, and is not the object of an adverse ruling or involved in current adverse proceedings.

After the Section 15 document has been filed, a cancellation can only be brought on one of the first seven exceptions listed in the section entitled "Marks Eligible for Registration." Your mark registration can't be cancelled because of the likelihood of confusion with another mark or a trade name or because the mark is merely descriptive or primarily a surname.

Renewing your registration

Your registration will last as long as you use the mark in commerce providing it's renewed every ten years. During the ninth year of each renewal period, you must file another Section 8 Affidavit, showing that your mark is still used in commerce. You must also request a renewal for another ten years.

You can combine Sections 8 and 15 Affidavits in a single document, and do all these required post-registration filings online. Log on to www.uspto.gov, go to the Trademarks section, choose the Filing Online option, find the File a Post-registration form, and then select the appropriate declaration.

Losing Your Commercial Identifier

You can lose your exclusive rights to a company identifier or mark under the following circumstances:

- ✔ **Failure to use.** If you don't use your commercial identifier for two or three years and show no intent to use it in the future, someone else can assume that you abandoned it and begin using it. To keep your identifier, you must show credible evidence that you intend to use it and were prevented from doing so by circumstances beyond your control. Proving these circumstances is difficult, if not impossible. Use it or lose it.

- ✔ **Authorizing uncontrolled use.** The law protects exclusive use of an identifier to give the public a reliable indication of quality. For example, you buy KODAK film because you know it's a quality product. Authorizing someone else to use your mark without controlling the quality of the products or services is considered fraud that creates a defense to allegations of infringement, and a ground for cancellation even after your mark has become incontestable.

✔ **Using the mark as a substantive.** A mark must always qualify a product or service. Never use it as a noun or, worse yet, as a verb, such as in "Drink SANKA" or "You can XEROX any documents." Your advertisement should say, "Drink SANKA brand of coffee" or "You can duplicate any document on our XEROX copier." If you don't treat your company name or mark as a valuable qualifier, others won't either. Your mark can lose its distinguishing character and become unenforceable.

Always type a mark in bold, uppercase letters, or some other way that makes it stand out in text, followed by a generic term — for example, "Our comfortable **TIPPYTOE®** slippers will keep your feet warm."

You can only use the ® symbol after obtaining a federal registration.

✔ **Unfair use.** You can't take advantage of your strong commercial identifier to impose obligations that go beyond your exclusive rights. A common example of misconduct is when a fast-food franchisor insists that all franchisees buy their disposable tableware from him. Other abuses of a mark include forcing a trademark licensee to also accept a license under a copyright or patent. Depending upon the degree of coercive conduct, the owner of the abused moniker can lose some or all of his exclusive rights.

✔ **Failure to go after infringers.** If you tolerate infringement, competitors may assume that you deserve a very narrow scope of protection. This clears the way for the copycats to use it. The longer you delay pursuing an infringer, the less likely you'll be able to stop him.

✔ **Genericness.** If you're lucky enough to have a successful and profitable product marketed under a strong mark, the public may eventually adopt your mark as the generic term for that kind of product. The court may then declare your mark generic and unenforceable. This has happened before — once upon a time, aspirin, linoleum, and cellophane were famous brand names.

✔ **Misuse of a certification mark.** Placing a certification mark on your own goods, using it for a purpose other than certifying another's goods or services, or losing control over its use subjects the mark to cancellation.

Part V
Exploiting and Enforcing Your IP Rights

The 5th Wave   By Rich Tennant

© RICHTENNANT

"Well, that's all very colorful, but in order to register your mark in this country you also have to fill out these forms."

In this part . . .

1 talk about what you can do after you've acquired your U.S. patent, copyright, or commercial identifier. If you're planning to do business abroad, your work isn't quite done yet. You need to know how to protect your IP overseas, so grab your passport, stow your carry-on bags, and get ready for an IP overseas getaway.

And now that you've spent a bunch of time and money (or blood, sweat, and tears) to get that protection, find out how you can use your intellectual property to increase profits. Finally, I show you what to do if someone infringes on your IP rights (stockade not included).

Chapter 18

All Aboard: Protecting Your IP Rights in Other Countries

"Travel is fatal to prejudice," wrote Mark Twain in *The Innocents Abroad,* a book relating the wanderings of a motley gang of American tourists through Europe and the Middle East. If you have a narrow-minded idea that foreigners are less industrious or entrepreneurial than Americans, filing patent applications overseas can quickly set you straight. Please, excuse the sarcasm — I'm simply trying to tell you that acquiring foreign patents or registering your mark abroad can be extremely costly, complex, and time-consuming. So, carefully ponder the pros and cons of obtaining foreign IP protection to chart a steady course before casting your money to wayward winds.

Because the patent process is the most complex of the IP rights, most of this chapter focuses on utility patents (see Chapter 4). But, I talk about plant and design patents, commercial identifiers, and copyrights at the end of the chapter.

Pros and Cons of International Patents

You're probably wondering whether you really want to go to all the trouble and expense of applying for international patents. A worthy question. And the answer is different for everyone. So, before you plunge ahead or slink away, take a look at the following reasons to file — and a reason to stay "local."

Counting the ways: Why file abroad?

If you have a good, solid invention, not just a pipe dream, but one that has a reasonable potential of being used outside the United States, filing abroad can give you a real competitive edge by protecting you from infringers, increasing your licensing payoffs, and getting licensees in the first place.

Stopping foreign infringers

With few exceptions, a patent offers no protection beyond the borders of the country that granted it. Although your U.S. patent lets you take anyone to court who makes, markets, or sells your patented gizmo anywhere from sea to shining sea, it has no sway in a foreign tribunal. Getting a foreign patent lets you police the world, or at least the most-developed nations.

Considering the universal high cost and uncertainties of legal proceedings, you probably can't afford to sue abroad. But, this works both ways — few can afford to be sued. So you gamble that your foreign patents will deter potential infringers.

Leveraging your licensing revenue

Getting a foreign patent helps you leverage your licensing clout and collect royalties on the overseas activities of an authorized party.

Here's an example. The good news is that you've been granted a solid U.S. patent and successfully negotiated a lucrative, exclusive license with Titanic Tools, Ltd. (TTL), a Fortune 500 company that agrees to pay you $1.00 for each of your two-handled flyswatters it makes or sells. The bad news — you didn't file for a patent abroad and now all application deadlines have elapsed. Don't be surprised if Titanic then has the swatters manufactured in China for sale all over the world. You're only entitled to royalties on units sold in the United States — nowhere else. The law forbids the use of your U.S. patent to extract royalties for your licensee's activities anywhere you don't have patent coverage. However, if you had patent protection in China, TTL would have to pay you royalties on its entire production, and you could've asked for a higher royalty rate. The greater the territorial coverage, the higher the royalty.

Attracting licensees

Having overseas patent coverage makes you more attractive to potential licensees. Most large companies shy away from an invention if they can't secure a monopoly in most industrial countries. Ever-expanding globalization of commerce discourages heavy investments in tooling, marketing, and other start-up costs for a product that competitors can freely copy outside the U.S.

Adding it up: Is it worth the money?

The substantial cost of obtaining and maintaining foreign patents is really the only factor that should prevent you from implementing an overseas patent program. Of course, cost is a pretty major factor, especially because most inventors seldom seek only one patent. As the technology is improved, they file additional applications and often have to file for multiple patents in each foreign country.

How much is substantial? As a rough estimate, plan to spend between $5,000 and $7,000 per patent per country. You're going to spend that much during the four years it takes to obtain the first generation of patents. Let's see: 12 countries, $60,000 here, $84,000 there, and soon you're talking real money.

After you get your patent, add about $300 or more in maintenance fees per patent per country per year, for the next 16 years. These figures are valid no matter which filing strategy you choose. (I discuss the different strategies in the "Charting a Course: Where Should You File Your Patent Application" section.) In some English-speaking countries like Canada or Australia, the costs may be less, but they're even higher in Japan, France, and Germany.

For example, if you file in the 12 major member nations of the European Union, plus Canada, Australia, Japan, China, South Korea, and Mexico (a relatively modest program), you need a pot-bellied piggy-bank holding between $90,000 and $125,000, the bulk of which you need up front.

I don't have ESP, but I can probably answer your next question. No, you can't handle your foreign application yourself. Even your U.S. patent attorney must hire a correspondent patent agent in every targeted country. I included all these guys' fees and other charges in my estimates.

Don't even think about starting an overseas application program unless you're certain that you can finance it to completion. In my experience, many folks and small businesses abandon their applications halfway through the process for lack of funds. The large sums they've already spent (and can't recover) would've been better spent on research and design (R&D) or marketing.

Try to be creative, and let someone else pay the piper. If you can license your invention early, be a tough negotiator and insist that the big guy, your licensee, pay for the acquisition and maintenance of foreign patents.

Making the decision

Your decisions boil down to the same basic consideration: Are benefits you and your business will receive by filing abroad worth the cost? It's a business decision only you can make. Your patent lawyer can only answer peripheral questions about the topics I just discussed.

I can tell you that the simpler the technology, the more foreign protection you need, because it's more likely to be copied.

In each country, look at the revenue potentials of each patent and the adverse consequences of not being covered. Do the math, carefully add up your resources, and then make your best educated guess. I'd be leading you astray by giving you more definite guidelines. Every business decision is a gamble. This could be your biggest one.

First Things First: Three Basic Rules of Filing for Foreign Patents

Before I get going on how to actually file a patent application abroad, I want to outline three basic rules you need to keep in mind from the start.

✔ **Keep your invention secret:** U.S. patent law gives you one full year to file a patent application after public disclosure, but most other countries don't allow you to have a patent if your invention was disclosed, without a confidentiality agreement, before you filed your patent application. Casually showing your homegrown prototype to Gus, your friendly neighbor, may constitute such a disclosure.

Treat your invention as a trade secret for as long as you can — at least until you file your U.S. application. Don't discuss it, show it, or generally disclose it to anyone except your attorney, and when you do, make sure it's under strict conditions of confidentiality spelled out in a written agreement. You don't need a confidentiality agreement with your attorney. She's already under a legal obligation of strict confidentiality.

✔ **Get a foreign filing license:** As a U.S. citizen or legal resident, you can't file for a patent application or generally disclose your invention abroad before you obtain a license (a permit to do so) from the U.S. Government. Such a license is routinely returned to you with your U.S. patent application receipt (see Chapter 9). You risk severe punishment, even prison, and the inability to obtain a U.S. patent if you file an unauthorized application abroad.

If your invention relates to nuclear energy or national defense, the license may be delayed or even formally denied. In some critical cases, the Department of Defense may request a secrecy order, and you could be denied the right to a patent that would disclose sensitive information. At that point, you can sue the government for reasonable compensation. For more information on this topic, see Chapter 9.

✔ **File foreign patent applications within one year from the filing date of your U.S. application:** This is critical if you want to claim a priority on invention based on your U.S. filing date under the *Paris Convention* as I explain later. If you don't take advantage of this, you may lose your chance of getting foreign patents if your invention becomes known, either through publication of your U.S. application or the issue of your patent.

The publication of an application or the grant of a patent constitutes a public disclosure of the invention. If this rule weren't enforced, any unscrupulous individual who reads the published document could claim to be the inventor and file her own application. Foreign patent authorities don't investigate priority of invention contests, as is done by the United States Patent and Trademark Office (USPTO) as I explain in Chapter 9.

As long as you keep your invention confidential, you can file applications abroad more than one year after filing your U.S. application. But you don't get the advantage of an early priority date and may lose the patent to someone filing overseas just ahead of you. The absolute deadline occurs when your U.S. application is published, about 18 months after its filing date or when your U.S. patent is granted, whichever comes first. To sum it all up: If you keep the invention secret, you have about 18 months to file abroad, but if you go public, you have only one year from your U.S. filing date.

Mark your calendar about ten months from your U.S. filing date to remind you that you only have two months left to start your overseas filing process, and also about five months thereafter to warn you of the publication deadline.

I'd like to add a fourth rule of my own: Let your patent attorney handle all your filing overseas through her own stable of foreign correspondents. Don't wait until the last month before any deadline. She or the correspondents may need time to prepare translations and obtain certified copies of assignments and other miscellaneous documents.

Charting a Course: Where Should You File Your Patent Application?

With the universal high cost of patents, few individuals or small businesses can afford a comprehensive foreign patent program. Even huge multinationals carefully select the countries in which they apply for patent protection. These decisions can be difficult in the early stages of your business venture as you teeter between the need to conserve financial resources and your desire to secure a broad marketing territory for your invention.

In general, give priority to countries that offer a good potential market over those that only have advanced manufacturing capabilities. When you control the most important markets, nobody else is interested in making the product. For example, if your product relates to surfing equipment, you should seek protection in the Western European nations, Australia, Brazil, and Japan. You can bypass Taiwan, South Korea, and China although these last countries are prime manufacturing candidates.

If the invention has worldwide applications, target the most prosperous countries rather than the most populous. The most popular choices, in order of preference, are: Western Europe, Japan, Canada, Australia, Mexico, Hungary, Taiwan, New Zealand, Israel, South Africa, South Korea, and Brazil. The nature of your invention dictates where you apply. Obviously, you can't sell many snowmobiles in Australia or surfboards in Hungary.

However, there are exceptions. For instance, if the manufacture of the product requires very sophisticated metallurgical techniques and machinery, get adequate patent protection in Germany, the United Kingdom, France, Sweden, Switzerland, China, India, and Hungary. Then don't worry too much about filing in other big market countries.

Research the population, average personal income, and manufacturing capabilities of the countries you're considering. Don't rely on your attorney's recommendations, except in connection with expenses for each foreign application. The attorney has a duty to help you obtain the maximum protection in as many countries as possible, but he's not a marketing expert. Most attorneys are reluctant to discourage you from filing in any particular country because that country may one day offer a lucrative market or be of particular interest to a potential licensee.

You can choose from two basic strategies to get the patent coverage you need. You can file individual patent applications in each country you choose, or you can file in several countries at once under the handy-dandy *Patent Cooperation Treaty.* I outline both options in this section and give you the pros and cons of each.

Filing separately under the Paris Convention

If you want to get a patent in only two or three countries or obtain a patent ASAP, you should apply directly with those countries. You must also apply directly with any country that isn't a member of a multinational patent-filing system, such as a good number of South American nations.

Most countries are members of the *Paris Convention for the Protection of Industrial Property* (Paris Convention), which outlines basic rules and IP protections. The Paris Convention gives you up to one year after the filing date of your first patent application in your own country to file a corresponding application in a member country and get the earlier filing date as your *Convention priority date* (often shortened to *priority date*).

That priority date defines both your priority of invention and filing. The Convention priority date is the best thing since the invention of the Swiss Army knife. If someone else has filed an application for the same invention in that country after your priority date and before your foreign application is filed, your application trumps that other guy's. Also, if any document describing your invention is published during that interim period, it won't be cited against your foreign application. The priority date for trademarks and design patents under the same convention is limited to six months. The Convention priority date can be claimed in a single country application as well as in the multinational patent applications discussed below.

A few countries haven't ratified this convention. For a list of Paris Convention signatories, go to www.wipo.int/treaties/documents/english/word/d-paris.doc. Taiwan is one exception, but don't fret! The United States and Taiwan have a separate treaty that provides the same filing convenience to American inventors.

In addition to providing a way to eliminate any interim patent application by another inventor, the Paris Convention makes it easy to meet two of the three basic rules in the section "First Things First: Three Basic Rules of Filing for Foreign Patents." If you take advantage of the Paris Convention, you only need to keep your invention confidential up to the date of your U.S. filing. You can start selling your "super-duper squabulators" the very next morning and file foreign applications, initiating them either at home or abroad, up to 364 days later. That's because your foreign applications are considered to have been filed on the same date as the U.S. one. You must specifically claim the benefit of your U.S. filing date in each foreign application.

Make sure that the foreign patent agent asks for this one-year convention-priority benefit when preparing your application, because it's not automatically granted. However, this benefit costs you — government authorities extract a few more bucks from your pocket. Your agent also wants his pound of flesh for checking the right box on the application cover letter. Then, you're also asked to provide a certified copy of your original U.S. application that the USPTO gladly sends you for an extra fee.

Hitting two (or more) birds with one stone: Multinational patent applications

Some small, mostly developing countries have established a common patent authority that can grant you a single multinational patent enforceable by the courts of all participant nations — a real bargain in terms of cost and time.

✔ **The Office Africain de la Propriete Industrielle (OAIP)** with headquarters in Yaoundé, Cameroon, groups the former French colonies of Benin, Burkina Faso, Cameroon, Central Africa Republic, Chad, Congo, Côte d'Ivoire, Equatorial Guinea, Gabon, Guinea, Guinea-Bissau, Mali, Mauritania, Niger, Senegal, and Togo. The OAIP accepts patent applications in English and French.

Currently, the OAPI doesn't conduct any substantive examination. An OAPI patent that's enforceable in all the member nations is granted without warranty of validity. The patent validity issue remains to be resolved at the time of trial when you sue an infringer.

✔ **The African Regional Industrial Property Organization (ARIPO)** located in Harare, Zimbabwe, covers the former British possessions of Gambia, Ghana, Lesotho, Malawi, Mozambique, Sierra Leona, South Africa, Sudan, Swaziland, Uganda, United Republic of Tanzania, Zambia, and Zimbabwe. The ARIPO language is English. The ARIPO conducts a formal examination of the application before granting a patent.

✔ **The Eurasian Patent Office (EAPO)** operating under the Eurasian Patent Convention (EAPC) in Moscow, Russia, gathers the former Soviet republics of Armenia, Azerbaijan, Belarus, Kazakhstan, Kyrgyzstan, Republic of Moldova, Russian Federation, Tajikistan, and Turkmenistan. Applications must be in Russian. The EAPO conducts a substantive examination only upon request. You must enter this request when you file your application.

Filing under the European system

The members of the European Union (EU) and a few candidate nations have instituted a well-rounded patent system, administered by the European Patent Office (EPO) located in Munich, Germany and in The Hague, Netherlands.

The contracting states are Austria, Belgium, Bulgaria, Cyprus, Czech Republic, Denmark, Estonia, Finland, France, Germany, Greece, Hungary, Ireland, Italy, Liechtenstein, Luxembourg, Monaco, Netherlands, Portugal, Romania, Slovakia, Slovenia, Spain, Sweden, Switzerland, Turkey, and the United Kingdom. That list will grow as other nations join the EU. For a nominal fee, an EPO application can be extended to Albania, Latvia, Lithuania, and Macedonia, in anticipation of their future admission.

The EPO accepts patent applications in English, French, or German. After the application has been approved in one of the three official languages, it must be translated into the other two. The patent can then be filed in any one of the designated countries to be issued by the local patent authority. If the country doesn't accept one of the three official languages, the patent must be translated into the national idiom. You get the same patent granted by all countries, but each in different national language.

You may wonder why the European Union didn't adopt a simple system similar to the OAIP, ARIPO, or EAPC, where one patent in a single language is valid in all member countries. First, there's an issue of national pride. Can you imagine the French giving full faith and credit to a patent document drawn in English? The other reason is more cynical. European patent agents outside Germany, where the first EPO opened, didn't want to be left out and insisted that the patent be provided in each nation and in each applicable national language. So after your patent application has been approved by the EPO, thanks to the good services of your German or Dutch patent agent, you must hire patent agents in member countries you selected on your application. They prepare translations in Italian, Portuguese, Finnish, or whatever. At this point, you've paid your U.S. patent attorney, the German patent agent, and agents in some other designated nations of the European gang. Also, you need to pay a plethora of government charges, and don't forget the translators — two more reasons to keep your application short and simple.

Filing under the Patent Cooperation Treaty

Under the *Patent Cooperation Treaty* (PCT), over 100 nations operate a common, uniform application process for utility patents. The PCT lets you submit a single patent application in your own domestic patent office to reserve the right to file that application in any contracting nation. Moreover, the PCT integrates the Paris Convention, and counts among its members the multinational patent authorities including the EPO.

By filing a PCT application in English with the USPTO in Washington, you can postpone entering your application abroad for about 2½ years from the priority date of your initial U.S. application. The World Industrial Property Organization (WIPO), headquartered in Geneva, Switzerland, administers the PCT.

This system lets you to postpone the heavy cost of filing overseas, giving you time to test-market your invention. By the 30th month, you should know whether you're going to get a worthwhile patent. By then, you either have your U.S. patent, or you've undergone a fairly complete examination. (See Chapters 4 through 10 for the whole patent story.) If it looks like you're not getting a good patent, you can abandon your foreign filing and save a bundle.

Membership in the PCT changes constantly. You can download a comprehensive list of contracting nations at `www.wipo.int/treaties/documents/english/word/m-pct.doc`.

A PCT application goes through four processing stages: the filing stage, the international stage, the regional stage, and finally, the national stage.

PCT procedures, regulations, and fees are in a constant state of flux. What I write today may change by the time you read this. Check the USPTO Web site frequently for the latest rules and forms.

Filling out the filing stage

You begin by filing your PCT application with the USPTO, which serves as the receiving office. Fortunately, you can file your PCT application in the same format as a regular U.S. utility patent application, but on A4 paper (the European version of standard 8½ x 11). See Chapter 7 for information on utility patent applications.

1. **Find the forms you need to fill out. You need:**

    • A Request form

    • A Transmittal Letter form

    • A Power of Attorney form (when applicable)

    The USPTO offers all the necessary forms and guidelines at its Web site www.uspto.gov. Just click on **Patents** and then on **Patent Cooperation Treaty.** Click on **Chapter I** for the forms.

2. **Fill out the Transmittal Letter and Power of Attorney forms, which are self-explanatory.**

3. **Next fill out the Request form. It comes with ample instructions, but here are some pointers:**

    • Follow the instructions to the letter or your application may be rejected.

    • Claim the filing date of your prior U.S. application — so long as it was filed no more than a year before the PCT application — in order to establish the earliest possible priority date.

    • Sit down before you tackle the Fee Calculation Sheet, which is part of the Request form. The total often exceeds $3,000 just for filing the application.

    • Keep in mind when selecting the countries to apply in that you never have to pay for more than ten designated countries. Most applicants designate all members of the PCT on the Request form, and then, before entering the regional and national stages, drop the ones they don't want or can't afford.

4. **Send in your application.**

    You may fax or mail your application, but you get a discount off the filing fee when you file electronically, and save even more if you use the PCT-EASY software. Check out the *PCT Applicant's Guide* on the USPTO Web site.

5. **The USPTO, acting as a receiving office, verifies that your application conforms to all applicable regulations and that you paid the necessary fees.**

    You also get some time to provide any necessary corrections or additions before the application is forwarded to the *International Bureau* at WIPO for the second stage of the procedure.

Going through the international stage

The International Bureau deals only with the multinational aspect of the application, which is the International Stage. Because the PCT was approved in two separate parts, the treaty is divided into two chapters. Member countries can observe the limited provisions of Chapter I, which includes an anticipation search but no examination of the merits of the invention, or adhere to the whole treaty, including Chapter II, which includes an examination of the claims based on the findings of the Chapter I search. Both chapters are processed during the International Stage. Currently, all PCT nations are bound by both chapters. Some future members may limit their participation to Chapter I. Check the WIPO Web site at www.wipo.org for the current members' status.

In Chapter I, a few months after your application reaches the International Bureau, your claims will be subject to an anticipation search, better known as the *international search,* which is conducted in your receiving office, in your case the USPTO, or the *International Searching Authority* at the International Bureau.

United States IP practitioners don't seem to agree on the best searching venue, but I suggest the USPTO — it's cheaper. However, if you've already filed a U.S. application, the examiner who handled that earlier application probably will conduct the international search. You're likely to see the same list of prior art references that were cited in your U.S. application, so you're not really getting a new search. Selecting the International Search Authority may offer a better opportunity to flush out prior foreign patents.

After you review the *International Search Report,* you have the opportunity to amend your claims. Exactly 18 months from the priority date, the application, search report, and any amendments will be published for the entire world to read.

The French made them do it

The PCT administration is essentially European in style and mentality. The French, who think the autocratic way is the only way and favor forms over substance, have had a major influence on these procedures. Every form must be filled out exactly as prescribed. Your last name must be entered first and your first name last. Your country of residence can't be listed as *United States of America, U.S.A.,* or *U.S.* No sir. It must be *US*

with no periods, period! And so it goes, with a multitude of meticulous rules that, just because they're so detailed, must be constantly updated. Fortunately, the good people in the USPTO bend over backwards to help you comply with all these PCT procedures. Most of the time, they graciously correct your minor mistakes, instead of returning the whole application.

Before the end of the 19th month from your priority date, you can initiate the Chapter II phase by filing a Demand for International Preliminary Examination of your application. *Note:* The Demand form must include your final list of the designated countries. (Get the form by clicking on **Chapter II** in the PCT section of the USPTO Web site.)

As I've mentioned, rules are forever changing among the members of the PCT. The list of countries that still observe the Demand and International Preliminary Examination requirement has shrunk to a point where many applicants don't bother filing the Demand. They accept filing of the application in their respective patent offices up to 32 months from the priority date. You can file your application in any of these countries that you elected in your Request. Consult your IP specialist to decide which way to go. You may not be interested in a patent in some of those holdout countries.

If you file a Demand, you should receive a report on the International Preliminary Examination a few months after you submit the Demand. You then have another opportunity to amend your claims before entering the regional and national stages.

Upon entering Chapter II with a Demand, you also have until 32 months from your priority date to file applications in the countries or groups of countries that adhere to Chapter II.

You must file your application before the expiration of the 19th month from your priority date in the countries that don't adhere to Chapter II.

Entering the regional stage

After the International Publication of your PCT application, you can move on to getting the actual patents by filing your PCT application with one of the three regional patent authorities mentioned earlier in this chapter: OAIP, ARIPO, and EAPO. These applications must be filed within the same time period as applications into individual countries. You can also file your application in the EPO under the same time constraints.

The EPO conducts a full-fledged examination and then issues a patent that can be entered in any designated country in the group. In most EPO countries, after the patent is issued, it only needs to be translated into the national idiom before it becomes locally enforceable.

During the regional phase, your attorney's local correspondent deals with the multinational organizations on your behalf. The office reports are sent to your attorney for your review and instructions on how to answer any objection or rejection. Don't be surprised if the process drags out over a year or two.

Entering the national phase

Some countries, including the U.S., Australia, Canada, China, and Mexico, don't belong to a regional group. You must send your PCT application to each one separately through your attorney's local correspondent. Your PCT application may be subject to a complete new examination, just as any domestic (non-PCT) examination. Some countries skip the new examination if you agree to accept the results of the Preliminary International Examination (if you haven't amended your claims after that examination).

You must have a local patent practitioner (in most cases a foreign correspondent of your U.S. attorney) at each level and pay local fees. This makes the whole process quite expensive, but cheaper than filing directly in the patent office of each country.

Selecting the proper filing protocol

The PCT and regional patent authorities offer you three domestic and foreign patent filing scenarios (two of which are slight variations of the one I already outlined):

- Instead of filing a U.S. application, you first file a provisional application in the United States (see Chapter 7). Within a year, file a formal application under the PCT and in non-PCT countries. Later, you can enter your PCT application in the USPTO as part of the national stage, as illustrated in Figure 18-1. This method is particularly effective if you're on a limited budget, or need to refine your invention before finalizing your applications.

- After you file a formal application in the United States, within one year you can file a PCT application and applications in non-PCT countries as illustrated in Figure 18-2. This approach postpones the big expenses associated with regional and national filings for up to 32 months, but expedites the issue of your U.S. patent.

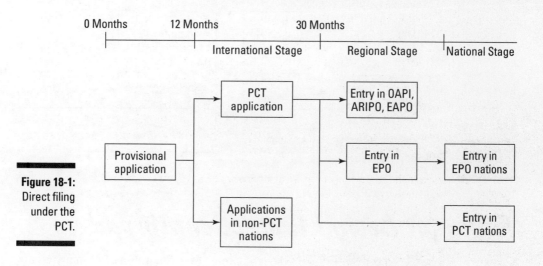

Figure 18-1: Direct filing under the PCT.

0 Months   12 Months   30 Months

International Stage   Regional Stage   National Stage

PCT application

Entry in OAPI, ARIPO, EAPO

Provisional application

Entry in EPO

Entry in EPO nations

Applications in non-PCT nations

Entry in PCT nations

> ✔ File a provisional application in the United States, and within one year, file a formal application in the United States, the PCT, and non-PCT countries, as illustrated in Figure 18-3. This hybrid filing strategy combines the two prior methods for maximum postponement of the all the big expenses, including the filing of your formal U.S. application. The downside is that the granting of your patent in the United States may be delayed.

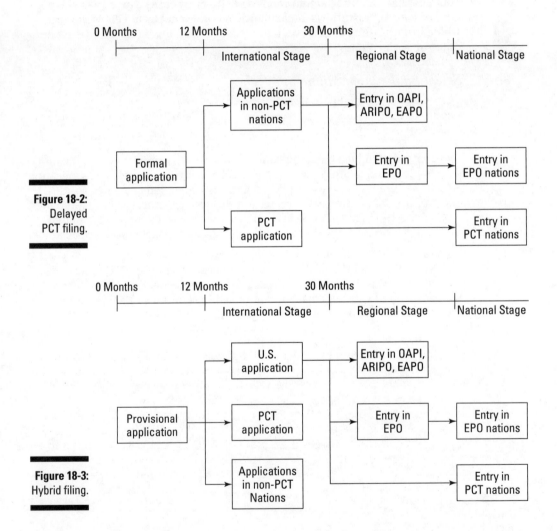

Figure 18-2: Delayed PCT filing.

Figure 18-3: Hybrid filing.

Filing for Design Protection Abroad

Only the United States offers design patents (see Chapter 4), but many countries offer similar protection for industrial designs and utility models. The scope protection is about the same. The major difference: In many countries, the duration of protection is less than the 14 years under a U.S. design patent.

The European Union provides *Community Design* protection for a new appearance of a product that exhibits "individual character." This patent requires lower standards of novelty and non-obviousness than a U.S. design patent does. The Community Design protection has a term of five years from the deposit of a graphic representation of the design, and can be renewed four times for a total span of 25 years.

Applications to register a Community Design are processed by the Office for Harmonization in the Internal Market (OHIM) located in Alicante, Spain. Download information about the OHIM registration process from their Web site at http://oami.eu.int/. After the registration is granted, it's enforceable in all 15 member nations of the EU without having to obtain a separate registration in each country. (In the near future, there should be approximately 25 members of the European Union.)

The Community Design protection is typical of what is available in most industrialized countries. You can register industrial designs in Africa with the OAIP and the ARIPO (see the section "Entering the regional stage," earlier in this chapter, for more info on these regional patent authorities). The conditions and procedures are similar to applying with the OHIM. These applications have to be handled by the local correspondents of your attorney.

You may also want to check out the *International Deposit of Industrial Designs Agreement* (The Hague Agreement). About 30 nations adhere to this agreement, which offers basically the same type of protection as the Community Design. Check the WIPO site or ask your attorney.

Any type of application for design protection abroad can claim a priority date upon a design patent application filed in the USPTO no more than six months before filing abroad, instead of one year for a utility patent.

Have a local IP practitioner handle your filing or deposit. Most U.S. practitioners maintain a network of correspondents upon whom they rely for that kind of filing. Requirements vary widely from country to country. A design doesn't usually disclose any kind of technological breakthrough and, consequently, isn't subject to the foreign filing license limitations imposed upon utility applications.

Protecting Your Plant Overseas

About 35 countries, including the United States, Japan, the United Kingdom, France, Germany, Canada, Australia, Italy, Spain, Argentina, and Mexico, are members of the *International Convention for the Protection of New Variety of*

Plants (UPOV). (The acronym is based on the French title.) Under this convention, a member country must give a plant breeder exclusive rights to the reproduction of a sexually reproductive or vegetatively propagated new plant for a minimum of 15 years. The new plant must be clearly distinguishable from commonly known varieties by at least one characteristic, and must be stable in its sexual reproduction or vegetative propagation. Under the U.S. implementation of the treaty, called the *Plant Variety Protection Act* (PVPA), administered by the *Plant Variety Protection Office* (PVPO) of the Department of Agriculture, the term of the protection is 25 years for trees and vines, and 20 years for other plants.

This protection is broader than that obtained under a U.S. plant patent (see Chapter 4). Note that in the United States, and theoretically in any other country with a plant patent system, a new plant can be protected in any particular country under either the UPOV registration or a plant patent, but not both.

When applying for registration in a member country, you may claim a filing priority date based upon either your U.S. application for a plant patent or your registration under the PVPA filed within the last twelve months.

Protecting Your Mark Abroad

At about the time this book goes to print, the United States will join the *Protocol Relating to the Madrid Agreement Concerning the International Registration of Marks* (The Madrid Protocol). After that happens, you'll be able to apply for registration of your mark in at least 57 countries with the click of a button and — by European standards — for a meager fee that will substantially reduce the overall costs estimated below.

The march toward global trademarks

The Madrid Protocol is a momentous event and a major step toward a global mark protection system. In the United States, unlike most other jurisdictions, we have a unique system of mark registration and protection that is predicated upon use of a mark rather than its entry in a government register. Many complex adjustments to the rules of the game had to be arduously negotiated by U.S. representatives to accommodate the peculiarities of our system. This is one of the reasons it took us 112 years to accede to this convention, first signed on April 14, 1891. As I write, the number of signatories to the Madrid Protocol is small, but should grow rapidly and include most industrialized countries within a few years.

Until now, a U.S. resident had to apply for registration of a mark in each country, at the average cost of $1,000 per country just for the original application, except when using the recently established European Community's Office for Harmonization in the Internal Market (OHIM) or the OAPI and the ARIPO in Africa to get a registration enforceable in all of their member states.

Oddly enough, OHIM is not currently a member of the Madrid Protocol, although all its adherents and postulants have joined.

OHIM, why bother?

Even though the United States will be joining the Madrid Protocol, filing with OHIM still has some advantages, because a European Community registration offers some special protection and doesn't carry some of the restrictions in the Madrid Protocol. For instance, a registration under the Madrid Protocol is totally dependant upon your U.S. application and registration during the first five years from application. If your application is refused or successfully protested, or your registration is cancelled during this five year period, all your Madrid Protocol registrations lapse. By contrast, OHIM doesn't even require you to file in the United States before you can register in the European Community. If you need to know more about the European Community mark, log on to the OHIM Web site at `http://oami.eu.int/`.

Let's all go to Madrid

The dust hasn't yet settled on the procedure to file a registration for the entire group of member countries under the Madrid Protocol, but I can give you a rough outline based on recently published proposed USPTO regulations. Applications for registration under the Madrid Protocol are handled by WIPO in Geneva, Switzerland, and must be based on a *domestic application* (you must first apply in your own country). The proposed procedure appears very simple:

1. **File your WIPO application online using the same electronic application program you used to file your U.S. application (see Chapter 17).**

2. **You don't even have to repeat the information from your domestic application.**

   Just enter your serial number, and the software combines your online entries with the information from your previously filed U.S. application and whisks the package to WIPO in Switzerland at the click of a button.

3. **The filing fee for all the designated countries can also be paid online to the USPTO.**

   Based on current practice and cost, a U.S. applicant designating about 25 countries in a Madrid Protocol application saves about $20,000 over the cost of filing in each country separately.

Visit `www.USPTO.gov` and `www.WIPO.int` for the latest information.

Copyrighting Overseas

International conventions and treaties, subscribed to by almost every country, mandate that each nation gives non-residents the same copyright protection it extends to its own citizens and legal residents, with no registration or other formality. So, in principle, there's no compelling reason to register your copyright abroad. However, some countries, like the United States, grant special procedural rights to owners of registered copyrights.

If you're concerned about infringement of your copyright in a particular country, have your IP specialist look at the copyright regulations in that jurisdiction to see if you could benefit from a local registration.

Chapter 19

Making 'Em Pay:
Licensing Your IP Rights

In This Chapter

▶ Exploiting your IP rights

▶ Avoiding tax and antitrust problems

▶ Marketing your assets

▶ Maximizing the income from your musical works

*I*f you have vision, you develop your IP assets with an eye towards letting these assets, and your IP rights to them, work like a lucrative investment. The royalties they generate, just like dividends and interest, can keep your wallet bulging — without you having to lift a finger except to hoist that frosty piña colada off the table by your poolside lounge chair. That dream has become reality for many astute entrepreneurs who took advantage of licensing opportunities that rewarded their creativity. You can license your invention, know-how, original work of authorship, or commercial identifier as long as it is protected by a patent, trade secret, copyright, or trademark. In this chapter, I explore the different kinds of licenses and the government requirements you need to comply with. I also touch on developing a licensing plan and dealing with the quirks of the music business.

Types of Licenses

A *license* is a contract between two parties. The *licensor* is the owner of an IP asset and its corresponding IP rights. The *licensee* is an individual or company that wants to use the IP assets in exchange for the payment of royalties or other valuable considerations. For example, if the IP asset is an invention and the IP right a patent, the licensee can practice the invention without being sued for infringement by the licensor.

A license doesn't actually transfer an asset or right — it just gives the licensee permission to use the IP asset, backed by the licensor's promise not to cancel that authorization as long as the licensee keeps up her end of the bargain by making required payments. A license is like the lease of a house, where the landlord gives the tenant permission to live there as long as he pays the rent on time. A license is different from an *assignment,* which is an outright transfer of an IP asset or right, which is like selling a house.

There are six types of licenses, according to the underlying type of IP right:

✔ **Patent license:** This license permits use of one of these IP assets:

- A technological breakthrough, such as a better mousetrap. In a license or other legal document, this is modestly referred to as an *improvement,* not as an invention.

- An ornamental design, such as an original perfume bottle.

- A variety of plant, such as a new species of cotton.

You can license your asset before you get your patent, because a license is a contract that stands independently from the patent. Courts recognize that when a manufacturer takes a license from an inventor, the former is buying insurance (with the royalties as the premium) against being sued for infringement when the patent is awarded. After the license agreement is signed, it doesn't matter whether the patent is granted. The manufacturer must pay royalties for the duration of the agreement.

✔ **Trade-secret license:** A trade-secret license is a contract to have the licensor disclose proprietary and confidential information to the licensee in exchange for a payment and a promise to keep the information under wraps. This is common in the chemical field where it's relatively easy to keep formulae and processes secret, and is more practical than getting a patent (see Chapter 5).

✔ **Copyright license:** A copyright license allows the licensee to enjoy one or more of the copyrights listed in Chapter 11. Copyright registration isn't a prerequisite to the granting of the license, but recommended for the reasons outlined in Chapter 13.

✔ **Trademark/Servicemark license:** This license authorizes someone else to operate under one or more of your commercial identifiers. The law requires that you keep some quality control over the activities of your licensee so that the customers who relied on the quality of your goods or services in the past will not be deceived.

Nowadays, many products aren't made by their original manufacturers but by firms that use the trademark under license from the original manufacturer and strict quality control conditions. A HANG TEN shirt may have been manufactured by one of many domestic and foreign licensees of Hang Ten International.

In the U.S., registration of a mark isn't a prerequisite to the license, but it's recommended (see Chapter 17). But mark registration is required in countries where the right to a mark isn't based upon a first use in commerce, but upon entry on a government register.

✔ **Merchandising license:** This is a copyright or trademark license, or a combination of both, where the range of goods upon which the mark or the copyrighted work is used goes beyond its original purpose. Certain commercial identifiers are so strong, recognized, and widely accepted that they can be rented out for use on a wide variety of goods. For instance, a movie studio may license the use of a cartoon character on a variety of children's products from toys to book bags.

Merchandising is pure name exploitation that depends on the value of the commercial identifier itself and the impression it conveys, and not the quality or reputation of the products or services originally provided under the mark. For example, the DIOR mark appears on a multitude of products, from garments and perfumes to sporting goods.

✔ **Combination license:** In a combination license, several IP assets and rights are bundled together, such as when a manufacturer is authorized to produce and sell a patented article under the licensor's mark and package it with copyrighted graphics. This type of license is subject to antitrust prohibitions. See "Avoiding illegal entanglements," later in the chapter.

A *franchise* is a trademark or servicemark license with rules about how the licensee (or *franchisee*) shall conduct the business according to a method imposed by the licensor, called the *franchisor*. This type of contractual relationship includes some transfer of know-how and technical assistance by the franchisor (coupled with a hefty down payment by the franchisee). Fast-food franchises are a familiar example, where a franchisee acquires a restaurant carrying the franchisor's servicemark and prepares and serves food under a set method and under strict quality control.

A servicemark license that involves some operating control (rather than just quality control) by the licensor is treated as a franchise — a critical distinction because, due to the large initial investment and high royalty rates, franchises are subject to special regulations by state and federal authorities.

Inspecting Basic Elements of a License

Before you can negotiate any type of license agreement, you must understand the important parts of an agreement and the specific legal clauses that you need to include — so I throw in examples from a patent license to give you some legal lingo to chew on. These clauses can be adapted to cover licenses for other types of IP assets and rights.

This outline of the basic clauses in a license agreement isn't exhaustive. Like any contract, the license agreement must include a number of additional clauses relative to future improvements, technical assistance, warranties, legal action against infringers, termination, notices, arbitration, and attorney's fees, just to name a few. My goal is to make you aware of the key issues you should address when exploiting your IP assets. You need the assistance of a competent IP specialist to negotiate and draft the license agreement.

Defining IP assets and rights

You must first clearly define the IP asset and/or right you're licensing:

> *Licensor is the sole owner of an improvement in an auto-focusing mechanism for cameras (The "Improvement"), disclosed in a pending U.S. utility patent application entitled Auto-focusing Mechanism for Outdoor Surveillance Video Camera under Docket No. 200-1 at the offices of Sue-Ann Dannoy, Esq. in Alexandria, Virginia (the "Application") from which and from continuation applications thereof a number of domestic and foreign patents are expected to issue (the "Patents").*

> *Licensee wishes to obtain the right to manufacture and sell several types of cameras using the Improvement.*

Note: The patent application isn't identified by its serial number — always keep that information confidential.

Granting permission to use your IP

This clause defines the scope of the permitted activities, and is the most important part of the license agreement.

Exclusivity

The *exclusivity clause* states who gets to use the invention.

- ✔ **Exclusive:** The licensor waives any right to practice the invention or to authorize anybody else to do so.

- ✔ **Co-exclusive:** The licensor reserves the right to practice the invention, but agrees not to license anyone but the licensee.

- ✔ **Non-exclusive:** The licensor reserves the right to practice the invention and can also license third parties in competition with the licensee.

The exclusivity clause determines other terms of the agreement, such as the amount of royalties, and the legal rights of the parties. For instance, an exclusive license carries higher royalties than a co-exclusive or non-exclusive license. Only an exclusive licensee can file legal actions against infringers.

The clause must be very specific in order to avoid future disputes. For the sake of illustration, this license contains multiple exclusivity provisions. Most licenses have a single exclusivity clause.

> *Licensor grants Licensee:*
>
> *a) an exclusive license and permission to manufacture, offer for sale, sell, and use digital still cameras incorporating the Improvement with right to sublicense others to do the same,*
>
> *b) a co-exclusive license and permission to manufacture, offer for sale, sell, and use analog and digital video cameras incorporating the Improvement without right to sublicense others to do the same; and*
>
> *c) a non-exclusive license and permission to manufacture, offer for sale, sell, and use analog still cameras incorporating the Improvement without right to license others to do the same.*
>
> *Licensor reserves the right to manufacture, offer for sale, sell, and use said analog and digital video cameras, without right to license others, and to manufacture, offer for sale, sell, and use said analog still cameras and license others to do the same.*
>
> *Licensor shall not use any IP right he may acquire over the Improvement to exclude Licensee from doing the acts authorized by this clause so long as Licensee complies with all the terms and conditions of this agreement.*

Territory and field of use

An owner of any type of IP assets and rights can divide and parcel the geographical areas and commercial fields where the invention can be practiced or applied. In this illustration, each license has a distinct territory:

> *Said exclusive license shall be limited to the consumer market in the United States and Canada and shall not extend to cameras primarily intended for professional or industrial use.*
>
> *Said co-exclusive license shall be limited to the United States and Canada in any field of use except geographical mapping and law enforcement surveillance cameras.*
>
> *Said non-exclusive license shall apply worldwide without any field of use limitations.*

Duration

To avoid allegations of abusive conduct, the duration of the license must be no more than the life of the patent or any other applicable IP right. A patent license agreement should specify that if no patent is issued, the duration should be no more than 20 years (the maximum life of a utility patent).

> *The term of the above licenses and the obligations imposed on the Licensee in this agreement shall not last beyond the expiration of the last of the Patents. In any territory where no patent has issued within ten years from the effective date of this agreement, said license and obligations shall expire on the tenth anniversary of said date.*

Getting paid: Remuneration

The law allows great flexibility in setting up the payment for the license. Payment may comprise

- ✔ One or more lump sums
- ✔ Royalties based on net proceeds, number of items made or sold, costs of goods, or any other readily verifiable parameter
- ✔ A combination of the above

Advances against royalties, delayed payments, stepped-up or stepped-down royalty rates based on sale proceeds or number of items sold, and guaranteed remittances can be used to fine-tune the agreement to the circumstances:

> *Licensee shall pay Licensor each of the following:*
>
> *A non-refundable lump sum of $5,000.00 on each anniversary of the effective date of this agreement.*
>
> *During the first 10 years of the term of this agreement, royalties at the rate of $10.00 per camera manufactured under said exclusive and co-exclusive licenses, and at the rate of $3.00 per camera manufactured under said non-exclusive license; plus 1% of the net proceeds from the sales of all types of cameras. After the 10th anniversary of the effective date of this agreement, said royalty rates shall be reduced by one half.*
>
> *A royalty advance of $25,000.00 upon execution of this agreement by all parties. Licensee shall not apply more than $5,000.00 per month out of said advance payment against royalties payable to licensor.*

The details of the remuneration clause are usually dictated by the business circumstances — the financial status and marketing clout of the licensor, the anticipated sales, the required investment in tooling and marketing, and so on.

A minimum performance clause should always be included in an exclusive license because you depend entirely upon the licensee's performance to exploit your IP asset. Such a clause may use a sliding scale to keep the licensed company on its best behavior. For example:

> *Licensor shall have the right to terminate this agreement by thirty day written notice to the Licensee in the event that the total amount of monetary remuneration received by Licensor does not exceed:*
>
> *$50,000.00 during the first full calendar year,*
>
> *$100,000.00 during the second calendar year,*
>
> *$150,000.00 or one half of the total monetary remuneration received by licensor during the preceding calendar year in any subsequent calendar year, whichever is greater.*

Reporting

Except when license fees are fully paid up front or by a fixed payment schedule, the licensee should be required to periodically report its sales and pay the applicable royalties:

> *Within thirty days from the end of each calendar year, Licensee shall provide Licensor with a report of the number of cameras manufactured under each of said licenses and of net proceeds collected by Licensee during said calendar year and shall tender payment of royalties applicable to said number and proceeds.*

Control

If the license authorizes the licensee to use or operate under your mark, you must include a clause allowing you to control the quality of the goods or services provided to the customer under your identifier.

> *Goods manufactured under this agreement shall conform with all governmental regulations and shall maintain a level of quality and merchantability equal to or better than the goods currently being manufactured and sold by Licensor. Licensor shall have the right to enter Licensee's manufacturing and storage facilities on any working day during regular business hours without prior notice to inspect said goods for compliance with this clause.*

As owner of the mark, you're liable for any losses suffered by the consumer as a result of any defect or failure of the product or inadequate service.

In a patent license agreement, the licensor is usually won't make any warranty that the invention is worth anything, will work as expected, or that the product or process made under it is effective and safe. There's no legal obligation imposed on the licensor to exert any degree of quality control over the activities of the licensee, making the licensor immune to liability for any of the licensee's failures or misdeeds.

Assigning Rather Than Licensing

Under certain circumstances, and for sundry reasons (such as tax considerations, wanting no further entanglement with the licensee, or because your prospective licensee wants it), you may decide to sell your IP asset and IP rights, under a written document called an *assignment.* Just like a grant deed on a piece of property, the assignment must be notarized (acknowledged before a U.S. consular officer if you reside abroad) to be readily admissible in court. This type of legal paper can be quite short and to the point:

> *For good and valid consideration, hereby acknowledged, I, Jeanne Doe, the owner of U.S. patent no. 9,999,999 for an improvement in motorcycle helmet, hereby assign and transfer my entire interest in said improvement and patent to John Deer, a U.S. citizen residing in Buckeye, Arizona.*

The same wording can be used to transfer a copyright or mark. Just make sure that the description of what's being transferred is complete and readily identifiable (attach a copy or photograph if necessary).

If you're John Deer, you want to record the assignment as soon as possible in the USPTO, or any other appropriate agency. In general, recording cuts off the transferor's right to assign the same asset or right to another person. If you don't record a patent or patent application assignment within three months from its signing, any subsequent assignment takes precedence over yours when it's recorded. Your sole remedy is to sue that weasel Jeanne and try to get some compensation for your losses.

Whether you license or assign doesn't necessarily dictate how you get your money — you can use a lump sum payment or royalty program for either method. However, a royalty program should include an agreement with all the payment and reporting clauses usually found in a license agreement.

Getting Down to the Government Stuff

You probably thought that after you got your registration, you were through with the government, right? Wrong —Uncle Sam is your partner. Both state and federal agencies regulate some types of license agreements, make sure that all taxes are paid, and act as an anti-trust watchdog.

Recording your document

In general, license agreements don't require filing or registration with government regulatory agencies. However, you can record (don't confuse recording with registering) a patent or trademark license with the USPTO, and a copyright license with the Copyright Office (see Chapter 13), just as you'd record an assignment or other transfer of title. An exclusive licensee wants to record the license to deter infringers and to prevent the licensor from granting a similar license to someone else.

The big exception is a franchise. In most states, you have to *qualify* (have it approved) your franchise scheme before you can offer it to prospective franchisees, proving that you can fulfill the promises you make. In some states, the qualification process is very strict and takes months. After your sell a franchise, it must be recorded with the appropriate agencies.

Franchising is a very complex operation best handled by an attorney specializing in that field.

Considering tax advantages

As you know, the government wants a chunk out of any exchange of money. So although I'm not a tax expert, I'd like to alert you to the tax consequences of licensing your IP assets and rights — versus assigning them (see above).

For tax purposes, proceeds from a license are usually considered ordinary income. Proceeds from an assignment of assets are treated as capital gains. The IRS may treat some exclusive patent licenses like assignments if the licensor retains little or no control.

When negotiating the transfer of IP assets or rights, consider the lower rate of taxation on capital gains compared to ordinary income. Section 1767 of the IRS Code provides that the lump sum or royalty proceeds from a sale or exchange of a patent are treated as a long-term capital gain. Sometimes, an assignment may be more lucrative than a license when taxes are plugged into the equation. All of these are touchy tax issues; rely on the expertise of a tax attorney or CPA.

Avoiding illegal entanglements

To a certain degree, patents, copyrights, and trademarks are monopolies and exceptions to many unfair competition and antitrust regulations. Therefore, the courts and government agencies monitor their use to prevent any coercive practices by IP right owners. The basic rule that will keep you out of trouble can be summarized: Don't leverage your IP rights to obtain advantages not directly related to those rights. The most common faux pas are:

- ✔ **Tie-ins:** An illegal tie-in obligates a licensee to buy something from you that lies beyond the scope of your IP rights. For instance, in the camera example I use in this chapter, you can't obligate the licensee to buy his lenses from you, because your patent doesn't cover the lenses.

- ✔ **Bundlings:** Questionable bundling occurs when you compel someone to take licenses based on several patents or other IP rights or when you bundle different IP assets or rights in a single license or in related ones. This practice is questionable rather than outright illegal because the nature of the wrongful conduct depends upon the circumstances.

    In the camera example, if you have a patent on a lens design and force the licensee to take a license for the lens along with the auto-focusing mechanism that he wants, and there are other sources of lens technology, the license violates antitrust law. However, if the licensee requests a license to make your lens because of its superior design, you're off the antitrust hook.

    It's also a no-no to obligate your patent licensee to also use your trademark, but if the licensee likes your trademark and asks you to license it along with your patent, there's no harm done.

The main reason to avoid anti-trust or anti-competition clauses in your license agreement isn't that Big Brother is gonna come breathing down your neck and charge you with violation of the Sherman Act. The government is too busy chasing the corporate big fish to play in your little pond. The problem is that your licensee may have grounds to attack the agreement in any future dispute, sue you, and bring Big Bro into the fray.

Adopting a Licensing Strategy

Many inventors and other developers of IP assets and rights don't have a clue about how to find a licensee to bring their creations to the market. They often fall victim to unscrupulous invention development companies (see my comments about these guys in Chapter 3). No magic formula will work for everybody, but the best way is to plan your licensing strategy before you pursue IP rights, but if you haven't, all is not lost. If you understand the marketplace, you can develop an effective and lucrative strategy.

The first step to developing a good licensing strategy is to understand market realities. Here are a few of my personal observations based on many years of service to fledgling entrepreneurs:

✔ The more you develop your project, the more you get for it. You generally can't sell an idea or concept. A patented but unproven invention may sometimes be sold or licensed, but not for much. An ongoing business, built around a product, process, or method protected by IP rights can be readily and lucratively sold.

✔ Few large companies respond to an unsolicited license offer or proposal.

✔ Most responsible companies don't accept the disclosure of your device or concept in confidence. Check the small print in any so-called non-disclosure agreement offered by a manufacturer. You'll find plenty of escape clauses that render any promise of confidentiality meaningless.

✔ Manufacturing companies that can directly benefit from your product or process are your most promising licensing candidates. Don't bother with firms that promise to market anything to anybody.

✔ Don't spend your resources on a product that carries a substantial risk of personal injury without making sure that you or your eventual licensee can obtain product liability insurance at a reasonable cost. This is especially important for medicinal products (especially those to be taken internally), infant toys, baby carriers, and power tools.

✔ Computer programs developed in response to a particular manufacturing or processing need are the most welcome.

Making Beautiful Music Business

The recording, sale, and performance of musical works is a huge, complex industry that relies heavily on copyright law to regulate most of its activities and large-scale licensing of copyrights to distribute its creations.

As a copyright owner, you control and can license reproductions of your song on sheet music or recordings under a *mechanical license,* and its public performance under a *performing license.* You can also authorize a motion-picture studio to use your creation as background music under a *synchronization license.*

You can't possibly enter into licensing agreements with all the record companies, theatres, radio and TV stations, and other organizations that you hope will record, perform, and broadcast your music. Instead, associations of songwriters, music publishers, and recording companies have established complex but very efficient systems to transfer the copyrights and channel a small part of the mechanical and performing royalties back to you.

Performing licenses and royalties

The bulk of the money you get for your musical creation is from performance licenses and royalties. Songwriter and author organizations collect your royalties every time a musical work is publicly performed or broadcast either live or by recording. The major players are:

- ✔ ASCAP, One Lincoln Center, New York, NY 10023-7142, phone 212-631-6000, Web site www.ascap.com.

- ✔ BMI, 320 West 57th Street, New York, NY 10019-3790, phone 221-586-2000, Web site www.bmi.com.

- ✔ SESAC, 55 Music Square Nashville, TN 37203, phone 615-329-9627, Web site www.sesac.com.

Each of these organizations maintains a list of all the works created by its members. They enter into license agreements with theaters and broadcasting companies to monitor, report, and pay performing royalties, which they then distribute to the authors and music publishers. One half of the royalty goes to the author and the other half to the publishing companies that created the recording or published the sheet music.

Your first step as a songwriter is to join one of these organizations and give it a list of your songs. Due to the instant popularity of your ballad, you can expect a trickle of royalty payments during the first few quarters to turn into a flood of huge checks as every DJ in America spins your CD every hour. You can get a complete application kit and song release forms from your chosen performing royalty association. Some offer online applications.

Mechanical licenses and royalties

Mechanical licenses allow a company to publish or record your music. There are two types of mechanical licenses:

- ✔ A standard, *voluntary license* is one you willingly negotiate and grant on your own to a specific music publishing or record company. Actually, there's very little to negotiate because the royalty rates and modes of payment are pretty standard throughout the industry.

- ✔ A *compulsory license* can be claimed by any recording company, without your consent, after you've authorized a company to produce and sell a recording of your work (see Chapter 11).

Most music publishing or recording companies have standard license agreements that don't give you much elbowroom to negotiate terms and conditions. They offer you a pittance for each record or piece of sheet music sold, because they have to pay a royalty to the recording artist, pay for the musicians and recording studio time, and assume other expenses associated with the packaging and sale of the recordings. Songwriters, in general, derive the bulk of their income from performing royalties and, to a lesser extent, from synchronization royalties for the chosen few who are lucky enough to have their music selected by a movie producer.

Your challenge is to maximize the performing royalties you receive. The music publishing company already collects half of your performing royalties — you as the author get the other half. This arrangement is a bit unfair, because the company already receives revenue from the sale of sheet music and recordings. To level the playing field, many songwriters create, their own music publishing companies that only deal with real music publishing and record companies. In turn, these other companies agree to give your fictitious company an equal share of the publisher's portion of the royalties. The net result is that you get 75 percent (your 50 percent and your paper company's 25 percent) of the performing royalties.

The creation of a sole proprietorship music publishing company is a mere formality in most states. Ask your performing royalty organization to provide you with a kit to form and register your music publishing company.

The Copyright Act requires the licensee in a compulsory license to provide a monthly report of sales to the copyright owner and also sets the royalty rate. Nobody wants to go through the cumbersome reporting procedure, so some agencies have been created to handle compulsory licenses and act as clearinghouses between the music publishing and recording companies. The royalty rate (slightly lower than the one specified in the statute) and payment schedule are standard. These organizations also handle synchronization licenses and licensing of foreign record companies.

The largest and most popular mechanical licensing organization is The Harry Fox Agency, Inc. created by the National Music Publisher's Association (NMPA), 711 Third Avenue, New York, NY 10017. Their telephone number is 212-370-5330, and their Web site is www.nmpa.org. This site is also a very convenient place to search copyright records.

Synchronization licenses

A *synchronization license* allows the licensee to use a musical work as background music in a movie, play, video production, or other performance. The name comes from the fact that the music score has to be synchronized with the images and other sounds on the film or other recording medium.

Copyrights in the electronic age

About every ten years, Congress introduces a major revision of the Copyright Act to keep up with advances in the music business. Congress doesn't necessarily respond to the needs of the songwriters, but to the whims of the big players — the recording and movie companies and the major broadcasters. Over the last 70 years, lobbyists have urged Congress to construct an elaborate legal structure that relies on compulsory license provisions with royalties imposed upon receiving and duplicating instruments, record making, and public transmission.

However, that system is becoming obsolete. The Internet and music sharing software is threatening the recording industry with near extinction. Peer-to-peer music sharing is a blatant violation of the Copyright Act that hurts the performers and record industry more than the songwriters. You can be sure that a solution will soon be devised; not by facilitating copyright enforcement, but by amending the law to legitimize electronic music sharing and compensating the record companies with royalties from taxes paid by computer equipment manufacturers and transmission service providers. After that, I'll rewrite this chapter.

If the job is substantial (an entire movie score), if there's an existing relationship between the copyright holder and the producer, or if the holder is a famous composer or songwriter, the copyright holder and the producer may enter into a negotiated license agreement. In other, more anonymous relationships, or when only a few minutes of music are at stake, the producer simply contacts a mechanical license organization and gets a standard license at a standard rate.

Chapter 20

Nailing the Bad Guys
(The Infringers)

. . . .

In This Chapter

▶ What is infringement?

▶ Enforcing your IP rights

. . . .

*F*rom a legal point of view, your patent, copyright, or distinctive commercial identifier does nothing more than give you permission to exclude others from doing something only you can legally do. However, this permission has many limits and restrictions. You can't take things into in your own hands and go shoot the meddler. You can't seize counterfeit merchandise. Come to think of it, you'd better not tell anyone that you suspect that person is doing anything wrong until you've jumped through a number of legal hoops held high by a clownish bunch of lawyers in the American legal circus — oops, I mean system. If you can't substantiate your allegations in court, you'll find yourself on the pillory being pelted with malodorous accusations of unfair practices, in the poorhouse, or both.

My goal isn't to discourage you from asserting your IP rights, but to explain some of the procedures particular to IP litigations and to point you toward the most expeditious and least expensive approaches.

Determining Infringement

Determining whether an IP right has been infringed requires a careful legal analysis of all circumstances. Going from the least to the most complicated IP rights, I describe their respective infringement tests and how to apply them.

Violating a copyright

A copyright may be infringed by copying or making adaptations of the protected work, distributing or displaying copies or adaptations, publicly performing a musical or dramatic work, or transmitting, and in certain case defacing, the work (see Chapter 11).

Only the act of copying requires special analysis. All other instances of infringement are simply based on cold facts. A recording of your song was played over the radio or it was not. Period. But even the test for infringement by copying is relatively simple. It only requires a review of the facts and a bit of legal analysis. The infringement test can be summarized in three words: access, expression, and substantial similarity. Ask these three questions:

- ✔ Did the alleged infringer have access to your copyrighted work?

- ✔ What part of your work constitutes a protected expression rather than a pure idea or material already in the public domain?

- ✔ If the answer to the first question is positive, do the similarities between that part of your work containing protected expression and the infringer's work indicate that partial or whole copying occurred?

If only part of the work was copied, make sure that the copied portion was copyrighted and isn't in the public domain. Here's an example: You design home furnishings and create an elegant pedestal made of a long, fluted Greek column with a Corinthian capital, capped by a square plateau. Sam Metoo, one of your competitors, comes out with a coffee table supported by a single foot in the shape of a squat and fluted Greek column with the same Corinthian capital as yours. You can prove that Sam visited your showroom, but you can't prove infringement. What he copied was the idea of a Greek column and the Corinthian capital used to support a piece of furniture. The concept of using an architectural column in a piece of furniture isn't protected by copyright. Corinthian capitals have been around since Alexander the Great was in diapers some 2,400 years ago. The copyrighted portion of your pedestal — its overall harmonious proportions — hasn't been copied. (For the infringement test of a computer program and other more complex works, review Chapter 11.)

Finally, you must make certain that the suspected infringement doesn't fall under one of the exemptions or exceptions listed in Chapter 11.

Imitating a commercial identifier

Determining whether your company identifier, trademark, or servicemark is being infringed is a bit more complex than assessing infringement of a copyright. The test is whether there's a likelihood of confusion between your identifier and the alleged infringer's. *Likelihood* doesn't mean possibility but a reasonable expectation that the public will be confused based on court-defined parameters.

Most courts use the test I go over in Chapter 16, with one additional factor: whether there have been instances of actual confusion. To document instances of actual confusion between the identifiers, keep records of any mistaken calls or inquiries you receive that were meant for the other guy. Also, note any instance where one of your customers ordered or bought goods or services from the infringer, thinking she was buying from you.

Establishing likelihood of confusion is fairly easy, and the penalties are severe. That's why imitating another's commercial identifier is a very risky choice.

Running afoul of a patent

Determining patent infringement requires very complex and costly legal analysis. I wouldn't expect you to conduct such an analysis, but I outline the gist of it here.

Don't worry if all the legal mumbo jumbo is a bit difficult to understand — like it or not, you'll have to shell out a few thousand dollars for an infringement analysis and written opinion from a patent attorney anyway.

A patent is infringed if the bad guy's device or process includes all the elements (or a substantial equivalent) listed in any one claim — in other words, the accused device doesn't have to infringe on all the claims, just one in its entirety (because each claim defines a different, distinct area of protected technology). So, the first step in determining patent infringement is getting the scope or coverage of your patent claims nailed down. The scope of a claim is strictly limited by its language. Of course, language can be open to interpretation, so both you and the bad guy get to propose your own interpretation of the claims to a judge, who decides the scope of each claim in a *Markman hearing* before the issue comes to trial.

If the claim language is ambiguous, the description, the drawing, and, if necessary, the application file of the patent are used to interpret the claim. (***Note:*** The specifications can't be used to add limitations to an otherwise clear and unambiguous claim.) Or the judge can receive expert testimony to interpret the meaning of a claim.

Patent owners have a friend in the *Doctrine of Equivalents,* a judge-made rule intended to protect the substance of the patentee's rights. You can establish infringement under this doctrine even if the accused device doesn't literally match the patent's claims, as long as the differences between your patented invention and the infringing one are insubstantial and there's a substantial similarity of function, method, and results.

The Doctrine of Equivalents requires that every component in a certain claim must be literally or equivalently present in the accused device or process. An element of little or no importance to the claimed invention can be satisfied by a wide range of equivalent elements not disclosed in the specification. These equivalents aren't limited to elements or process steps that were available when the patent was issued, those equivalents can also arise after the patent was issued and before it was infringed. Another important factor to be considered is whether persons reasonably skilled in the art would know that the part contained in the patent was interchangeable with one that was omitted. For example, if an element in the claim of an 18-year-old patent recites a telephone handset connected to a wall unit, and the accused device uses a cellphone, the Doctrine would wipe out the difference.

In a recent and very controversial decision, the Court of Appeals for the Federal Circuit (see Chapter 9) has drastically curtailed the application of the Doctrine. The last chapter hasn't been written yet. Ask your patent attorney for the latest on that topic, if you really care.

Another tricky aspect in interpreting the scope of a claim is "means plus function" language. Here are some guidelines:

- If a claim expresses a way to perform a specified function, for example, a means for attaching A to B, without describing how to attach the elements or with what, the means are construed to cover the elements described in the specification and its equivalents. For example, if the "means for attaching A to B" is disclosed as a hinge, the means will cover any flexible link that could act like a hinge.

- If the "means," or way of performing a function, discloses a physical structure insignificant to the claimed invention, there may be many more equivalent structures than if the characteristics of the structure are critical in performing the claimed function. For example, if an element claimed in the preferred embodiment as a "means for securing together" two pieces of wood is a set of nails, then screws, dowels, dovetails, and other types of joints would constitute equivalent elements if nails aren't critical to the invention's function.

- When interpreting "means plus function" language, an equivalent structure or act cannot embrace technology developed after the patent was issued (as permitted under the Doctrine). Comparison between the proposed equivalent and what's disclosed in the specification must consider the overall structure or process. Accordingly, the accused device may have more or fewer parts than the structure disclosed in the specification, as long as the same function is performed in a substantially similar way.

During the prosecution of a patent, the inventor or his attorney may make concessions, such as restricting the meaning of a term, to avoid rejection because of a prior disclosure. For instance, the phrase "tubular sleeve" may be restricted to tubular elements that are open at both ends, and exclude tubular sleeves that are closed at one or both ends. This kind of concession could only be discovered by careful examination of the application file.

A patent claim that addresses a combination of two or more elements or components can be infringed if one of the elements or components is offered, sold, or imported in the United States with the intent to infringe a patent. Note that even if the elements or components are combined outside the United States, there may be infringement.

Stopping Infringement Cold

You've done your homework. You are convinced that Tom is copying your copyrighted poster, Dick is using the *Kitty Love* trademark on toastable tarts in derogation of your federally registered *Puppy Love* fast-food restaurant servicemark, or Harry is making, importing, and selling cameras that incorporate your patented auto-focusing mechanism. Now what? Here's what you can do:

- ✔ Take the high road — go to the nearest federal district court and file an infringement action. Don't forget to bring your checkbook.

- ✔ Look for a special procedure short of full-fledged litigation.

- ✔ Send a *cease and desist notice* threatening the infringer with a lawsuit if the unlawful activities are not promptly stopped.

- ✔ Negotiate a friendly settlement that accommodates both parties.

Taking the high road and going for broke

Suing the infringer is the most effective way to stop an infringement. However, it can be very expensive and may drag out over two or more years, especially if a patent is involved.

Outline of the proceedings

IP litigation is conducted under the same rules as any other civil matter. The proceedings can be broken down into five phases:

- ✔ **Temporary relief phase:** You try to obtain a temporary court order restraining the defendant from doing some act that can't be corrected (like cracking Humpty Dumpty), pending further proceedings.

✔ **Discovery phase:** Both parties bombard each other with *interrogatories* (formal or written questions to a witness) requiring an answer under oath, request admissions and documents, and *depose* (ask to give evidence or testimony under oath) the other guy's prospective witnesses.

✔ **Summary proceeding phase:** One or more of the parties tries to get a judge's decision on some key issues or an *injunction* (court order prohibiting someone from performing a specific act) against an infringing activity. The parties may also submit to voluntary or court-mandated arbitration.

✔ **Trial phase:** During the trial phase, the matter goes before a judge or jury.

✔ **Appeal phase:** The party who's dissatisfied with the outcome of a summary proceeding or trial takes the case to a higher court. The outcome of appeal may be a remand for a new trial.

Expending a lot of resources and effort up front to win a temporary relief order or prevail in a summary proceeding may bring the issue to a close before you ever get to trial. For instance, if you win a temporary restraining order or injunction compelling the defendant to stop using your mark pending the outcome of the trial, what other option does that defendant have but to use a different mark? He has no reason to pursue the case because, even if he wins, he doesn't want to go through the trouble and expenses of changing his mark again.

Watching the calendar

The *statute of limitations,* the time you have to file a lawsuit in a federal court after an infringement, is six years for patents and three years for copyrights. In trademark cases, the grace period varies as the U.S. court follows the law of the state where the suit is brought. That means that you can sue someone for infringing your patent five and one half years after the patent expires and recover damages for any infringing activity that took place within the last six months of the life of the patent.

Selecting a venue

You usually file the infringement lawsuit in the nearest U.S. district court, but the defendant may try to get the action moved to his district. The laws controlling the venue of a lawsuit are complex and vary depending upon the type of infringement. Things can get very complicated when your complaint includes different types of infringement, multiple defendants living in separate districts, or infringements that occurred in different places. You may sue a retailer or buyer of counterfeit goods who lives in your district and obligate a distant manufacturer to come to his defense. You always want to litigate in your own backyard, for a number of reasons: convenience, reducing costs, the fact that you may find local law more favorable to your case (even federal law varies from circuit to circuit), and other unmentionable reasons (your legal gun knows the judge).

Praying for paying remedies

Your goal in a lawsuit is a court order that ends the infringing activities. Depending upon the type of action and the statute under which you filed your complaint, you may ask for and recover your losses due to the infringer's activities; you may also ask to recover the infringer's profit, your attorney's fees, and court costs. If the conduct of the defendant has been particularly egregious, such as an intentional patent infringement, you may recover up to three times the amount of your losses.

What's the cost?

Here's my very rough estimate of the average cost to litigate or defend an infringement action all the way through trial, but short of appeal:

- Copyright: $250,000 to $325,000
- Trade secret: $275,000 to $450,000
- Company identifier or mark: $200,000 to $450,000
- Design or plant patent: $250,000 to $500,000
- Utility Patent: $500,000 to $2,000,000

You can use these average figures for budgetary purpose, although actual cases can deviate substantially from these estimates. In some complex and dragged-out patent cases, courts have awarded over $20 million in attorney's fees to the prevailing party. If the defendant doesn't have the resources to fight, he'll cave in very early. Even large companies try to avoid the cost and the drain of human resources caused by IP litigation. That's why a large majority of patent cases are settled before trial.

Insuring against litigation

If you just read the list of costs in the previous section, you're probably thinking, "I could never afford to sue someone for infringing. Should I really even bother applying for a patent (or some other IP right)?" Good question. For a reasonable premium, you can purchase a policy that pays the cost of defending a claim of infringement brought against you or your company and also pays your attorney to pursue infringers of your copyright or patent. What's the catch? If you win your case, the insurance company is entitled to a percentage of any reward granted to you by the court. But because the most important thing is stopping the infringer, giving up part of any monetary award you get from the court is worth it. And if you lose the case, you don't find yourself in the poorhouse or working as your attorney's chauffeur for the next ten years. Refer to Chapter 24 for a source of litigation insurance information. The premium for that kind of insurance depends on many factors and is a matter for negotiation with the carrier.

Taking advantage of special remedies

Because of the high cost of a full-fledged litigation, I want to go over some alternate and less costly ways to stop copycats.

Criminal statutes

State and federal laws provide criminal penalties for some infringements of IP rights.

> ✔ **Federal law:** The federal anti-piracy law provides for punishment of copyright infringement for commercial advantage or private financial gain (so what's the difference?), as well as the reproduction of recordings, or the trafficking in counterfeit recordings, computer programs, and motion pictures. The penalty can be as high as six years in prison and a fine up to $250,000.
>
> The penalty for trafficking in counterfeit goods or services (using a counterfeit mark) can be up to ten years in prison and $5,000,000 in fines for an individual and up to a $15,000,000 fine for a company.
>
> ✔ **State law:** Some states have criminal statutes against the misappropriation of trade secrets and industrial espionage.

Ask your attorney whether you can take advantage of these criminal statutes by asking for the intervention of the local U.S. attorney, district attorney, or state consumer protection agency instead of filing a civil action. Sometimes, U.S. attorneys or district attorneys can deputize your hired gun to prosecute the infringer on behalf of the people. Imagine your infringer being dragged, handcuffed to the federal pen. I'd do anything to get out of this predicament.

AntiCybersquatting statute

If you find a domain name on the World Wide Web that's confusingly similar to your mark, you may invoke the *AntiCybersquatting Act* to get the name cancelled. You must prove that the name was selected and used in bad faith, which means that the infringer knew about your mark and intended to profit from or disparage your mark. You must file this action in a U.S. district court.

If you discover a domain name that is confusingly similar to your registered mark, you also have recourse to the *domain name dispute-resolution* procedure administered by the Internet Corporation for Assigned Names and Numbers (ICANN). For general information and a copy of the name-dispute rules, log on to www.icann.org/udrp/udrp.htm.

Getting help from U.S. Customs

U.S. Customs can seize counterfeit merchandise that violates your registered copyright or mark or bears your company trade name. If you suspect an unlawful importation, you can register your copyright, mark, or company identifier with the U.S. Customs service, so that they can seize the targeted goods. You and the goods' owner will be "invited" to appear at a hearing to determine whether the goods should be destroyed or released to their original addressee.

This is a much more efficient and less expensive method to bar imported goods than waiting until they appear on the U.S. market and suing the U.S. distributor in a court of law.

Running to the International Trade Commission

If the infringer is importing the counterfeit merchandize into the United States, you could seek relief from the *International Trade Commission* (ITC) by asking for an order banning importation. The ITC investigates by looking at the validity of your patent, registered copyright, or mark, and then decides whether the importation has an anticompetitive impact on U.S. commerce by infringing your IP rights. For more on the subject, check out the Information Center at www.usitc.gov or consult your IP specialist.

The ITC proceedings are considerably quicker than in a court of law and consequently tend to be less expensive.

Threatening litigation

Rather than making a beeline for the courthouse as soon as you find out someone is infringing on your rights, first have your attorney send a stern *cease and desist letter* that demands an immediate stop to all acts of infringement, gives an accounting of all illegal sales, and requests payment to reimburse your losses. What happens next can run from a great disappointment to a big surprise. The infringer can

- ✔ Ignore your letter (the most frequent occurrence). Move back to "Taking the high road and going for broke."

- ✔ Contact you to seek an amicable solution, where you forego the payment of damages and the infringer agrees to cease all infringing activities.

- ✔ Drag you to court to defend a declaratory relief action, forcing your attorney to counterclaim (counter sue) for infringement. Oops — you're back in the litigation circus.

  In a *declaratory relief action,* the alleged infringer becomes the plaintiff and asks for a judgment on the grounds that either he's not infringing your IP right or that your IP right is invalid. You, the defendant, find yourself no better off than if you'd filed a suit for infringement. Worse, the declaratory relief action will probably be filed in the infringer's district, forcing you to hire a local attorney and doubling your litigation costs.

Covering your derrière

Accusing anyone of infringing your IP rights on your own judgment without obtaining a written opinion from a knowledgeable attorney is *prima facie* (decisive) evidence of reckless behavior, if not willful harassment of your target. If you lose the case, your cavalier act will be used against you to increase the damages you have to pay. Never accuse anyone without jumping through the infringement analysis hoop — with a qualified IP attorney. Be sure to get your IP lawyer's opinion in writing. That opinion should refer to, and be based on, a thorough analysis of your patent or trademark application file.

Only someone with a reasonable apprehension of being unjustly sued can file a declaratory relief action. You can avoid triggering that kind of action by drafting the cease and desist letter in a non-threatening manner, offering a settlement in the form of a license, or some other equitable arrangement.

Negotiating a compromise

In most situations, your most sensible approach to resolving an infringement issue is through skillful negotiations. That's where attorneys are at their best. The result may be the grant of a very narrow non-exclusive license to the infringer if the case doesn't involve a commercial identifier. In the case of a trademark infringement, you could offer concurrent use of the identifier in distinct territories or markets. Trust your attorney to balance all the legal and business aspects of the case and guide you to some safe haven, free of tempestuous litigation.

Part VI
The Part of Tens

In this part . . .

This part contains some great information, if I say so myself, in easily accessible and digestible lists. Want to know the most common mistakes people make when doing the patent thing? You can check them out here, along with other useful info like frequently asked copyright questions, the ten worst ways to go about naming a company or product, and additional resources that you can use when entering the IP jungle.

Chapter 21

Top Ten Patent Application Pitfalls

In This Chapter

▶ Avoiding the most common preparing and filing mistakes

▶ Choosing the right approach

The following list covers the most common and most damaging errors committed by inventors. Because of them, many great inventions never make it to the market. Over the last 30 years, I've seen too many inventors torpedo their own patent applications or get into serious legal trouble when an ounce of knowledge and a bit of caution could have saved the day. Forewarned is forearmed — if you've read this book, you know how to avoid these problems.

Choosing a Utility Patent When Other Protection Will Fit the Bill

A utility patent takes lots of time and money to obtain and even more to enforce against an infringer. Sometimes, you can adequately protect many IP assets by less costly IP rights, such as a design patent, plant patent, copyright, trade secret, or trademark. Check out Chapter 5 for information on when and why another type of IP protection could be right for you.

Filing When You Can't Afford It

I've seen too many people abandon their patent application mid-stream for lack of funds. Take a good look at the overall cost (check out Chapter 3 for some handy cost estimates) *before* you begin preparing the application. If you're not sure where the money will come from, and you're not planning to just sell your invention, forget about a utility patent. It's more important that you develop a good product and get some early sales. Use your limited resources for developing an effective marketing program, including a blockbuster of a trademark, and look at an alternate and cheaper form of IP protection.

Going It Alone

Unless you received special training, don't think that you can file and pursue a utility patent application without the help of a professional — what you end up with likely won't be worth the paper it's printed on. The worst part is that you won't even know you've messed up on the application until you try to sue someone for infringement.

Reading this book is an excellent first step, but it's not going to make you a competent patent attorney. What it will do is provide you with a basic knowledge base from which you can confidently communicate with the experts, make informed decisions, evaluate the commercial potential of an idea, work with others to protect your businesses IP rights, and do much of the IP legwork, such as gathering a complete background file for your invention and laying out a sensible IP protection strategy. Most importantly, you'll know to avoid some very damaging faux pas. In some uncomplicated cases, you may be able to conduct preliminary patent and trademark searches and obtain copyright registrations on your own.

Concealing the Past

Too many patents are declared invalid during an infringement trial because the inventor failed to tell the patent examiner everything he or she knew about the background and history of the invention, including prior technology that may be relevant to the issue of patentability. Even if the invention seems entirely new and non-obvious, you have a duty to disclose everything you know. See Chapter 7 for the information you need to disclose to your IP professional.

Showing Your Hand

In the United States, you have only one year to file your patent application after you make the invention public. Most foreign countries give you no leeway at all — you have to file before the invention is public. See Chapter 8 for all the important deadlines to filing a patent application.

Be careful — making an invention public doesn't take much: Bragging about it to your neighbor Clyde may be enough of a public disclosure to blow you out of the game. So get on the ball and file your application as soon as possible — in the meantime, keep your invention under wraps. Treat it as a trade secret, as I explain in Chapter 2, as long as you possibly can and at least until you have a complete patent application on file.

Naming a Non-Inventor

Purposely listing someone who didn't contribute to the invention as an inventor is a misrepresentation that can invalidate a patent. The same goes for failing to name a bona fide inventor. Some inventors feel obligated to name their spouses as co-inventors on the mistaken belief that this makes them equal owners of the invention. An employer will want to be listed as an inventor because the employee who came up with the invention was working for him and using his or her facilities, therefore automatically making him or her a contributor. An employee sometimes names the supervisor just to score some brownie points. Some believe that the technician who built the prototype is automatically a co-inventor, although that technician didn't contribute anything beyond standard engineering knowledge. If you faithfully provide your IP professional with all the information listed in Chapter 8, she'll know how to identify the correct inventors.

Disclosing Too Little

You must describe your invention with enough detail to allow a person who's skilled in the field to practice (implement) it without undue experimentation. That's called the *enabling disclosure requirement*. You must also describe what you believe is the best way to actually use the invention, not necessarily the way you built your original prototype. Failure to disclose a critical element of the invention, such as where to purchase a hard-to-find component, can be fatal. For example, if you think your new sander works best with a diamond powder coating, but you only described it using a cheaper glass powder coating, you aren't disclosing the best way to practice the invention.

Disclosing Too Much

Some applicants, fearful of failing the *enabling disclosure* requirement (see Chapter 7) because they didn't provide enough information, go overboard and describe everything including the kitchen appliances. Anything that a person skilled in the field of the invention can figure out on his or her own is nonessential. I'm not talking about the person of ordinary skill defined in Chapter 7, but about a sophisticated expert in the field who understands the technology, is familiar with all the common acronyms, and knows how to anneal a metal, reduce a chemical solution, or modulate a carrier with a waveform without further explanation.

Adding superfluous descriptions and drawings to your application ends up costing a lot when you file corresponding applications abroad because in some countries, you pay according to the number of pages and the number of drawings in your application.

Waiting Too Long

Preparing a patent application takes time. Consulting your IP professional close to a filing deadline forces her to rush the drafting of the application at the expense of completeness and accuracy. Attorneys aren't magicians — give her a few weeks to do the job right. It's all to your benefit.

Accepting Money in Exchange for a Share of the Profits

Accepting money in exchange for a percentage of your future earnings from the invention or patent is illegal. That's called selling a security. If the state or the Fed doesn't come after you, you can bet that your investor will at the first hint of a downturn. What you can safely do is sell a portion of your invention and patent for cash under a written assignment. In this case, the buyer gets instant value in the invention and patent, not a mere promise of eventual financial return. You and the co-owner can then enter into an agreement about how the invention and patent will be jointly exploited.

Chapter 22

Ten Common Copyright Questions

In This Chapter
▶ Clearing up most common misconceptions
▶ Addressing what you can and can't borrow

I couldn't tell you how many times I've heard clients come up with the same misconceptions about copyrights, such as thinking that it's legal to copy less than 30 percent of a copyrighted work, or believing that they can use a recording as background music for an aerobics class because they bought and paid for it. The questions they often ask are the same ones that I answer in this chapter.

I Wrote a Children's Story: Can I Get a Copyright?

You don't need to. Like all authors, you automatically acquired a copyright when you wrote it down — or dictated it into a recording machine, if you want to get technical about it. However, registering your copyright is a must if you need to take action against a copycat, and you can get greater compensation if you register your work before it's copied. If you want to register your copyright, read Chapter 13 to find out how.

I Coined a Campaign Slogan for the Next Election: Can I Copyright It?

No. Names, titles, slogans, and short phrases aren't considered substantial enough to deserve copyright protection. A limerick or other short poem will pass the threshold. In music, a single original measure may have enough substance. So will a simple line drawing.

I Have an Idea for a TV Show: How Do I Get It Copyrighted?

Sorry, but you can't. You can't copyright ideas, concepts, systems, procedures, principles, methods, or discoveries. Copyright protects only the original *expression* of an idea and not the idea itself, so you have to at least write a treatment in order to get a copyright. As you develop the script, copyright attaches as soon as you describe a scene that's a choice among other possibilities. Check Chapter 11, where I talk about the copyright golden rule.

How Much of a Copyrighted Work Can I Copy without Infringing the Copyright?

None. Unless you get permission to use the work from the copyright owner, any copying is infringing. You can't copy a little bit any more than you can be a little bit pregnant. However, with proper permission, you can even modify and adapt the preexisting copyrighted material.

I'm Designing a Web Site: Can I Use Graphics Copied from a Magazine?

Yes, but there's a catch. You need to get permission from the copyright owner of the material you borrow. Check out Chapter 12 and the section on music in Chapter 19 to find out how and where to get the permission that you need. No permission, no use.

Can I Use a Popular Song in a Video Clip of My Dog to Send to America's Funniest Animals?

No. Copying a song from a CD to your videotape would be your first count of copyright infringement. Then every time your tape is played in public or broadcast constitutes another act of infringement. I can hear you thinking that everyone does it, and you may be right. But how many tax cheats are in the federal pen, even as we speak? Check Chapter 11 for exceptions and exemptions.

I'm a Teacher: Can I Copy a Page from a Book and Give the Copies to My Students?

Yes. This is one of the *fair-use limitations* to a copyright, meaning exactly what it implies. See Chapter 11 for a list of fair-use limitations.

How Long Does a Copyright Last?

It depends. A copyright's life depends on when the copyrighted work was first published or registered. The safe rule is 70 years beyond the life of the author. In the case of an anonymous author, it's the shorter of 95 years from original publication or 120 years from creation.

Where Can I Get Permission to Copy a Protected Work?

You can find out in this book. To be more precise, read about investigating the status of a copyright in Chapter 12. If you're talking about a musical recording, read about the music business in Chapter 19.

Can I Protect Software with a Copyright and a Patent?

Yes. The copyright only protects the ways in which the underlying process is presented by the program instructions, and the patent protects the process itself. While you're at it, you can keep a good part of the program instructions confidential and protect them as a trade secret. (Find out how to preserve the trade secret in a computer program in Chapter 13.) You may also give a distinctive name to your software and get some trademark protection. (Check out Chapter 15 for tips on creating distinctive names.)

The Ten Worst Naming Blunders

Contrary to conventional wisdom, the most popular ways of selecting a company name or a product brand are the worst approaches, and they often spell disaster. On the other hand, the best way to choose the commercial name by which you'll be known is to follow the methodical approach outlined in Chapter 15. You want to coin the most motivating, memorable moniker possible that nobody can copy or imitate, a name that will gain you a loyal customer base and may even provide you with a new and independent source of income. In other words, *avoid* the wildly popular routes for selecting a commercial identifier that I outline in this chapter.

Using Your Family Name

Family pride may drive me to name my new enterprise the CHARMASSON Company, but I'd limit myself in many ways. Problems with similar names may lurk in unexpected places. For openers, a surname isn't easy to register as a trademark or servicemark, or to protect against copycats, unless it has some alternate meaning (for example, if you're a scooter manufacturer with the name Dash). Unless your name is unique and memorable, it contains minimal promotional value, and the valuation and transfer of the name upon the sale of the business is often problematic. And in my case, how many customers dislike Frenchmen?

Mimicking Another Company's Brand

Imitation may be the sincerest form of flattery, but why flatter your competitor? Worse, there's liability for infringing upon another's commercial identifier. Copying is stealing, and penalties can include a seizure of your goods and a court order to change your counterfeit brand name. Copying is the lazy way to avoid the discipline of naming. Be unique. Move to the head of your industry, rather than dissolve in the crowd.

Describing Your Product or Service

This is the most frequent and serious mistake. Do you want to name your company DIGITAL PRODUCTS (among dozens of Digital This and Digital Thats) or would you rather display uniqueness, brilliance, and creativity with a name like APPLE? Should your beer be known as LITE and lose its identity to a gaggle of imitators or sport a shining tiara like CORONA? A commercial identifier must be unique and distinctive, and not a mere description of your product that could apply to all other similar products.

A descriptive name is a ticket to the courthouse and to endless, expensive, and time-consuming litigation because it's bound to be imitated eventually by your competitors. The courts have determined that you can't monopolize any part of the language. You can either create a new word out of nothing, such as KODAK, or give a totally new meaning to an existing word, like CREST for toothpaste. See Chapter 14 for more info on descriptive versus distinctive names.

Having Brainstorming Sessions

Brainstorming monopolizes expensive management time and generates more arguments than deciding on the merits of chocolate versus vanilla ice cream. The result is a predictably colorless compromise that lacks the marketing punch and legal clout you need.

Group interaction in naming has its place, but such endeavors need method, structure, and common goals to be effective.

Holding a Naming Contest

Holding a public or employee contest to coin a name makes as much sense as practicing medicine by popular vote. It's haphazard at best. And a contest requires a winner, even if the best entry is unsuitable. Have a company picnic instead.

Ignoring the Customer

Insiders are too close to the product and its history to be open-minded. A commercial identifier that's effective in the marketplace looks outward; it speaks the customer's language, not the engineer's or designer's. It should motivate your prospect, catch his or her fancy, and be long remembered. Don't focus on your achievement. Consider what will attract the public.

Creating Techno-Babble

Cold and unpronounceable combinations of Zs and Xs, or meaningless and pseudo-scientific monikers like CHLORASEPTIC and HYBRINETICS just don't communicate. The minor technical gloss doesn't make up for the lost opportunity to carry a high-impact message to the market several times a day.

Choosing Availability over Exclusivity

Just because a name's not already registered doesn't necessarily make it a good candidate for your product or company. If the name isn't strongly enforceable in court, you'll soon be copied and lose goodwill and market share, to the despair of your investors. (Check out Chapter 14 for more info on making your name hold up in court.) Go for the gold, not the tinfoil of an ordinary identifier.

Relying on the Logo

A creative ad and a snazzy logo help the customer remember your commercial identifier. When he or she decides to buy a widget, your name will pop out first. A logo should enhance the impact of a name, but great graphics won't save a weak name. Do your best when coining your identifier, and *then* take it to the graphic artist.

Leaving Your Mark Unprotected

When the time comes to stop a copycat, would you rather limp into court with a wet noodle or swagger in with a bazooka? Registration is your most powerful weapon and should be your top priority. Chapter 17 tells you everything you ever wanted to know about registering your mark. Your registered mark can eventually become incontestable if, after five years, no one has challenged you and you file an affidavit to that effect. Having an incontestable mark gives you an invaluable defense when your success squeezes all those prior name users out of the woodwork.

Chapter 24

More Than Ten Great IP Resources

• •

In This Chapter

▶ Finding out where to get more information

▶ Diving into Web sites about IP rights

• •

Although I've packed this book full of useful information, the subject of intellectual property rights can fill thousands of printed volumes and millions of Web pages. So I include this chapter to help you check out additional sources of information, resources, and forms, which you can use to find out more about various topics that I discuss in this book.

Contacting the USPTO for General Info

You have a couple of options for contacting this organization for general information and inquiries about patents and trademarks:

✔ **Online:** Go to www.uspto.gov. The amount of information you can access on this site is huge, which is great. But, because of all that info, navigating the site can be a challenge if you're not sure what you're looking for. I provide detailed navigational instructions throughout this book to help you get to specific areas you need quickly. To familiarize yourself with the site on your first visit, check the First Time Visitor box and the Need Help tab on the first page. I also suggest you make yourself a copy of the Glossary of Terms and keep it as a handy reference.

✔ **Mail:** USPTO Contact Center, Crystal Plaza 3, Room 2C02, P.O. Box 1450, Alexandria, VA 22313-1450

✔ **Phone:** 800-786-9199 or 703-308-4357

The USPTO is a huge organization that can't practically respond to mail and phone inquiries. The Web site is your best bet to find what you need.

Contacting the U.S. Copyright Office

Information about copyright matters is available via these three modes:

- ✔ **Online:** Go to www.copyright.gov.
- ✔ **Mail:** Copyright Office, Library of Congress, 101 Independence Avenue, S.E., Washington, DC 20559-6000
- ✔ **Phone:** 202-707-3000

You can access an information specialist by phone during working hours and recorded information 24 hours a day. I suggest you first check the Web site and call only for information you can't find there.

Accessing Online Applications

The USPTO is quickly moving toward a full electronic filing system. You can already file your utility patent application online, but not a design or plant patent application yet. The electronic filing system (EFS) is still in a state of flux and is often being modified; watch the USPTO Web site for new info.

- ✔ **Domestic patent applications:** On the USPTO Web site, click on Patents, and then on File. On the EFS page, click on the How to File tab and you're on your way.
- ✔ **Foreign patent applications:** To file an application under the Patent Cooperation Treaty (PCT), visit the World Intellectual Property Organization site at www.wipo.int. On the home page, click on Activities and Services, PCT System, and then on PCT Applicant's Guide in the Shortcut box. For direct filing abroad, consult your IP professional.
- ✔ **Domestic copyright registration applications:** You can't file electronically for copyright registration yet. However you can get a great deal of information by visiting the Copyright Office Web site at www.copyright.gov. You can also download or fill out application forms online and then mail with the copyrighted material.
- ✔ **Domestic trademark registration applications:** Applying online for the registration of a mark will be the only way to go. Visit the USPTO Web site and click on Trademarks File to get the latest scoop on e-filing.

✔ **Foreign trademark registration applications:** To file an application for registration of a mark in a number of foreign countries under the Madrid Protocol, visit the USPTO Web site. Click on Trademarks File, then on Madrid Protocol. To file an application for European registration of a mark, visit the WIPO Web site at `www.wipo.int` and check out the European Union's Office for Harmonization in the Internal Market site at `http://oami.eu.int`. Click on OHIM, then on The Community Trademark.

Old-Fashioned Application Access

You can still file your patent or mark registration the old way by mail. However, you'll soon be penalized with an extra filing fee if you don't file your application for mark registration online. At least, that's what I heard on the USPTO very unofficial grapevine. You can get all the necessary forms to send in by visiting the USPTO and the Copyright Office Web sites.

Getting Down with Government Manuals

Each dealing with the USPTO and the Copyright Office must be in accordance with official laws and regulations. Those laws and regulations are interpreted and amplified in a series of manuals, which IP professionals rely on in their daily practice. If you want to gain some expertise in IP law and practice, consult these manuals either online or by getting your own copies.

✔ ***Manual of Patent Examining Procedure* (MPEP):** This manual contains detailed instructions to patent examiners on how to examine an application, PCT application rules, and copies of patent statutes. This huge manual is periodically updated. It's available by subscription from the Superintendent of Documents, U.S. Government Printing Office (see the contact information in the next section). Or consult the MPEP online or download the manual from the USPTO Web site. Just go to the Patent section and look under Guidance, Tools, and Manuals.

✔ ***Compendium of Copyright Office Practices:*** This slightly out-of-date guide, available from the Government Printing Office, is used by the Copyright Office in examining applications for registration of copyright.

✔ ***Trademark Manual of Examining Procedures* (TMEP):** This manual contains detailed instructions to trademark examining attorneys on how to examine an application. It's periodically updated and available by subscription from the Superintendent of Documents, U.S. Government Printing Office. Or see the TMEP online or download it from the USPTO Web site. Just go to the Trademarks section. It's under Publications.

The Government Printing Office

Besides the manuals mentioned above, you can find a variety of treatise and code books related to IP matters at this government store.

Government Printing Office, Washington, DC 20402. Phone: 866-512-1800 (202-512-1800 in the Washington, D.C., area). Internet: `http://bookstore.gpo.gov`.

Inquiring about IP Litigation Info

All patent and copyright cases and the majority of trademark and service-mark disputes are litigated in federal courts and under federal rules. If you want to know more about how the game is played, check out the code book listed here. These lawsuits are complex, expensive, and beyond the means of individuals and small businesses. However, litigation insurance can cover the cost of both defensive and offensive legal actions. Here is a source of information about this type of coverage.

- **Litigation rules:** *Federal Civil Judicial Procedure and Rules* (West Publishing Co., Saint Paul, Minnesota). This book contains all the rules relating to litigation in federal courts. The same rules are followed in *inter partes* proceedings before the USPTO (proceedings where two parties are involved, such as patent interferences and trademark oppositions and cancellations).

- **Litigation insurance:** Intellectual Property Insurance Services Corporation, 10503 Timberwood Circle, Suite 114, Louisville, KY 40223. Phone: 800-537-7863. Internet: `www.infringeins.com`. This is where you can find and purchase litigation insurance.

Further Reading for the IP-Addicted

If you can't get enough of IP after reading this book, I feel for you. But I also understand (it's my life's work). Here are a few basic and inexpensive books:

- *This Business of Music* by M William Krasilovsky (Billboard Books, Watson-Guptill Publications). This book offers a comprehensive discussion of all aspects of the music industry.

- *Drafting Patent License Agreements* by Harry R. Mayers and Brian G. Brunsvold (Bureau of National Affairs, Inc.).

- *Franchising For Dummies* by Dave Thomas and Michael Seid (Wiley Publishing, Inc.).

Appendix

(12) **United States Patent**

Soproni

(10) **Patent No.:** **US 6,329,033 B2**

(45) **Date of Patent:** *Dec. 11, 2001

(54) **IMITATION WAX SEAL**

(76) Inventor: **Zoltan Soproni**, 7887 Dunbrook Rd., Suite C, San Diego, CA (US) 92126

(*) Notice: This patent issued on a continued prosecution application filed under 37 CFR 1.53(d), and is subject to the twenty year patent term provisions of 35 U.S.C. 154(a)(2).

Subject to any disclaimer, the term of this patent is extended or adjusted under 35 U.S.C. 154(b) by 0 days.

(21) Appl. No.: **09/227,727**

(22) Filed: **Jan. 8, 1999**

Related U.S. Application Data

(60) Provisional application No. 60/074,035, filed on Feb. 9, 1998.

(51) Int. Cl.^{7} **B32B 27/00**
(52) U.S. Cl. **428/40.1**; 40/616; 428/40.9; 428/41.3; 428/42.1; 428/42.2; 428/915; 428/916
(58) Field of Search 428/40.1, 41.3, 428/42.1, 42.2, 40.9, 915, 916; 40/616

(56) **References Cited**

U.S. PATENT DOCUMENTS

4,149,738	* 4/1979	Illos	283/8
4,595,351	* 6/1986	Dickson	425/114
5,154,448	* 10/1992	Griffin	283/102

FOREIGN PATENT DOCUMENTS

2593952	* 8/1987	(FR) .
58-8774	* 1/1993	(JP) .

* cited by examiner

Primary Examiner—Nasser Ahmad
(74) *Attorney, Agent, or Firm*—Henri J. A. Charmasson; John D. Buchaca

(57)   **ABSTRACT**

An imitation wax seal suitable for application to a document, package or container is injection-molded out of a semi-rigid plastic, then coated in the back with an adhesive temporarily protected by a peelable film. The fabrication mold accepts a variety of substitutable center escutcheon that can carry a variety of letters, symbols, and logo types. The seal is flexible enough to pass through post office automatic sorting and canceling equipment without breaking or coming loose. The seal is impregnated with a bee-wax scent or other pleasant fragrance.

8 Claims, 1 Drawing Sheet

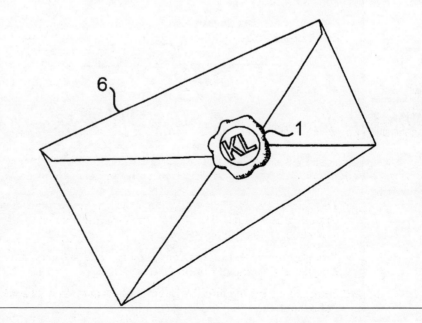

Figure A-1: Sample utility patent, Page 1.

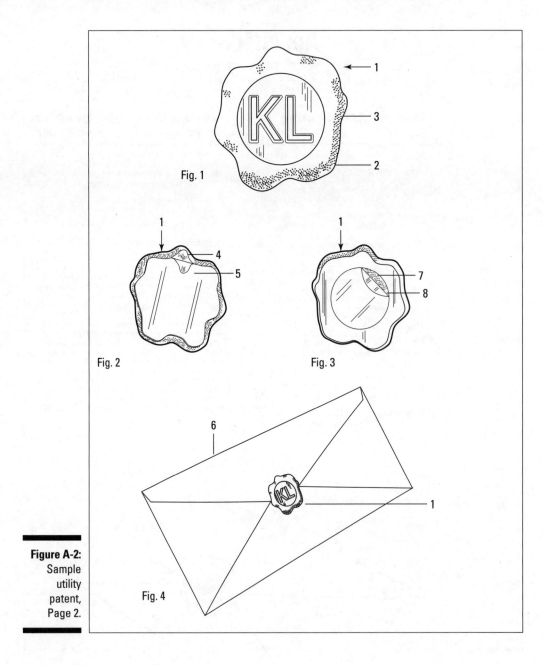

Fig. 1

Fig. 2

Fig. 3

Fig. 4

Figure A-2:
Sample
utility
patent,
Page 2.

US 6,329,033 B2

1

IMITATION WAX SEAL

PRIOR APPLICATION

This is a continuation of provisional application Serial No. 60/074,035 filed Feb. 9, 1998.

FIELD OF THE INVENTION

This invention relates to insignias, seals, decorative buttons and more particularly to plastic substitutes for natural wax seals.

BACKGROUND OF THE INVENTION

Wax seals have been used since antiquity to guarantee the integrity and authenticity of documents The traditional beewax or tallow-wax seal is formed by applying a glob of melted wax on a document, ribbon or fastener, then stamping the melted glob with a brass seal engraved with a mirror image of the desired design.

Nowadays, this type of wax seal is seldom used to certify a document, but survives only as a decorative element that lends class and distinction to a diploma, award certificate, or personal missive.

Traditional wax seals are very brittle, and cannot survive the sorting and canceling machines used in most post offices Their debris can interfere with the good operation of that type of equipment. Accordingly, envelopes bearing a natural wax seal must be hand-delivered to a post office where they are manually canceled and sorted.

Brass seals are relatively expensive. Moreover, the whole process of melting the wax, applying a glob of it to the document, then stamping it is awkward for most people and is often botched.

SUMMARY OF THE INVENTION

The principal and secondary objects of this invention are to provide a customized decorative seal of pleasant appearance and fragrance that has the exact appearance of a traditional wax seal, can be conveniently applied to a document without heat, and is flexible enough to pass through the handling, sorting and canceling equipment of the post office without breaking or coming loose.

These and other valuable objects are achieve by a thin plastic slug formed in an injection mold and having a central part decorated with lettering, a blazon or logo type. A section of double-sided adhesive tape temporarily protected by a peelable film is applied to the back of the slug. The plastic material is impregnated with a pleasant fragrance essence

BRIEF DESCRIPTION OF THE DRAWING

FIG. 1 is a top plan view of a seal according to the invention;

FIG. 2 is a back perspective view of the seal showing the adhesive layer;

FIG. 3 illustrates an alternate adhesion method; and

FIG. 4 shows a seal applied on an envelope.

DESCRIPTION OF THE PREFERRED EMBODIMENT OF THE INVENTION

Referring now to the drawing, there is shown in FIG. 1 a slug made in an injection mold from a choice of colored and scented plastic material such as polypropylene. Alternately, the slug may be made of a metal-resin composite such as those available from LuminOre, Inc. of Encinitas, Califor-

2

nia. The slug **1** has the random outline **2** and general profile of a traditional wax seal. The central portion **3** which is formed by a substitutable coin in the injection mold carries a design which can be one or a set of initials, a blazon, or a logo type or other informative sign. Accordingly, the seal can be readily customized. In addition the surface of design design carried by the seal may be pad-printed or hot-stamped to impart special shapes or colors. A double-sided adhesive tape **4** temporarily protected by a peelable film **5** is applied to the flat back of the slugs as shown in FIG. 2. In lieu of the double-sided adhesive tape, a dot **7** of high-tack adhesive, such as an acrylic glue, also protectively covered by a peelable film **8** may be applied to the back of the slugs as shown in FIG. 3.

After having peeled the film, the user simply applies the seal with a thumb pressure.

The thickness of the slug should not exceed 1.58 millimeters (62 mils), and is preferably kept around 1.2 millimeters (45 mils). These dimensions yield a slightly flexible seal that can pass through post office handling, sorting and canceling equipment without breaking or coming loose. Accordingly, as shown in FIG. 4, the seal **1** can be conveniently used to seal a letter **6**. A similar seal can be used on other types of documents such as a diploma, an award certificate, or a ribbon and similar fasteners. The seal can also be used to personalize a gift by applying it to its container, accompanying tag, or on the gift item itself.

What is claimed is:

1. An imitation wax seal which comprises:

a slug of molded synthetic material shaped and dimensioned to resemble a stamped glob of hot wax, said slug having a top face embossed with a sign, a substantially flat bottom face and a thickness of no more than 1.58 millimeters; and

means for securing said bottom face on a receiving surface without heating said slug.

2. The structure of claim **1**, wherein said means for securing comprise:

a double-sided portion of adhesive tape having a first side applied against said bottom face, and a second opposite side; and

a peelable protective film applied to said second side.

3. The structure of claim **1**, wherein said means for securing comprise:

a layer of adhesive applied to said bottom face; and

a peelable protective film covering said layer.

4. The structure of claim **1**, wherein said material is a polypropylene.

5. The structure of claim **1**, wherein said material is a metal-resin composite.

6. The structure of claim **4**, wherein said material includes a fragrant essence.

7. The structure of claim **1**, wherein said sign comprises initials.

8. The combination of a document with an imitation wax seal wherein said imitation wax seal comprises:

a slug of molded synthetic material shaped and dimensioned to resemble a stamped glob of hot wax, said slug having a top face embossed with a sign, a substantially flat bottom face and a thickness of no more than 1.58 millimeters; and

means for securing said bottom face on said document without application of heat to said slug.

* * * * *

Figure A-3: Sample utility patent, Page 3.

(12) **United States Design Patent**
Dehaan

(10) Patent No.: **US D435,884 S**

(45) Date of Patent: ** **Jan. 2, 2001**

(54) **PAINTBALL GUN BARREL MUZZLE**

(75) Inventor: **David J. Dehaan,** San Diego, CA (US)

(73) Assignee: **Dye Products, Inc.,** San Diego, CA (US)

(**) Term: **14 Years**

(21) Appl. No.: **29/126,128**

(22) Filed: **Jul. 7, 2000**

(51) LOC (7) Cl. **22-01**
(52) U.S. Cl. **D22/108;** D22/100; D22/199
(58) Field of Search D22/100, 108, D22/199; 42/76.01; 89/14.3, 14.4; 181/223

(56) **References Cited**

U.S. PATENT DOCUMENTS

D. 296,350 * 6/1988 Cellini .... 89/14.3 X
1,130,609 * 3/1915 Jones 89/14.4
2,712,193 * 7/1955 Mathis 89/14.3
5,305,677 * 4/1994 Kleinguenther et al. .... 89/14.3 X
5,425,298 * 6/1995 Coburn 89/14.3
5,675,107 * 10/1997 Ledys et al. 89/14.3

* cited by examiner

Primary Examiner—Louis S. Zarfas
Assistant Examiner—Monica A. Weingart
(74) *Attorney, Agent, or Firm*—Henri J. A. Charmasson; John D. Buchaca

(57) **CLAIM**

The ornamental design for a paintball gun barrel muzzle, as shown and described.

DESCRIPTION

FIG. 1 is a back, bottom left side perspective view of a paintball gun barrel muzzle showing my new design; and, FIG. 2 is a front, top right side perspective view thereof.

1 Claim, 1 Drawing Sheet

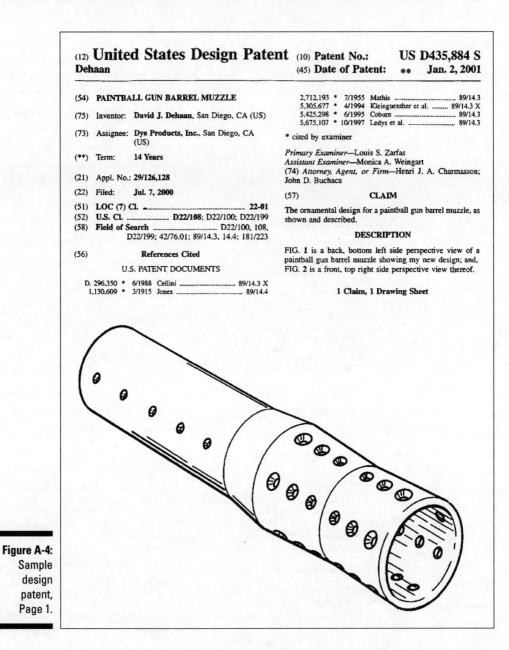

Figure A-4:
Sample
design
patent,
Page 1.

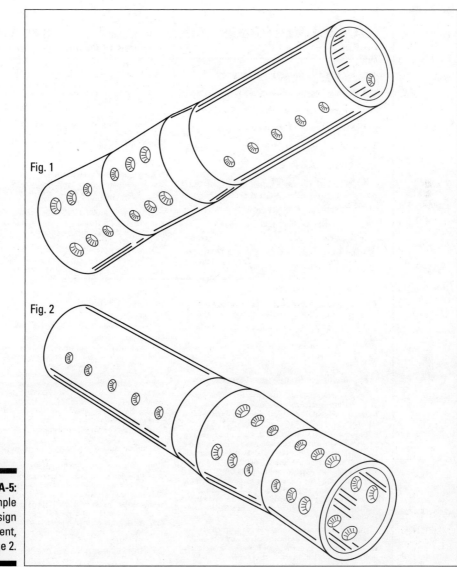

Fig. 1

Fig. 2

Figure A-5:
Sample
design
patent,
Page 2.

---

(12) **United States Plant Patent**
Kos

(10) **Patent No.:** **US PP13,741 P3**
(45) **Date of Patent:** **Apr. 29, 2003**

---

(54) **LILY PLANT NAMED 'FUTURA'**

(75) Inventor: **Pieter Jan Kos**, Anna Paulowna (NL)

(73) Assignee: **World Breeding, B.V.** (NL)

(*) Notice: Subject to any disclaimer, the term of this patent is extended or adjusted under 35 U.S.C. 154(b) by 0 days.

(21) Appl. No.: **09/834,748**

(22) Filed: **Apr. 13, 2001**

(65) **Prior Publication Data**

US 2002/0152528 P1 Oct. 17, 2002

(30) **Foreign Application Priority Data**

Apr. 14, 2000 (NL) 2000/0595

(51) **Int. Cl.**^{7} A01H 5/00
(52) **U.S. Cl.** Plt./313

(58) **Field of Search** Plt./313

(56) **References Cited**

PUBLICATIONS

The New Royal Horticultural Society Dictionary of Gardening, vol. 3, editor-in-chief Anthony Huxley, The Royal Horticultural Society, 1992, pp. 68–80.*

* cited by examiner

Primary Examiner—Bruce R. Campell
Assistant Examiner—Anne Marie Grünberg
(74) *Attorney, Agent, or Firm*—Klarquist Sparkman LLP

(57) **ABSTRACT**

A new and distinct variety of upright Oriental×Aurelia hybrid lily plant, named 'Futura', characterized by large, yellow flowers.

1 Drawing Sheet

1

LATIN NAME OF THE GENUS AND SPECIES OF THE PLANT CLAIMED

Genus: Lilium. Species is unknown.

VARIETY DENOMINATION

'Futura'.

BACKGROUND OF THE INVENTION

The present invention relates to a new and distinct variety of Lilium hybrid referred to commercially as an upright Oriental×Aurelia lily hybrid and given the cultivar name 'Futura'.

This new variety is the product of a controlled breeding program using embryo culture and was carried out in the municipality of Breezand, The Netherlands, using the proprietary Oriental type hybrid lily E-890-19 as seed parent and the proprietary Aurelia type hybrid lily OR-90.058-8 as the pollen parent. The resulting plants were evaluated for cut flower production. Compared to the typical characteristics of common Oriental or Aurelia lily hybrids, this new variety has larger flowers, taller overall plant height and taller stems, and blooms earlier.

This new variety has not been observed under all possible environmental conditions. The phenotype may vary significantly with variations in environment such as temperature, light intensity, day length, and nutrient availability, without, however, any variations in genotype.

BRIEF SUMMARY OF THE INVENTION

The following traits have been repeatedly observed and are determined to be the basic characteristics of this invention that in combination distinguish this lily as a new and distinct variety:

1. floriferous habit;
2. large yellow flowers;

2

3. vigorous growth habit;
4. tall plant;
5. good virus tolerance; and
6. excellent vase-life.

Bulbs of this plant may be pre-cooled and forced out of season for very uniform cut flower production.

The primary distinguishing feature of 'Futura' is its numerous, large, yellow flowers. The seed parent, an Oriental type hybrid, does not produce yellow flowers, and 'Futura' can be bred approximately 25 days more quickly than the seed parent. The pollen parent, an Aurelian type hybrid, has a different inflorescence and calyx-like flowers. Furthermore, the flowers of the 'Futura' variety are larger than those produced by the pollen parent.

BRIEF DESCRIPTION OF THE DRAWING

This new variety of lily plant is illustrated in the accompanying photographic drawing, which shows the upper half portion of the flowering stem of a potted plant in the full face view of the flowers together with some foliage. The accompanying photograph, showing the 'Futura' variety, was taken in a studio and illustrates the typical flower and foliage form, with color as true as reasonably possible in this type of color illustration.

DETAILED BOTANICAL DESCRIPTION

This detailed description of the invention is based on plants approximately 80–90 days old produced in greenhouses in Breezand, The Netherlands. Bulbs were planted in (and the resulting plants cultivated in) trays with peatmoss. Plants were grown at a minimum temperature of about 15° C. without supplemental fertilization or supplemental lighting. Color references are provided according to The R.H.S. Colour Chart published by The Royal Horticultural Society of London, England, except where the context indicates a term having its ordinary dictionary meaning.

Figure A-6:
Sample
plant patent,
Page 1.

US PP13,741 P3

3

Origin: Resulting from a hybridization.

Parentage:

Seed parent.—Oriental type hybrid lily E-890-19 (proprietary owned).

Pollen parent.—Aurelia type hybrid lily OR 90.058-8 (proprietary owned).

Commercial classification: Upright Oriental×Aurelium hybrid lily, cut flower type.

Classification: Division VIII, all hybrids not provided for in any previous Division according to the Horticultural Classification of Lilies by The Royal Horticultural Society.

Form: Single erect stem from each bulb bearing terminal cluster of flowers.

Height: To about 140 cm. from the top of the soil to the top of the inflorescence.

Stem: Green in color (RHS 141B).

Growth: Vigorous, upright, and very strong. Plants grew about 120 cm over a span of about 80 to 90 days.

Foliage:

Arrangement.—Spiral.

Quantity.—Many fine leaves, with approximately 40 to 45 leaves per plant.

Leaf size.—To about 18.5 cm. long and to about 3 cm. wide.

Leaf shape.—Lanceolate.

Leaf margin.—Entire.

Aspect.—Glossy.

Texture.—Leathery.

Color.—Upperside of leaves: Green (RHS 137A). Underside of leaves: Green (RHS 139C). Leaf venation: Yellow-green (RHS 145A).

Bulb:

Type.—Concentric.

Size.—About 5.5 to 6.0 cm in diameter and about 16 to 18 cm in circumference.

Color.—Yellow-white (RHS 158C) and greyed-purple (RHS 184D).

Bud:

Size.—To about 13.5 cm. long and to about 3.5 cm wide, just prior to opening.

Shape.—Lanceolate, with the apex commonly having three obtuse tips.

Color.—Very Light Yellow (RHS 12C) at first opening turning into a Yellow (RHS 14C) when unfurling, blushed with Orange (RHS 35C).

Opening rate.—The mature bud opens slowly in response to light.

Flower:

Blooming habit.—Annually, once and profusely.

Days to bloom.—Flowers approximately 80 to 90 days after greenhouse planting under typical flower forcing conditions at minimum temperature of 15° C.

Outdoor blooming time.—Bulbs planted in mid-March bloom about mid-June.

Greenhouse blooming time.—Bulbs can be planted year-round and forced to bloom approximately 80 to

4

90 after planting. Greenhouse bloom lasts about 12 to 15 days.

Flower number.—About 4 to 5 flowers per plant.

Flower size.—Very Large.

Diameter.—To about 23 cm.

Depth.—To about 7 cm.

Borne.—Cluster of about 3 to 5 flowers from bulbs of about 14 to 16 cm. in circumference.

Shape.—The flower is funnel shaped. After opening, the tepals recurve at the top.

Tepalage.—Number: 6. Arrangement: Imbricated. Shape: Oval. Texture: Leathery. Aspect: Satiny. Size: Length: Inner tepals to about 13.6 cm. Outer tepals to about 14.5 cm. Width: Inner tepals to about 6.6 cm. Outer tepals to about 4 cm. Nectary: Green (RHS 145B), about 4.5 cm along vein. Spots: Orange-brown (RHS 171B) covering bottom one-third of tepal to halfway down nectary. Blush: None. Color, adaxial surfaces: Outer tepals are Yellow (RHS 12D) with midrib Yellow (RHS 4D). The inner tepals are Yellow (RHS 12C) with midrib Yellow (RHS 4D). Color, abaxial surfaces: Yellow-orange (RHS 14C) on the outer edge portion and yellow-orange (RHS 17B) toward the midrib. Some greyed-orange (RHS 170D) spots. Yellow-green (RHS 151B) keel. Fragrance: Weak.

Lasting quality.—Excellent. Each flower lasts about 14 days, with a vase life of about 12 to 15 days. Orientation: Ascending upwardly off the stem, the first flower to about a 40 degree angle, the last flower to about 90 degrees (horizontal).

Pedicel.—Length: About 8 to 9.5 cm. Color: Green (RHS 139C).

Reproductive organs:

Stamens.—Number: Six, typical of the genus Lilium.

Anthers before dehiscense.—Length: To about 4.2 cm. from mature bud. Color: Orange-brown (RHS 166A).

Filaments.—Length: To about 8.9 cm. Color: Yellow-green (RHS 145C).

Pollen.—Color: Orange (RHS 168B).

Pistil.—Number: One.

Style.—Length: To about 8.3 cm. Color: Green (RHS 145C) on top half, bottom half Lighter Green (RHS 145C).

Stigma.—Color: Dark Brown (RHS 200A).

Fruit:

Fertility.—Fruit is produced.

Shape.—Ovoid.

Fungal resistance: Some resistance to Pytium species. Color at maturity: Green (RHS 144B).

I claim:

1. A new and distinctive variety of Oriental×Aurelia hybrid lily plant, substantially as herein illustrated and described.

* * * * *

Figure A-7: Sample plant patent, Page 2.

U.S. Patent   Apr. 29, 2003   US PP13,741 P3

Figure A-8:
Sample
plant patent,
Page 3.

Index